T0330259

The Dynamics of Change in EU Governance

STUDIES IN EU REFORM AND ENLARGEMENT

Series Editors: Thomas Christiansen, *Senior Lecturer, European Institute of Public Administration, Maastricht, The Netherlands*, Anne Faber, *formerly of University of Cologne, Germany*, Gunilla Herolf, *Stockholm International Peace Research Institute, Sweden* and Wolfgang Wessels, *Jean Monnet Professor, University of Cologne, Germany*.

This exciting new series provides original contributions to one of the key debates about the European Union: the relationship between the twin processes of 'widening' (EU enlargement) and 'deepening' (EU reform). Arising largely from a European-wide research consortium, the books published in this series will deal with the important issues emerging from these twin challenges facing the European Union at a crucial period in its history. Individual books will focus either on the broader questions of European governance that are raised by the widening/deepening debate, or will look in more detail at specific institutional or sectoral areas. Containing cutting-edge research with a multi-disciplinary approach, the books in this series will be of great interest to scholars of European Studies, politics, economics, law and contemporary history.

Titles in the series include:

The Institutions of the Enlarged European Union
Continuity and Change
Edited by Edward Best, Thomas Christiansen and Pierpaolo Settembri

The Dynamics of Change in EU Governance
Edited by Udo Diedrichs, Wulf Reiners and Wolfgang Wessels

The Dynamics of Change in EU Governance

Edited by

Udo Diedrichs
Wulf Reiners
Wolfgang Wessels

University of Cologne, Germany

STUDIES IN EU REFORM AND ENLARGEMENT

Edward Elgar
Cheltenham, UK • Northampton, MA, USA

Published by
Edward Elgar Publishing Limited
The Lypiatts
15 Lansdown Road
Cheltenham
Glos GL50 2JA
UK

Edward Elgar Publishing, Inc.
William Pratt House
9 Dewey Court
Northampton
Massachusetts 01060
USA

A catalogue record for this book
is available from the British Library

Library of Congress Control Number: 2009941249

MIX
Paper from
responsible sources
FSC
www.fsc.org FSC® C018575

ISBN 978 1 84844 886 5

Typeset by Servis Filmsetting Ltd, Stockport, Cheshire
Printed and bound by MPG Books Group, UK

Contents

Contributors

Holger Bähr is a Research Fellow at Saarland University and the University of Applied Sciences in Saarbrücken, Germany.

Kálmán Dezséri is Senior Research Fellow of the Institute for World Economics of the Hungarian Academy of Sciences.

Udo Diedrichs is Senior Lecturer at the Department of Political Science of the University of Cologne, Germany.

Gerda Falkner is Director of the Institute for European Integration Research of the Austrian Academy of Sciences and Associate Professor for Political Science at the University of Vienna, Austria.

Jörg Monar is Director of European Political and Administrative Studies at the College of Europe in Bruges, Belgium and Professor of Contemporary European Studies at the University of Sussex, UK.

David Natali is Associate Professor at the University of Bologna-Forlì, Italy and Research Director at the European Social Observatory (OSE) in Brussels, Belgium.

Anne Peters is Professor of Public International Law and Constitutional Law and Dean of Research of the Law Faculty at the University of Basel, Switzerland.

Wulf Reiners is Research Fellow at the Jean Monnet Chair of Professor Wessels, University of Cologne, Germany.

Colin Shaw is Research Fellow in the field of Social Policy at Queen's University, Belfast, UK.

Oliver Treib is Assistant Professor in the Department of Political Science and Sociology at the University of Salzburg, Austria.

Krisztina Vida is Senior Research Fellow of the Institute for World Economics of the Hungarian Academy of Sciences.

Wolfgang Wessels is Jean Monnet Professor of Political Science at the University of Cologne, Germany.

Preface

The entry into force of the Lisbon Treaty in December 2009 has enriched and enhanced the opportunities for using modes of governance in the European Union. By introducing new provisions on decision-making and policy-shaping, the member states have defined new rules of the game and triggered a fresh dynamics of intra- and interinstitutional interaction. This volume examines the transformation of governance in the European Union over recent years by mapping, analysing and evaluating the emergence, execution and evolution of 'new modes of governance' across policy fields. It brings together the results of research conducted in the context of the integrated project 'NEWGOV – New Modes of Governance', coordinated by the European University Institute, Florence. As a key issue in studying European politics in general and not least of the evolution of the European Union, this book is published in the 'Studies in EU Reform and Enlargement' series embedding governance into a macro approach of analysis of the construction of the EU system.

For this purpose, the volume combines the research undertaken by political scientists, economists and lawyers, engaged in collecting data, mapping and analysing innovations and transformations in the legal and living architecture of governance operating at the multiple levels and arenas of the evolving and enlarging European polity and economy. A particular focus has been placed on the ways in which these innovative mechanisms and practices relate to each other both horizontally and vertically; how they relate to 'old methods' of governance; and what their implications are both for the effectiveness and efficiency of policy-making. These questions are followed in a number of policy areas which cover all three pillars of the European Union and their development over recent years. The findings of the chapters are finally integrated into an explanatory framework that explains the dynamics of EU governance by a 'integrative spiral' which is driven by the interrelation between the legal and the living architecture of the EU.

The editors are grateful for the contributions and the active support from the different authors and their co-authors which have made this publication possible. We would like to thank the editors of the series as well as Joanne Betteridge, Caroline Cornish and Jenny Wilcox at Edward Elgar for their extremely friendly, supportive and patient cooperation. Finally, our special thanks go to Marlene Gottwald for her excellent assistance in compiling the final manuscript.

The Editors
Cologne, March 2011

Abbreviations

AFSJ	Area of freedom, security and justice
ATHENA	The mechanism for financing military operations
BEPG	Broad Economic Policy Guidelines
CARDS	Community Assistance for Reconstruction, Development and Stabilization
CDM	Capability Development Mechanism
CEN	European Committee for Standardization
CENELEC	European Committee for Electrotechnical Standardization
CEPOL	European Police College
CFSP	Common Foreign and Security Policy
COMP	Competitiveness (Council formation)
COREPER	Committee of Permanent Representatives
CSCE	Conference on Security and Cooperation
DFCR	Common Frame of Reference
DG	Directorate General
DRC	Democratic Republic of Congo
EASA	European Advertising Standards Alliance
EBB	Electronic Board Bulletin
EC	European Community
ECAP	European Capabilities Action Plan
ECJ	European Court of Justice
ECOFIN	Economic and Financial Affairs (Council formation)
EDA	European Defence Agency
EDC	European Defence Community
EEC	European Economic Community
EES	European Employment Strategy
EFP	European Foreign Policy
EFTA	European Free Trade Area
EIB	European Investment Bank
EMCDDA	European Monitoring Centre for Drugs and Drug Addiction
EMU	Economic and Monetary Union
ENV	Environment (Council formation)
EP	European Parliament

EPC	Economic Policy Committee
EPC	European Political Cooperation
ERDF	European Regional Development Fund
ESDP	European Security and Defence Policy
ETSI	European Telecommunications Standards Institute
EU	European Union
EUFOR	European Union Force
EUMC	European Monitoring Centre on Racism and Xenophobia
EUPM	European Union Police Mission
EYC	Education Youth and Culture (Council formation)
FRA	EU Agency for Fundamental Rights
GDP	Gross domestic product
IASB	International Accounting Standards Board
IFRS	International Financial Reporting Standards
IGC	Intergovernmental Conference
IMF	International Monetary Fund
JHA	Justice and home affairs
MA	Managing Authority
MC	Monitoring committee
NGO	Nongovernmental Organization
NMG	New mode of governance
NSR	National strategy report
NUTS	Nomenclature of Territorial Units for Statistics
OECD	Organisation for Economic Co-operation and Development
OLP	Ordinary legislative procedure
OMC	Open Method of Coordination
OP	Operational programmes
QMV	Qualified Majority Voting
R&D	Research and Development
SDP	Sustainable Development Policy
SEA	Single European Act
SGP	Stability and Growth Pact
SMV	Simple Majority Voting
SOC	Employment, Social Policy, Health and Consumer Affairs (Council formation)
SPC	Social Protection Committee
TEU	Treaty on European Union
TFEU	Treaty on the Functioning of the European Union
TNC	Transnational corporation
TREN	Transport, Telecommunication and Energy (Council formation)

UK	United Kingdom
UNAN	Unanimity Voting
VEA	Voluntary Environmental Agreement
WEU	Western European Union

1. The dynamics of change in EU governance

Udo Diedrichs, Wulf Reiners and Wolfgang Wessels

THE PROFILE OF THE VOLUME

The examination and debate concerning modes of governance in the European Union (EU) has belonged to the most interesting and stimulating issues of relevance for both the academic as well as the political world in the last decade. Still, there is little consensus on what modes of governance exactly are and how far they have changed over recent years (Diedrichs et al., 2011; Peters and Pierre, 2009; Kohler-Koch and Larat, 2009; Kohler-Koch and Rittberger, 2009; Tömmel, 2008; Wallace, 2005). Some crucial questions have been posed which still wait for answers. Have new modes of governance replaced older, more traditional patterns, or have they simply complemented the procedural and institutional landscape of the EU without revealing a major impact on pre-existing types?

It seems rather difficult to explain in which way new modes of governance are related to 'old' modes and to which ones in particular. While it is true that old and new modes can only be distinguished with some difficulty, they are still useful for heuristic reasons. The contributions to this volume will take this debate as an incentive to describe the dynamics and changes of and within the EU system.

The relevance of this endeavour is underlined by the dynamics of the EU's institutional and constitutional development which has found a new stage with the conclusion and coming into force of the Lisbon Treaty. The new provisions on the legal architecture of the EU, particularly with regard to the definition of areas of competences and the decision-making procedures, offer a number of opportunities which the EU institutions and member states will be able to use in the coming years (Hofmann and Wessels, 2008). While the implementation of the Lisbon Treaty remains a subject for future analysis – at least for the foreseeable future – the treaty provides a concluding step in the process of shaping and reshaping the basic constitutional framework of EU governance. Thus, it may be seen as the result of experiences and lessons learned from the past for which the contributions to this volume present some empirical and conceptual insights in a number of key policy areas.

Having these developments in mind, our main focus will be on the changing fabric of governance in the EU up to the Treaty of Lisbon as the result of a productive tension between the legal and the living architecture of the EU. Our key question is: What changes have taken place in EU governance, and which factors can be identified that account for such change?

This question will serve as the overall guiding perspective of the volume, which will help us to analyse the dynamics of EU governance in a number of key policy areas over recent years and to define explanatory variables for these processes. Starting from this general mission, the volume addresses three more specific tasks:

- It will link the research on modes of governance to the analysis of the basic legal, institutional and procedural features of the EU system over recent years. How have changes to the legal architecture such as treaty reforms promoted the emergence of new modes of governance?
- It will offer empirically dense analyses of different policy areas in a comparative perspective, enhancing our understanding of the real forms and patterns of EU governance. Which patterns and trends can be identified, and do we observe divergence or convergence?
- It will relate the results of the research undertaken to a coherent explanatory approach on the evolution of the EU system as a whole. Is there an overall cross-pillar mode of evolution for the whole EU system?

To begin with, Anne Peters (Chapter 2) explores the different types and forms of soft law in the EU from a legal perspective, providing a systematic overview for mapping modes of governance. While new modes of EU governance are regularly associated with a growing use of non-binding, informal and unorthodox instruments and procedures of decision-making, her chapter reveals that soft forms of governance are not so radically new and recent, but have been used in different shapes and constellations by the EU since its inception. She distinguishes in particular different (pre-legal) functions of soft law and their relationship with binding legal acts, further institutionalization and 'hardening' of decision-making, thereby depicting a more complex image of the EU's legal repertoire. As a prominent expression of such 'soft' mechanisms Colin Shaw (Chapter 3) presents a comprehensive overview of the Open Method of Coordination (OMC) which has been labelled as paradigmatic for new modes of governance. He discusses different approaches to OMC, categorizes them in a systematic manner according to their institutional features, their performance and deficiencies, and hints at their path-finding function, testing the ground for further steps in institutionalization. David Natali then focuses on the OMC in the field of pension reform which has been widely regarded as weak and rather under-institutionalized, and he looks for the factors that account for the emergence of the process by using a 'window of opportunity' approach, which identifies relevant actors and mechanisms (Chapter 4). More classical European Community (EC) areas, social policy and environmental policy, are dealt with by Oliver Treib, Holger Bähr and Gerda Falkner (Chapter 5) who compare the emergence and evolution of these two fields, which both started from a similar point outside the EC/EU Treaties, but then took rather different paths of development with regard to their modes of governance. They use a threefold model for modes of governance, which includes the analysis of decision-making procedures and the quality of legal acts, placing high importance on the question of binding versus non-binding instruments over time. Kálmán Dezséri and Krisztina Vida (Chapter 6) adopt a multi-level governance approach in order to describe the changes that occurred in implementation of the EU's cohesion policy in the new member states. They define modes of governance as a concept which relates to the interaction between the EU and member states.

In order to cover all relevant EU pillars, Udo Diedrichs (Chapter 7) follows the development of the Common Foreign and Security Policy (CFSP) and the Common Security and Defence Policy (CSDP) in an attempt to identify the dynamics which have taken place in the shadow of intergovernmentalism, leading towards a number of innovative forms of governance beyond or below the conventional Community model. In particular, he identifies trends regarding the introduction of softer forms of intergovernmentalism, in the shape of a weak coordination mechanism for military capability improvement and a nascent regime for cooperation in the defence industry.

Jörg Monar (Chapter 8) covers the area of freedom, security and justice, which has undergone impressive changes, particularly after the coming into force of the Amsterdam Treaty; here, we find a number of different soft and hard instruments at work, the use of which is related to the dynamics in the legal architecture of the EU, offering new incentives for decision-making. Taking the legal quality of instruments as a key indicator for changes taking place in the field of justice and home affairs (JHA), the author reveals a highly mixed picture with regard to different subareas.

Finally, Udo Diedrichs (Chapter 9) presents an analysis of the legal and the living architecture of the EU from the 1950s until the Treaty of

Lisbon, comparing the formal provisions for decision-making, their actual use over time and the shifts that have taken place between different modes. This chapter underlines the close link which we establish between the evolution of the EU system as a whole and the emergence and evolution of modes of governance, which we assume are closely interrelated. Thus, with all the nitty-gritty details accumulated in the single chapters, the general perspective will be kept on the 'big picture' – or even 'big movie' – of the EU system, capturing the broader development.

Before finally presenting an explanatory approach for the dynamics of EU governance, integrating the trends and patterns visible in the single policy fields into a consistent model for the evolution of the EU system, we draw general conclusions by assessing and evaluating the results of research of the individual chapters by relating them to the general and conceptual questions of the volume.

OUR APPROACH TO EU GOVERNANCE

In the last decade governance has become a prominent and widely debated concept in social sciences whose precise meaning remains unclear, however, as there is no consensus on its features and contents (Kohler-Koch and Rittberger, 2009). Generally speaking, governance refers to patterns of interaction and coordination of social and/or political actors for the purpose of adopting and implementing collectively binding decisions (Peters and Pierre, 2009: 91–3). It includes the preparation, adoption, implementation and control of decisions, revealing both a structural and a process dimension. Thus it is embedded into institutional structures defining the rules of the game, as well as specific interaction principles guiding the actors' capacities, behaviour and orientations. For our purpose, we have to specify the notion of governance in a way which allows us to analyse the features of EU policy-making and the changes that have occurred over time. Therefore we will use it as a framework for the description and analysis of the procedures and output of EU decision-making in the context of the EU's legal and living architecture. Thus, we distinguish our understanding from those approaches that focus primarily on the implementation of decisions and in particular from those focusing on impact of the EU at the national level.

While the concepts of governance and of modes of governance used by the authors in this volume offer a range of different perspectives, which is mainly due to the particular policy areas and conceptual preferences in play, they still fit into this framework and make it available for comparative research. Mapping modes of governance is a key element taken up in each chapter. At the same time, our key point of orientation is the 'supranational method', also referred to as the 'Community method', as the conventional mode of EU governance, characterized by supranational decision-making procedures and the production of legally binding instruments (Kohler-Koch and Rittberger, 2009: 7; Wallace, 2005; Scharpf, 2003). We are fully aware that the Community method has never been the one and only way for policy-making in the EC/EU, and that it exists in a number of variants concerning the precise institutional and procedural provisions, but it can be used as an ideal-type model against which other forms and patterns may be compared and evaluated. At the other extreme stands the model of classical intergovernmental cooperation outside the treaties, while in between we find different mixtures and combinations, such as the OMC, which was the paradigmatic model for 'new' modes of governance (Borrás and Jacobsson, 2004; de la Porte and Nanz, 2004). In this perspective, the question about new versus old modes of governance will be addressed in a way that takes the co-existence of different modes of governance for granted and tries to assess the shifts and reforms that have taken place and which have been particularly fuelled by institutional and constitutional reforms (see Chapter 9 by Udo Diedrichs on the legal and living architecture).

In this regard, innovation of governance refers to a complex matter. In a particular policy area, new modes may be identified as innovative in the sense that they have not so far been experienced and are untested. But it may also mean that already familiar ways of decision-making in certain policy areas are introduced in other areas, that old modes are incrementally adjusted, or that the mix of modes has changed over time (Diedrichs, 2005).

Thus, modes of governance are regarded as 'new' (Diedrichs et al., 2011: 23) if and when:

- innovative modes of decision-making, at least initially outside the existing treaty provisions, are introduced, such as the OMC;
- 'old' institutional and procedural provisions on decision-making are transformed or further developed, particularly by up- or downgrading existing modes;
- the mix between different old and/or innovative ways of decision-making is changed by enhancing certain modes in favour of others;
- the nature of the policy instruments (binding/non-binding decisions) is shifted in the direction of either hard law or soft law.

These assumptions may warn us again against using the idea of new modes of governance in a too homogeneous and narrow sense, hinting at only one direction of innovation. It requires a contextual perspective that takes into account the composition and configuration of different features of a policy area over time. At the same time, it hints at a tension between the developments at the policy level, which may reveal rather peculiar trends and features, and the EU system level. The question arises as to whether it is possible at all to put all the findings together into a coherent analytical and explanatory framework which gives new insights into the process of European integration.

As a common point of reference the set of two basic expectations may be contrasted and tested in order to help us sharpen an overall perspective:

1. The evolution of the EU system is increasingly tending towards a diversification of modes of governance, making it ever more difficult to identify common institutional features and an overall dynamics which could be described and explained by integration theory. New modes are considered as innovative attempts to find methods for decision-making which may not fit the conventional forms of the supranational method, but still try to enhance the set of common approaches in order to tackle problems arising from growing interdependence among the member states. While reflecting a high degree of variety and differentiation, the forms they take are regarded as temporary and transitional, open to further upgrading and enhancements at later stages. Here, some kind of 'circular relationship' (Peters and Pierre, 2009: 102) or 'integrative spiral' is at work: new forms of governance in the real world lead to adaptations in the legal architecture which, in turn, provide opportunities again for new forms. Though not fully consistent with the traditional forms of EU decision-making, these forms are nevertheless compatible with the broader trends of the EU system, serving as a pathfinder for further communitarization. In other words, new modes can be observed in the form of a shift in the pattern of institutional interaction. They take place when the states' problem-solving instinct is initially stopped for a certain period by the sovereignty reflex, which is then eroded. Despite the emergence and evolution of different modes of governance in the EU, there are common features and even an overarching dynamics at play, reflected by a growing convergence of modes of governance towards supranational modes.

2. A second expectation, which is opposed to the first, sees new modes of governance as a reflection of the loss of an overall trend in the institutional development of the EU, leading to a high degree of differentiation and even fragmentation between and among policy areas. In general, they are regarded as a weakening of the supranational method, whose attraction for the member states has lost consider-

ably in value and weight over recent years, reflecting not necessarily a reversal of the basic integrationist dynamics, but a need for peculiar institutional and procedural solutions within distinct areas of political and legal action, thus breaking up the familiar set-up of the Union and leading to a new range of fuzzy and often confusing provisions.

The tension between these expectations may not be settled once and for all, but it could at least be determined in which direction the balance is leaning. We will take up these assumptions and try to offer an answer by putting the pieces of empirical findings together into a conceptually and theoretically inspired explanatory approach on the dynamics of EU governance.

THE LEGAL AND THE LIVING ARCHITECTURE OF THE EU: FORGING MODES OF GOVERNANCE

Basically, we assume that the emergence and evolution of governing modes are interrelated with the legal and living architecture of the EU whose interplay adds new dynamics to the integration process. This also means that we cannot separate the discussion about modes of governance from the overall evolution of the EU system, as has become apparent particularly in the treaty changes over recent decades, with the Lisbon Treaty as – probably – the final stage in this process for the years to come (Hofmann and Wessels, 2008). Those treaty reforms, adopted formally by the European Council, reflect basic demands for the institutional and procedural landscape of the EU to be adjusted, in response to major internal and external challenges.

Thus, as a starting point, it is important to describe the dynamics of the overall development of the EU system as a whole, as laid down in the treaties (Wessels, 1997, 2001, 2005). Traditionally, the Community has been marked by a high degree of supranational decision-making, accompanied by the production of legally binding output. The supranational method became the paradigmatic way of decision-making, distinguishing the EC from other more traditional variants of international organizations (Wallace, 2005). The evolution of the EU system over time has brought an expansion of policy areas, but the more fields were covered, the more difficult did it prove to maintain the supranational method as a predominant pattern of decision-making.

The changing legal architecture of the EU has opened windows of opportunity for the further development of the EU system. New forms of governance distinct from the classical Community method were introduced without replacing older patterns of decision-making from the repertoire of procedural and institutional provisions.

The analysis of treaty-based provisions for the shaping of governing modes is undertaken by Udo Diedrichs in his concluding chapter on the perspectives of the legal and the living architecture of the EU, which identifies a number of trends in the strengthening of supranational decision-making powers across all EU policy areas. The legal architecture has strengthened the foundations for the use of supranational decision-making, while at the same time opening up the space for combinations of different institutional and procedural provisions. Fundamentally, the treaty reforms since the Single European Act opened ways for Qualified Majority Voting (QMV) in the Council, and the Treaties of Maastricht, Amsterdam, Nice and Lisbon were even more crucial for extending opportunity structures for supranational decision-making, particularly via the co-decision procedure. Since the mid-1990s, this trend has been accompanied by a differentiation process, expressed in the introduction of the OMC and a further increase in combinations of decision-making procedures. Some of the new modes, such as forms of the OMC, have been included in the Lisbon Treaty (for example Art. 168 and 173 TFEU).

While treaty changes provide opportunities, incentives and constraints for decision-making in the EU, the analysis of the living architecture of the EU system reveals that the treaty provisions have been intensively used by the actors. Since Maastricht, supranational policy-making has been dynamically expanded, and the stronger engagement of the European Parliament in co-decision and consent – although still not constituting the majority of EP activity – shows the growing importance of the new provisions on enhanced parliamentary participation. As regards policy output, the adoption of instruments by soft law is much less of an overall development: it depends instead on the specific nature of the policy area, the political will of the member states, and the resistance of domestic social, economic and political structures to European solutions.

These general findings are complemented by the contributions of the authors in their respective policy areas. Of particular importance is the case of justice and home affairs (JHA), where the creation of the area of freedom, security and justice in 1999 through the Treaty of Amsterdam and the communitarization of fields such as immigration and visa policy have opened new opportunities for decision-makers to use more efficient decision-making procedures and adopt more binding instruments. A major further step in the legal implementation might come from the new supranational basis in the Lisbon Treaty. Also in EC policy areas such as social and environmental policy, the provisions of primary law have been intensively used by the EU in order to adopt legal acts, leading particularly in social policy to a growing role for co-decision and an increase of binding legal acts.

Colin Shaw highlights different levels of institutionalization which distinguish OMCs from each other. While a treaty base is considered as a necessary condition for OMCs to develop fully, the entry into force of the Lisbon Treaty could widen the constitutional foundation for a number of OMCs. In all cases a key role is ascribed to the European Council in defining the objectives of the process, so that a link with the overall institutional framework of the EU is preserved. In Shaw's view, OMC may be regarded not only as a substitution of the supranational method, but also as complementary to it, and could even be seen as a 'pathfinder for new areas of communitarization' (see Chapter 3 by Colin Shaw).

THE EMERGENCE, EVOLUTION AND EVALUATION OF GOVERNING MODES: PATTERNS AND TRENDS

While the legal architecture is regarded as a major source of dynamics for the EU system, it does not provide for a single model of governance. Change in EU governance does not take place homogeneously across all areas of EU activities; therefore it is necessary to take the specific conditions of the different policy fields into account. The empirical analysis identifies different stages in which modes of governance appear and develop. Starting with the emergence of different modes, it follows their progress over time, and thus aims to describe and explain the evolution of EU governance.

THE EMERGENCE OF MODES OF GOVERNANCE

The emergence of modes of governance has been driven by a number of factors which push and pull the process. On the one hand, specific policy objectives have been in play; on the other the institutional concerns of the member states and EU institutions and windows of opportunity have been highly relevant. Economic competitiveness, social protection as well as internal and external security appear as the key driving motivations, while the preservation of sensitive or sovereignty-loaded areas which should not fall under the full rule of EC Treaty law, served as a major source of institutional concern against supranational decision-making. This rationale has been particularly assumed to be in play for the establishment of OMC. Common wisdom suggests that new modes of governance have emerged in order to solve policy problems without resorting exclusively to the conventional supranational method, which is considered too costly for member states in terms of concerns over national sovereignty and autonomy, the preservation of individual countries' historical legacies, or protecting sensitive issue areas where uncertainty over EU decision-making has prevailed.

As Colin Shaw and David Natali point out, the Lisbon strategy has been a major driving force for the introduction of OMC. Ever since, coordination processes have seen a phase of expansion and differentiation. Ever more fields have been covered by coordination, while the specific wording of the procedure has been adjusted for each particular case. The authors also hint at the crucial role of the European Council in initiating coordination mechanisms and in defining their policy objectives (see Chapters 3 and 4 by Colin Shaw and David Natali). In the areas of pension reform or social inclusion, coordination processes describe rather diffuse goals, coupled with the use of legally non-binding commitments for achieving them, while in employment policy or in research policy at least the targets are more specific (although still without legally binding commitments).

Policy failures or policy gaps have also been adduced as leading to the introduction or improvement of modes of governance when it comes to tackling the major challenges facing modern welfare systems (employment flexibility, ageing societies or declining environmental standards). Furthermore, the external standing and role of the EU has also played a major role in driving the development of modes of governance, both in economic terms under the Lisbon heading and with regard to the CFSP and the ESDP, whose development is not least a reaction to the changed international security environment (Diedrichs, 2008). In the intergovernmental pillars of Maastricht, the CFSP and JHA, modes of governance came into play basically as a reaction to the deficiencies of classical intergovernmental bargaining and its limitations for solving policy problems, while avoiding a move towards traditional and fully-fledged patterns of communitarization (see Chapter 7 by Udo Diedrichs on CFSP and Chapter 8 by Jörg Monar on JHA).

While in the CFSP modes of governance were mainly located in the sphere of intergovernmentalism, adding elements of differentiation through the cautious introduction of other variants, JHA can be taken as an example of a policy area which has been transferred – only with some still persisting exceptions in the Lisbon Treaty – from intergovernmental cooperation to more supranational oriented policy-making through treaty change. In this regard, a major juncture has been the Amsterdam Treaty, providing for the communitarization of visa, asylum, immigration and other policies concerning the free movement of persons, which in itself has had rather diverse impacts on the modes of governance resulting from this transfer, revealing a dividing line between sovereignty-loaded areas, where mainly non-binding measures have been taken, and those areas that are amenable to more binding instruments. Pressure and demands for more effective problem-solving, of spillover and of EU enlargement, account for this process. The member states have tried to open a window for higher levels of supranational decision-making in certain policy sectors of JHA, not least out of fear that the accession of new member states might lead to a dilution of the *acquis*. The Lisbon Treaty has then moved nearly all intergovernmental articles into the supranational mode of the 'ordinary legislative procedure'.

In total, the emergence of new modes of governance has followed a particular pattern: new modes have rarely replaced traditional patterns of decision-making, but rather have been used in a complementary way. They emerge in order to cover policy areas where coordinated action by all member states is regarded as necessary and useful, but where there is no explicit reference or only a rather weak reference within the EC Treaty as originally existing – for example, in the case of the introduction of the OMC on pension reform (rather disperse references in the EC Treaty), social policy or environmental policy (see Chapter 5 by Oliver Treib, Holger Bähr and Gerda Falkner). More centralized forms of decision-making co-exist along with less hierarchical modes and less binding instruments.

THE EVOLUTION OF MODES OF GOVERNANCE

On a macro-level of the EU system as a whole, we come to the conclusion that the use of specific legal instruments has undergone changes, primarily with the entry into force of the Amsterdam Treaty, while no major shift from binding to more non-binding acts on the overall EU level can be detected. The more policy-specific chapters of this volume add up to this analysis by referring to the still growing use of binding legal acts, even in broader policy areas where in general less binding instruments are at work (see Chapter 8 by Jörg Monar).

Shifts in modes of EU governance are subject to dynamics which appear more incremental than 'revolutionary', leading to new institutional and procedural solutions triggering a process of differentiation. We find elements of mixture and combination, with trends in the direction of more supranational, hierarchical modes in the context of complexity and evolutionary enhancement. The evolution of modes of governance thus reveals a complex and multicoloured picture which is characterized by an overall systemic dynamics and as well as policy-specific trends that reflect specific conditions in play.

The expansion of OMC processes since the 1990s shows some major trends. Almost all of these mechanisms have been triggered and pushed by European Council decisions taking the lead in shaping these modes, confirming its role as the 'architect' of modes of governance in the EU (Wessels, forthcoming). Second, the Lisbon strategy of 2000 has been a key factor in policy terms for creating new cases and has served as a model of inspiration for a number of policy areas where an 'export' of coordination mechanisms has been observed. The treaty base is rather disparate for coordination processes (the legal base may be strong or weak in the sense that references in the primary law are in some cases explicit and in others more diffuse), but it is hardly ever really absent, which means that the coordination mechanisms introduced have not simply been developed as parallel structures in isolation from the legal framework of the Union, but refer to key objectives and provisions of primary law. In most cases common objectives for all member states have been defined. Thus coordination processes, although deviating from the conventional supranational method, regularly take up elements of it in order to provide for coherence and consistency across member states.

In social and environmental policy (see Chapter 5 by Oliver Treib, Holger Bähr and Gerda Falkner), although their starting conditions were similar, the original mode of intergovernmental negotiations was progressively replaced by more supranational decision-making forms in the wake of institutional reform starting as early as with the Single European Act. However, each policy has developed a particular profile due to different conditions as regards the domestic heritage, regulatory requirements and the transnational problem pressure. In social policy, core areas of national welfare states, such as social security, funding for employment policy and collective interest representation, have remained subject to unanimity, while health and safety in the workplace, working conditions and information for workers have been opened for QMV. This division has been further differentiated by the rather fuzzy relation between procedural mode and legal instrument, particularly with respect to the binding nature or otherwise of legal acts. However, it also becomes clear that binding instruments are not in decline, but are rising in number, although the trend is not so strong. The EU is thus continuing a highly intensive use of instruments, using binding and non-binding tools in parallel.

On the other hand, in environmental policy, the picture appears to be the opposite: binding instruments have been adopted increasingly since the 1990s, whereas the rise of non-binding policy output has been less steep. However, developments in both social and environmental policy reveal the mix which is in play where the use of different policy instruments is concerned, as well as the fact that there is an overall dynamics in the evolution of the legal output, so that the issue of new and old modes of governance in the EU – with regard to the policy dimension – may be taken not as a sign of an overall stagnation of the classical methods of steering but rather as a reflection of a differentiation of the toolset available for integration.

In the Second Pillar, the CFSP, major dynamics in governance have been delivered by the establishment of the European Security and Defence Policy since 1998 (St Malo) and 1999 (Cologne Summit), which led to the introduction of (cautious) incentives for coordination (in the area of improvement of military capabilities, which is subject to a regular review) and for delegation (by the creation of the European Defence Agency), in the shadow of intergovernmental negotiations (see Chapter 7 by Udo Diedrichs on CFSP). These were rooted in institutional agreements among the member states deliberately choosing options outside the formal framework of the treaties, before being partially included in the legal architecture of the Union by the Treaty of Lisbon.

In the field of justice and home affairs, the rise in numbers of binding legal acts reflects a major shift in EU governance since the times of the Maastricht Third Pillar. Jörg Monar reveals that the provisions of the Amsterdam Treaty have been seriously exploited by the EU. Its rhythm of intensity has been marked by the European Council's programme documents (Tampere, The Hague), by the respective deadlines set for the implementation of measures, and by enlargement, when the old EU member states tried to realize as much of their programme schedule as possible.

While in general the use of non-binding instruments exceeds the binding acts, in specific sub-areas the record is highly surprising. Trends away from intergovernmentalism are particularly relevant in fields such as civil law cooperation and visa policy, while they have been more limited in others such as police cooperation. Monar attributes these differences to the sensitivity of the area involved, the executive nature of some particular fields of cooperation, and to the overall concern about sovereignty. Of particular interest is the fact that the use of binding versus non-binding instruments in JHA crosses the pillar lines; areas of the former Third Pillar such as judicial cooperation in criminal matters are more intensively handled by binding legal acts, while communitarized matters such as immigration reveal a higher proportion of non-binding instruments. This trend is labelled by Monar as a growing hybridization of governing modes, overcoming the traditional legal divide of the EU pillars.

To sum up, the development of modes of governance in the former Second and Third Pillars has been moving prudently 'closer' to the supranational method, including innovative mix and combination of policy sectors, while in the area of the (former) European Community the conquest of new spheres of action for the EU has also tried to evade the supranational method as too costly for the member states in economic, institutional and political terms. In the CFSP, where new instruments have remained mainly intergovernmental, the supranational method is still further away, while in JHA different modes and trends towards hybridization co-exist much more frequently, and tight forms of legislation have had a strong impact. So far, new modes of governance thus represent the changing composition of governance in particular policy areas rather than fully innovative phenomena. Furthermore, this changing composition is less a mix or combination in the strict sense than the co-existence or parallelism of different modes of governance which is to be observed across policy areas. The supranational methods thus play a twofold role: as an obstacle or threshold (which the member states first try to avoid), and at the same time as a longer-term line of convergence (when transformations become visible in the direction of more Community-related modes). In all these cases, therefore, the supranational method may serve as the point of orientation for the dynamics of modes of governance in the EU and the legal provisions of the Lisbon Treaty generally support this trend (see Chapter 9 by Udo Diedrichs).

THE EVALUATION OF GOVERNING MODES IN THE EU: REVIEWING THE RESULTS

When it comes to the evaluation of different governing modes, a stable pattern appears across the contributions to this volume; softer modes suffer from a lack of effectiveness and efficiency and face problems in legitimacy. Colin Shaw describes the record of OMC procedures as generally disappointing due to the modest fulfilment of self-defined targets in terms of achieving benchmarks among the member states, sketching a rather gloomy outlook for the future of such coordination processes. While member states favour the rather convenient way of coordination, they do not seem to respond to adaptational pressures affecting their policies. In a similar way, David Natali reaches a sober judgement on policy learning in pension reform, for which there is little room and poor hope. Jörg Monar arrives at a similar conclusion with regard to non-binding instruments used in JHA, where the soft modes are facing obvious problems in achieving sufficient discipline among the member states when it comes to the implementation of decisions. In CFSP, as non-coercive measures are the normal case, commitments by the member states in achieving certain benchmarks (particularly on military capabilities) remain frail and uneven. Oliver Treib, Holger Bähr and Gerda Falkner attribute the different evolutionary paths in social policy and environmental policy basically to member states' interests and preferences resulting from structural conditions at the domestic level, and Kálmán Dezséri and Krisztina Vida identify a number of structural problems among the new member states as underlying reasons for problems in implementing partnership-based modes of governance in cohesion policy.

A conclusion that may be drawn from these findings is that without formally binding commitments it remains extremely difficult to set coherent and effective policies in place. Expectations on voluntary and peer-based processes of learning and mutual persuasion do not provide for the necessary impetus needed either for efficient decision-making or effective policy-shaping. In our view, these deficiencies create demands for change and reform, which may be taken up at the European level and be translated into revisions of the legal architecture of the EU. A particular field where this may be identified concerns the coordination of economic and social policies, explicitly mentioned in the Lisbon Treaty as an area of EU competence. This wording does not take up the label OMC, but tries to establish a closer link between a number of coordination mechanisms and the treaty framework.

A second conclusion concerns the role of the member states in the initiating and shaping of EU modes of governance. Their relevance, not only in the traditional *domaine reservé* of the former Second and Third Pillar, but also in OMC and in Community-based policies, is highlighted by the analyses in this volume. Colin Shaw describes the weakness of OMC as a function of member states' interests in protecting themselves from Community interference, while David Natali highlights Belgium and Italy as political entrepreneurs which are considered as essential for using windows of opportunity when it comes to initiating the OMC on pension. Oliver Treib, Holger Bähr and Gerda Falkner point out that the development of new modes in social and environmental policy depends primarily on the interests and preferences voiced by member states. In CFSP and JHA, the impetus of reform and change has been driven by national governments which have reshaped the institutional and constitutional architecture of the Second and Third Pillars since the conclusion of the Maastricht Treaty.

However, their impact can only be fully understood in the context of the institutional framework of the EU. Member states may express preferences for or against certain modes of governance, but when it comes to creating and revisiting those forms, they need to coordinate their actions within the Council and particularly in the European Council. An underlying assumption to be found in all contributions of the volume relies upon the European Council as the principal and architect of modes of governance in the EU (Wessels, forthcoming). Its relevance is reflected basically in the role as key institution for treaty revisions, thus providing the basis for the use of governing modes, furthermore as the most frequent initiator and watchdog of OMC processes, as well as the final decision-maker not only in CFSP and JHA, but also in a growing amount of Community policy-making. The European Council thus serves as the institutional interface for modes of governance, outside and inside the EU, within or across different pillars.

LINKING RESULTS TO THE EVOLUTION OF THE EU SYSTEM: RATCHET FUSION AT WORK?

Taking up the set of two opposing guiding expectations on fragmentation and innovation, we finally aim at presenting an explanatory framework for relating the development of new modes of governance to the evolution of the EU system in general, moving beyond the specific patterns observed in a number of policy areas in all three pillars. These provide empirical evidence for the main trends and directions which allow us to assess the role and impact of new modes of governance for the integration process.

We argue that new modes of governance may well fit an overall institutional and procedural dynamics of the EU system, in which the basic trends over the last 50 years have not been substantially reversed or become subject to fragmentation and break-up. Though not fully consistent with the traditional forms of decision-making, they are nevertheless compatible with the broader trends of the EU system and can be understood as implicit steps to further integration.

It does not come as a surprise that new modes have emerged at a crucial phase of the integration process, linked to policy expansion and the 'conquest' of new areas of competence and responsibility for the EU, and reflecting specific tensions which arise from the member states' interest in tackling problems that are common to the modern welfare states while preserving a high degree of autonomy and capacity for national governments. The key question thus lies in the interpretation of such developments as either a case of productive innovation or of a degeneration and fragmentation of the EU.

Following the metaphor of a 'treaty-based ladder', new modes of governance are emerging and evolving within a general upward trend on the systemic level of the EU (Wessels, 2005, 1997). The steps of this ladder represent stages in the evolution of the legal architecture of the EU, from intergovernmental cooperation outside the treaties at the lowest level, up to shared or exclusive competencies and the supranational method at higher levels. These changes are finally agreed by the member states at the IGCs where treaty reform is concluded. The translation of the legal architecture into political decision-making within the living architecture of the EU is a process which runs in close interrelation with the legal architecture, but is generally smoother and highly pragmatic. Modes of governance come into play when formal provisions based upon the treaties are used in a way which reflects the actual interests and needs of the actors involved who try to secure their influence in the process. In the end, we expect that the experience gained in the living architecture leads to a drive towards 'climbing up the ladder', that is deeper integration. In this manner, the introduction of mechanisms such as OMC highlights the wish of the member states to preserve their influence while allowing for common approaches in certain policy areas. The actual perceived failure of OMC in terms of effectiveness reinforces the trends towards communitarization.

In line with the first guiding expectation from the outset, we regard new modes of governance as transitional and temporary phenomena, which aim at the inclusion of new policy areas or at the strengthening of existing cooperation without – initially – employing the traditional Community method.

This interpretation holds that modes of governance reflect stages of approximation towards the supranational method, although at different speeds and in differentiated stages, leading to a certain degree of fuzziness and a lack of transparency when it comes to describing the transition between one already reached plateau of the integration ladder and the next. It is here that an 'integrative spiral' (Diedrichs et al., 2011: 25) shows its impact. Discussions and decisions on new steps in the integration process are a result of experience gained and lessons learned at earlier stages. These stages are not neatly distinguished, but include a range of highly mixed, differentiated and hybrid arrangements in various policy areas which are open to upgrading and deepening at a later stage, but do not neatly fit all demands for a clear-cut set of intra- and interinstitutional as well as procedural provisions. The rule of thumb could even be formulated as follows: the higher the ladder goes in the transfer of competencies, particularly reaching those of a sensitive nature – be it in economic, social, political or security terms – the more complicated the transition becomes and the more likely member states will be to look for innovative interim solutions, not primarily in order to block further developments of problem-solving, but for the sake of retaining control and gaining experience. Our empirical research has confirmed that this is the window of opportunity for new modes of governance, whose concrete shape depends upon the policy area in question and the features of the policy issues in play. There may be spillover, but the new modes of governance do not provide an unequivocal institutional and procedural solution. The supranational Community method represents a long-term goal and serves as an orientation point against which changes and reforms are often measured.

Shifts in modes of EU governance are thus subject to dynamics which are more incremental than revolutionary, leading to new institutional and procedural solutions that trigger off a process of differentiation. Instead of a consistent, clear-cut architecture we find elements of mixture and combination, with trends in the direction of more supranational modes in the context of complexity and evolutionary enhancement. New modes of governance have emerged and evolved as a result of policy demands, particularly in areas that have been transferred from intergovernmental cooperation in spheres where sovereignty concerns are particularly pronounced to more Community-oriented fields of policy-making without always adopting the traditional supranational method. The Lisbon Treaty has reinforced this direction. This transfer, taking place along with an increasing upgrading of the decision-making procedures, has not necessarily changed the mainly intergovernmental nature of particular areas, but has rather opened up dynamics where either close relations to EC policies exist (defence industry) or policy gaps have had to be addressed. However, older modes have rarely been replaced by more innovative ones. Instead, different modes and trends towards hybridization co-exist much more frequently. So far, therefore, new modes represent the changing composition in modes of governance in particular policy areas.

In other words, new modes of governance do not modify the EU system in the sense of breaking the general trend towards further integration, but rather have to be understood as an integral element of the EU integration process. They have been introduced by establishing innovative mechanisms of decision-making whose impact and effectiveness have been generally weak in policy terms but rather successful in preserving member states' autonomy and discretion of action. The power allocation should therefore also be seen in the light of the competencies which have been opened for the EU at the cost of temporarily accepting new modes as transitional means for handling these competencies. The temporary deviation from the supranational Community method may be regarded as a weakening of the EU institutional and procedural framework, particularly at the expense of the European Commission, the European Parliament and the European Court of Justice, and to the benefit of the member states. On the other hand, it may also be seen as a creative and innovative answer of the member states to the problem of achieving institutional solutions where consensus is frail, policy objectives are not broadly shared, and the political will to transfer further competencies is uneven.

The evidence collected in this volume mainly covers the last decade from the end of the 1990s onwards – that means between the entry in force of the Amsterdam and the Nice Treaty to the start of the Lisbon Treaty. As it could not take into account the financial and economic crisis from 2008 onwards, the task is now to study how the reformed legal architecture and provisions affect the living architecture in a changed economic and social environment. Here, member states – caught in the dilemma between a problem-solving instinct and the sovereignty reflex – are expected to use extensively the institutional offer of the Lisbon Treaty. By dealing concretely with a problem on the agenda of public policies they might also face the need to further develop several modes of governance with a rising proportion following the conventional supranational method, thus laying the ground for dynamics of further change of EU governance.

REFERENCES

Borrás, Susanna and Kerstin Jacobsson (2004), 'The open method of coordination and new governance patterns in the EU', *Journal of European Public Policy*, Special Issue, **11**(2), 185–208.
de la Porte, Caroline and Patrizia Nanz (2004), 'The OMC: a deliberative-democratic mode of governance? The cases of employment and pensions', *Journal of European Public Policy*, Special Issue, **11**(2), 267–88.
Diedrichs, Udo (2005), 'New modes of governance: preliminary remarks about an ambiguous concept', paper presented at the NEWGOV Conference, May 2005, Cluster One Meeting.
Diedrichs, Udo (2008), 'Neue Dynamik in der Europäischen Außen- und Sicherheitspolitik: auf dem Weg zu einer Security Governance', in Ingeborg Tömmel (ed.), *Die Europäische Union. Governance und Policy-Making*, Politische Vierteljahresschrift Sonderheft (40), Wiesbaden: Verlag für Sozialwissenschaften, pp. 343–64.
Diedrichs, Udo, Wulf Reiners and Wolfgang Wessels (2011), 'New modes of governance: policy developments and the hidden steps of EU integration', in Adrienne Héritier and Martin Rhodes (eds), *New Modes of Governance: Governing in the Shadow of Hierarchy*, Basingstoke, UK and New York: Palgrave.
Hofmann, Andreas and Wolfgang Wessels (2008), 'Der Vertrag von Lissabon – eine tragfähige und abschließende Antwort auf konstitutionelle Grundfragen?', *Integration*, **1**, 3–20.
Kohler-Koch, Beate and Fabrice Larat (2009), 'Introduction: research on EU multi-level governance', in Beate Kohler-Koch and Fabrice Larat (eds), *European Multi-Level Governance*, Cheltenham, UK and Northampton, MA, USA: Edward Elgar, pp. xix–xxviii.
Kohler-Koch, Beate and Bertold Rittberger (2009), 'A futile quest for coherence: the many frames of EU governance', in Beate Kohler-Koch and Fabrice Larat (eds), *European Multi-Level Governance*, Cheltenham, UK and Northampton, MA, USA: Edward Elgar, pp. 3–18.
Laffan, Brigid and Colin Shaw (2005), 'Classifying and mapping OMC in different policy areas', NEWGOV Paper 02/D09.

Monar, Jörg and Anya Dahmani (2007), 'Specific factors and developments trends of modes of governance in EU justice and home affairs', NEWGOV Policy Brief 3.

Peters, B. Guy and Jon Pierre (2009), 'Governance approaches', in Antje Wiener and Thomas Diez (eds), *European Integration Theory*, 2nd edn, Oxford: Oxford University Press, pp. 91–104.

Scharpf, Fritz W. (2003), 'Problem-solving effectiveness and democratic accountability in the EU', Max Planck Institut für Gesellschaftsforschung, Working Paper 03/1.

Tömmel, Ingeborg (ed.) (2008), 'Die Europäische Union. Governance und Policy-Making', *Politische Vierteljahresschrift*, Sonderheft (40), Wiesbaden: Verlag für Sozialwissenschaften.

Wallace, Helen (2005), 'An institutional anatomy and five policy modes', in Helen Wallace, William Wallace and Mark Pollack (eds), *Policy-Making in the European Union*, 5th edn, Oxford: Oxford University Press, pp. 49–93.

Wessels, Wolfgang (1997), 'An ever closer fusion? A dynamic macropolitical view on integration processes', *Journal of Common Market Studies*, **35**(2), 267–99.

Wessels, Wolfgang (2001), 'Nice results. The Millenium IGC in the EU's evolution', *Journal of Common Market Studies*, **39**(2), 197–219.

Wessels, Wolfgang (2005), 'The constitutional treaty: three readings from a fusion perspective', *Journal of Common Market Studies*, Annual Review 2004/2005, The European Union, pp. 11–36.

Wessels, Wolfgang (forthcoming), *The European Council*, Basingstoke and New York: Palgrave.

2. Soft law as a new mode of governance

Anne Peters[1]

INTRODUCTION

From the beginning, European Community (EC) and European Union (EU) practice has relied on a range of instruments which were not as such legally binding or whose legal status was unclear. Nevertheless, until the turn of the millennium, the concept of European 'soft law' was hardly discussed in the legal scholarly literature.[2] Although some attention has been paid to interinstitutional agreements (Snyder, 1996 and Hummer, 2004), the overall phenomenon of soft regulation has been much less thoroughly explored on the EU level than it has in public international law. Textbooks and general courses on European Union law still either do not mention soft law at all or only treat it in an extremely cursory fashion with only a few standard examples.

Interest in European soft law mounted with the new millennium's debate on European governance and better regulation (European Commission, 2001a). Soft law and self-regulation are meanwhile envisaged by the European institutions themselves as regulatory alternatives (for example in the Commission's 2002 Action Plan Simplifying and Improving the Regulatory Environment; European Commission 2002a: 11–12).

EU modes of governance can be analysed along the two dimensions of steering methods and of actors. Modes may be called (relatively) 'new' when their steering function is characterized by (1) informality and (2) lack of hierarchy, and when private actors (both profit-making and non-profit entities) are systematically involved in policy formulation and/or implementation (Börzel et al., 2005). Joanne Scott and David Trubek highlight the following characteristics of new modes of governance: (a) participation of civil society/of the private sector and therefore a greater degree of power sharing than traditional legislation (process of mutual problem solving); (b) multi-level integration (involvement of various levels of government); (c) diversity and decentralization (acceptance of coordinated diversity instead of creating uniformity across the Union); (d) extended deliberation among stakeholders which serves to improve problem-solving capabilities and to provide some degree of democratic legitimation; (e) flexibility and reversibility (open-ended standards, flexible and revisable guidelines and other forms of soft law); and (f) experimentation and knowledge creation (Scott and Trubek, 2002: 5–6; see also Héritier, 2003; and Treib et al., 2005: 13 ff.).

The juridical concept of soft law is often framed as displaying these features and therefore in a way aligns with those 'new' modes of governance. Of course, both in international law and on the EU level, governance by means of soft law is nothing new. However, two novel features have emerged and evolved only recently. First, soft forms of international and European governance are proliferating dramatically. Note, however, that in EU social policy, for example, 'the proliferation of soft governance mechanisms does not crowd out more traditional hard governance. Although the open method of coordination very much dominates both public and academic discourse nowadays on EU-level social affairs, the number of binding legal instruments (Directives and Regulations) has not yet declined' (Falkner et al., 2005: 350). Second, new forms of governance increasingly involve non-state actors. These novel quantitative and qualitative aspects justify considering soft law (notably private or hybrid – public–private – soft law) as a 'new mode of governance' (NMG) as defined above.

CONCEPTS AND *PROBLÉMATIQUE*

The notion of soft law is quite vague. The European Parliament considers it 'ambiguous' and even 'pernicious', and has recommended 'that the expression of soft law, as well as its invocation, should be avoided at all times in any official documents of the European institutions' (European Parliament 2007: paras A. and AA. 19).[3] Some preliminary conceptual clarification is therefore required.

Soft laws are unquestionably norms (prescriptions/'ought' phrases).[4] However, there is disagreement over whether these norms belong to the realm of law.[5] If they do not, the norms in question would be non-legal, notably political or moral norms. Two fundamentally contrary assessments have been formulated by lawyers: the binary view and the idea of graduated normativity (often called the continuum view). Dinah Shelton summarizes the scholarly debate as follows.

> In respect to 'relative normativity' scholars debate whether binding instruments and non-binding ones are strictly alternative or whether they are two ends on a continuum from legal obligation to complete freedom of action, making

some such instruments more binding than others. If and how the term 'soft law' should be used depends in large part on whether one adopts the binary or continuum view of international law. (Shelton, 2006: 180–81)

The binary view leads to the rejection of the concept of soft law for reasons of legal logic. In contrast, the continuum view holds that normativity may be graduated, and that therefore soft law is conceptually possible (Fuller, 1969: 122–3; Chinkin, 2000: 32; Neuhold, 2005: 47–8; Mörth, 2006: 120). I subscribe to the graduated view and presuppose that soft law is (as the noun in the compound term suggests) a special kind of law. The graduated view best explains reality, because there is no parameter, such as precision of content, formal features such as registration or publication, the intention to be legally bound, or a norm's sanction potential, that allows for a precise delimitation between legal and non-legal norms, or between hard and soft law. No relevant parameter is fully conclusive, and most of the usual criteria may be more or less satisfied. Generally speaking, law (hard and soft) seems to be a phenomenon which cannot be recognized and identified on the basis of an enumeration of predicates. The examination of parameters only makes it possible to identify a prototype of law, with the outer realm of the law being blurry. We can recognize (hard) law more or less readily, depending on a text's closeness to the prototype. The famous dictum of US Supreme Court Justice Potter Stewart on pornography, 'I know it when I see it',[6] illustrates this technique of recognizing a blurry phenomenon and the concept going with it.

Building on the idea of graduated normativity and on the prototype theory of concepts, I submit that *soft law is in the penumbra of law* because it deploys specific legal effects apart from outright legal bindingness, and not merely political or otherwise factual effects.[7] Soft law texts may, in the words of international courts and tribunals, 'even if they are not binding, sometimes have normative value' (International Court of Justice 1996: 226, para. 70).[8] While they have 'a certain legal value, this legal value differs considerably, depending on the type of resolution and the conditions attached to its adoption and provisions'.[9] Soft law should and can more or less readily be distinguished from purely political documents, depending on its closeness to the prototype of law. On the other hand, there is no 'bright line' between hard and soft law. Legal texts can be harder or softer.

The claim that these effects are legal and not merely factual need not be based on the idea that soft law protects legitimate expectations and binds actors on the basis of the principle of good faith. On that argument, soft law is presented as a source of legal obligation through acquiescence and estoppel, perhaps against the intention of the parties (Chinkin, 2000: 31).

However, this appears to be a circular reasoning. The parties involved deliberately 'only' adopt a soft legal instrument. Consequently, only limited expectations are created by such an instrument. Reliance, in the style of Munchhausen pulling himself up from the swamps by his own hair,[10] cannot create legal obligations of strict bindingness.

Rather, I hold European soft law to have legal effects which *flow from the general duty to cooperate* (Art. 4(2) TEU [-Lisbon]). The legal duty of cooperation is the source of a legal obligation of the member states to take European Union soft law into account in some way or the other – without being directly bound by it. The duty of cooperation relates not only to the content and the scope of the obligations but also to the form or their legal effect.

So far, the term '(European) soft law' has not been defined in official EU documents. Scholars usually rely on the definitions elaborated in public international law. Along these lines, soft law in the European realm can be defined as '[r]ules of conduct that are laid down in instruments which have not been attributed legally binding force as such, but nevertheless may have certain (indirect) legal effects, and that are aimed at and may produce practical effects' (Senden, 1994: 112, 456; also Wellens and Borchardt, 1989: 28; Beveridge and Nott, 1998: 290–91; Trubek et al., 2005: 5). Many authors also place the non-binding acts provided for in Article 288 TFEU, namely the European recommendation (by the Council or the Commission) and the opinion (usually issued by the Commission), under that umbrella, as a special, 'formalized' or 'legal' type of soft law (Senden, 2004: 158–89; Bothe, 1981: 761; Beveridge and Nott, 1998: 290; Falkner et al., 2005: 178–9). Recommendations and opinions have, as Article 288 TFEU clearly states, 'no binding force'. These acts will not be dealt with in this chapter, because their formal legal status is not unclear: it is explicitly defined in the Treaty on the Functioning of the European Union (TFEU). The same goes for directives, which are partly 'soft' in terms of substance in that they leave the means of implementation to the member states.

Moreover, this chapter does not deal with soft law under the *EU Treaty*. In the field of the Common Foreign and Security Policy (CFSP) under Title V the EU Treaty provides for a host of instruments whose exact legal effects are diverse and which are less than simply and fully legally binding on the member states.[11] For instance, in the CFSP, the Council shall adopt joint actions and common positions (Article 24 TEU [ex-Arts 14 and 15 TEU]). As this two-policy area has not yet been integrated into the supranational framework, and as the instruments appear to differ sharply from ordinary Union acts under the TFEU, the question of non-supranational EU soft law requires special investigation.

THE EMERGENCE OF EU SOFT LAW

Typology of EU Soft Law

The European documents which may be brought under the heading 'soft law' as defined above are numerous and various. They may be classified along different lines (Senden, 2004: xxxi–liv). We can roughly orient ourselves along the lines of the authors of the instruments – the Commission, the Council, the Parliament, the member states, joint acts of EU institutions, and private actors. In particular the acts adopted by the institutions themselves (institutional soft law) can usefully be further systematized according to their function.

Institutional soft law
A functional typology of institutional soft law establishes the following categories.[12]

1. Preparatory and informative instruments:
    One type of preparatory documents is *action programmes* (European Commission, 2001b) (produced by the Commission and at a later stage also by the Council). Some observers also include *green* and *white papers* (issued by the Commission) among the informative instruments and qualify them as soft law. The green and white papers form part of the legislative drafting process. It is, however, questionable whether these have any legal effect at all. Probably they only serve to initiate and structure the legislative debate, and to some extent resemble communications. *Purely informative communications* are issued by the Commission, eventually with the involvement of other institutions. Finally, there are *interinstitutional communications*.
2. Interpretative and decisional instruments:
    Instruments whose function is to interpret and to decide are most frequently called 'communications'. They are linked to primary or secondary EU norms. A specific legal basis is therefore apparently not considered necessary. Generally, interpretative communications and notices are issued by the Commission (European Commission, 2004a: 2), but they are occasionally also issued by other institutions. An important sub-group is administrative rules, which are not legally binding as such but indicate the way in which a European institution will interpret and apply EU law (Senden, 2004: 138–43). Probably the first case, and still the primary example of administrative rules, is two communications concerning the application of (ex) Article 85, first

paragraph (the 'Christmas communications' of December 1962).[13] Among the decisional instruments also come the decisional notices and (less frequently) communications issued by the Commission. Another type of decisional instrument is decisional guidelines, codes and frameworks, likewise issued by the Commission. Their objective is to furnish decisional rules in areas where the Commission is entrusted with the power to decide on individual cases, primarily in the area of state aid. Addressees are the member states (as a third party) and potential beneficiaries.

3. Steering instruments:

    The final major group is steering instruments. Under this umbrella, we might group Council conclusions, Council declarations, (Council of the European Union, 1998b: 1) joint declarations (European Parliament et al., 1999: 1) and Council resolutions. Interinstitutional agreements (European Parliament et al., 2003: 1) may be binding (on the participating institutions, or even for third parties) (Bieber, 1992: 189–92). But in cases where their legal basis and their wording speak against a binding character those agreements constitute only soft law. A final and important type is Council and Commission *codes of conduct or practice*. Examples are the 1999 Code of Conduct for improved cooperation between authorities of the member states concerning the combating of transnational social security benefit and contribution fraud and undeclared work, and concerning the transnational hiring out of workers (Council of the European Union et al., 1999: 1); the 1998 Code of Conduct on Arms Exports (Council of the European Union, 1998c); or the 1993 Code of Conduct concerning public access to Council and Commission documents of an internal nature (Council of the European Union and European Commission, 1993: 41).

Member states' European soft law

The member states themselves may jointly promulgate, within the scope of Union law, non-binding documents which are not totally devoid of (indirect) legal effects. One example was the Charter on Fundamental Rights of the European Union of 7 December 2000 (European Parliament et al., 2000: 1), which acquired a 'hard' legal value on an equal footing with the treaties only with the entry into force of the Lisbon Treaty (Article 6(1) TEU). Although this charter was formally signed only by the presidents of the EU organs, and published as an act of the organs, it seems fair to attribute it to the member states, whose representatives participated in its elaboration in the Charter Convention.

Another controversial example is the so-called Luxembourg Agreement of 1966. This agreement was not a formal treaty, and therefore did not have the legal effect to formally amend the EC treaties. On the basis of the agreement, Council decisions were, with a few exceptions, taken without any vote between 1966 and 1974.[14] This practice foreclosed the possibility of majority votes that was provided for in the treaties, and thus in an informal way did modify them.

Private self-regulation and co-regulation

One type of European soft law that is proliferating is soft law issued by private (mostly economic) entities. Although for certain sectors (for example, the media, advertising, the environment) scholarly writing on self- and co-regulation is abundant (Peters et al., 2009 and Hennebel and Lewkowicz, 2007), a legal assessment of the private or semi-private instruments on the EU level is only just emerging. The analysis of alternative practices cannot directly draw on scholarship on self-regulation and private standard-setting developing outside EU law, because with the Interinstitutional Agreement on Better Lawmaking (European Parliament et al., 2003) the European Union chose to adopt its own special concepts and to institutionalize the use of the private practices in accordance with European constitutional principles. For this reason, a comprehensive legal evaluation of these alternatives to legislation is of particular importance.

The most relevant (co-)regulating entities are Europe-based transnational companies on the one hand and trade and industry associations in Europe on the other hand. These European private (business) actors are increasingly engaging in 'autonomous' self-regulation. The Commission has defined self-regulation as follows:

> [I]t concerns a large number of practices, common rules, codes of conduct and, in particular, voluntary agreements which economic actors, social players, NGOs and organized groups establish themselves on a voluntary basis in order to regulate and organise their activities. Unlike co-regulation, self-regulation does not involve a legislative act. Self-regulation is usually initiated by stakeholders. (European Commission, 2002b: para. 4.1)

Self-regulation often happens in form of a code of conduct, defined in a relevant directive as: 'an agreement or set of rules not imposed by law, regulation or administrative provision of a Member State which defines the behaviour of traders who undertake to be bound by the code' (European Parliament and Council of the EU, 2005: Art. 2, lit. f).

A prime example is the self-regulation of advertising. In this field, we even find meta-norms on self-regulation, such as the 2004 Advertising Self-regulation Charter, signed by representatives of the advertising industry of Europe, in which advertisers, agencies and media, and the European Advertising Standards Alliance (EASA), re-committed themselves to effective self-regulation across the European Union.[15] An equally relevant field is that of unfair commercial practices. For instance, the EU Unfair Commercial Practice Directive of 2005 does not exclude the control of unfair commercial practices by business codes of conduct, but deems it appropriate to provide a role for such codes which enable traders to apply the principles of the directive (European Parliament and Council of the EU, 2005: Arts 10 and 2, lit. f and preamble para. 20).

An interesting variant of the privatization of soft law is the emergence of *mixed public–private acts*, sometimes referred to as 'hybrid', or 'multi-stakeholder' acts or *co-regulation*. An example is the Social Dialogue under which the initiative for proposing legislation rests with the social partners (representatives of employers and employees). They are allowed to enter into voluntary agreements which are subsequently enacted as directives by the Council.

It must be pointed out that self-regulation and co-regulation are not necessarily soft in all respects. Private actors may, among themselves or together with EU institutions or with member states, conclude agreements which are binding on the participants (Röthel, 2007).

Currently the most important space for so-called voluntary agreements is in environmental policies (European Commission, 1996; European Commission, 2002b). Under the umbrella of voluntary environmental agreements (VEAs) we find both legally binding ones and non-binding ones (Bailey, 1999: 172). Only the latter variant is soft-law-like and therefore relevant for this inquiry.

A very important feature of self-regulation and co-regulation is the (potential) involvement of formal law-making institutions. In particular, the Commission may indicate its intent to act in a particular area if the social partners cannot reach agreement on their own. This 'threat to legislate' is a highly effective stimulus for self-regulation.

Technical and financial standard-setting by or with private bodies

A very important form of private or semi-private regulation which overlaps with self-regulation as described above is standard-setting (Schepel, 2005; Mattli, 2003; Nobel, 2005). Standard-setting currently happens most intensely in the areas of production, engineering and finance. These technical and financial standards are, crucially, established by private bodies, either solely or in collaboration with government institutions.

The European body with the broadest mandate is the European Committee for Standardization (CEN). The CEN is a multi-sectoral organization producing standards in numerous business domains ranging from chemistry, food and health care to transport and packaging. Another example is CENELEC (the European Committee for Electrotechnical Standardization), which seeks to achieve a coherent set of voluntary electrotechnical standards as requested both by the market and by European legislation.[16] Another case in point is the European Telecommunications Standards Institute (ETSI), which produces telecommunications standards.

Finally, financial standards may be incorporated into (European) 'hard' law. For instance, the International Financial Reporting Standards (IFRS), adopted by the International Accounting Standards Board (IASB), have been incorporated into a Commission regulation of 2003, the annexes to which, containing the standards, are continual being amended (European Commission, 2003b: 1; Kirchner and Schmidt, 2005: 67–82).

The relation between standards and (hard) law is complex and raises problems similar to those raised by soft law. Notably, standards have – as soft law does – *indirect legal effects*. The typical way in which they are referred to and incorporated by businesses is that observance of 'private' standards will give rise to a presumption of lawfulness. Within the European Union, conformity with the technical standards elaborated under the so-called 'new approach' to technical standard-setting triggers the presumption that a product is in conformity with the relevant European directives and is therefore allowed to circulate freely in the Common Market (Röthel, 2007: 759).

Soft Law as a Core Element of the Open Method of Coordination

The proliferation of soft law is paralleled by the emergence of the Open Method of Coordination (OMC) (Schäfer, 2005; Zeitlin and Pochet, 2005; see also Hodson, 2001; Telò, 2002; Regent, 2003; Ashiagbor, 2004; Schäfer, 2004a; 2004b). Despite important differences between the 'old soft law' and the 'new' OMC which will be pointed out below (Borrás and Jacobsson, 2004; Jacobsson, 2004; Diedrichs, 2005), they have common features. The OMC has been used since the European Council of Lisbon in 2000. Legal bases can be found in the provisions of Article 121 TFEU (ex-Article 99 TEC) (member states' economic policies as a matter of common concern) and Article 148 TFEU (ex-Article 128 TEC) (member states' employment policies) taking into account Council guidelines and action plans, as in the case of employment and social exclusion. The OMC relies on regular monitoring of progress towards meeting those targets, allowing member states to compare their efforts and learn from the experience of others (Borrás and Jacobsson, 2004; Laffan and Shaw, 2005). On the basis of ex-Article 128 TEC, the European Employment Strategy (EES) was developed as the first and still the most important OMC. In the 2001 white paper on European Governance, the Commission explains the OMC as follows: 'The open method of co-ordination is used on a case by case basis. It is a way of encouraging co-operation, the exchange of best practice and agreeing common targets and guidelines for Member States, sometimes backed up by national action plans' (European Commission, 2001a: 21–2). Putting it differently,

> the OMC aims to coordinate the actions of the several Member States in a given policy domain and to create conditions for mutual learning that hopefully will induce some degree of voluntary policy convergence. Under the OMC, the Member States agree on a set of policy objectives but remain free to pursue these objectives in ways that make sense within their national contexts and at different tempos. (Scott and Trubek, 2002: 4–5)

Mere cooperation within the framework of the OMC is a less intrusive strategy than harmonization, let alone unification of law and policy. Member states therefore participate more readily. It is hoped that in the long run this soft strategy might achieve a similar or even greater degree of policy convergence than the traditional modes of European governance. However, the OMC risks upsetting the institutional balance, diluting the achievement of common objectives, and excluding the European Parliament from the European policy process, to name only a few problems. Overall, the OMC may constitute a significant step back to intergovernmentalism as opposed to supranationalism. This is not the place to assess the benefits and shortcomings of the OMC in a comprehensive fashion, but only to examine the potential links between soft law and the OMC.

Notably Borrás and Jacobsson (2004: 188) have distinguished between the OMC and traditional soft law, as follows. The Open Method of Coordination is an intergovernmental approach which the Council monitors politically at the highest level. It systematically links policy areas, and interlinks EU action and national public action. It seeks the participation of social actors and aims at enhancing learning processes.

In contrast, traditional European soft law has been employed within the supranational sphere. The Commission and the Court of Justice had a dominant role. It was monitored only in the sense of administrative monitoring. It did not explicitly seek to link either policy areas or the EU level with national levels, and did not explicitly state enhancing learning as an objective. The authors stress that the OMC functions differently from the previous uses of soft law in the EU, *inter alia*, in being a political rather than a legal process, building on a different set of actors, and being an ongoing process entailing a refined system of monitoring and follow-up (Borrás and Jacobsson, 2004: 197).

Noting these differences, I find that these are differences in degree, not in kind. Both modes of governance consist of law-like and other elements. Even if the OMC may be situated more in the political than in the legal sphere ('soft governance') (Jacobsson, 2004), traditional soft law is also characterized by its dubious status in the grey zone between law and politics. Both modes share the feature of non-bindingness. The open and 'soft' method of coordination is to a great extent realized through instruments which resemble soft law. My conclusion is therefore that soft law is one important component of the OMC (cf. Senden, 2004: 22, 179; Trubek and Trubek, 2005: 344).

Explaining the Emergence of Soft Law as a New Mode of Governance

The following factors accounted for the emergence of soft law as a new mode of governance (NMG). First, there is a growing bureaucratization of European institutions. Many of the new institutional actors (sub-units, programmes and so on) lack formal law-making capacity. This situation is naturally leading to an explosion of soft law.

A second factor is the increasing complexity of global problems and scientific uncertainty about causalities. This complexity makes it more difficult to build a consensus of member states. Effective legal responses are often not clearly identifiable, while at the same time civil society demands that something must be done. In these fluid situations, a 'soft' response appears particularly useful, as it preserves the freedom of action of the political elites. Environmental protection is one issue area where this calculus plays a part.

Third, member states are cautious about committing themselves legally. In that perspective, the rise of soft law can be interpreted as a sign of

> respect for hard law, which states and other actors view cautiously. They may use the soft law form when there are concerns about the possibility of non-compliance, either because of domestic political opposition, lack of ability or capacity to comply, uncertainty about whether compliance can be measured, or disagreement with aspects of the proposed norm. (Shelton, 2000: 12)

Firm commitments are likewise avoided when it is difficult to predict factual developments. This is typical for certain subject areas, for example, monetary policy.

Finally, a very important motive of governments is that the endorsement of soft agreements is more rapid and simpler than the adoption of binding EU instruments, and that they are more flexible and easy to revise, precisely because they are less binding.

EXECUTION: UNDECLARED POLICY GOALS OF EUROPEAN SOFT LAW

The NMG under investigation involved a mix of private and/or public actors. The emergence of *mixed public–private acts*, sometimes referred to as 'hybrid' or 'multi-stakeholder'-acts or co-regulation, is especially important. The following seem to be the policy goals of resort to soft law, although governments do not declare them.

Competence Creep

First, European political actors' reliance on soft law may be motivated by their lack of legal powers (competences) and may result in 'competence creep'. As far as the powers of the Union as a whole are concerned, European institutions have frequently regulated in a soft manner areas in which the EU lacked legal authority vis-à-vis the member states, or where the division of competences between the EU or former EC and the member states was unclear. The European institutions were thereby able to initiate new policies which had no legal basis in the treaties. Classic examples are environmental policy, research and technological development, culture, and public health issues, which were tackled mainly by means of action programmes, research programmes, framework programmes and declarations, until the respective competences were transferred to the Union (or former Community). For instance, only in 1986 were competences in the field of environmental policy and in research and technological development transferred to the then European Community by the Single European Act. Before 1986, four environment action programmes had been adopted (Council of the European Communities et al. 1973; 1977; 1983; 1987). They were later implemented through the development of hard law (directives). The same happened in research and technological development. Before 1986, the first soft instruments were research programmes – from 1983 the framework programmes. Competences in culture and public health were transferred to the then European Community in 1992 by the Treaty of Maastricht. The new competence for public health policy was ex Article 129 (then Art. 152 TEC, now Art. 168 TFEU). Before 1992, public health action programmes and declarations had been adopted. Soft law here performed its promoting function and indeed paved the way to hard law. Today, the OMC is applied without any treaty basis in the fields of social exclusion and pensions.

Sovereignty

Using soft law instead of hard law lowers 'sovereignty costs'. As soft instruments are not legally binding as such, they entail a smaller loss of autonomy for the cooperating (member) states than hard legal acts. Thus soft law offers a compromise between sovereignty-autonomy and order.

Alleviation of Private Actors' Lack of Formal Law-making Capacity

The resort to private or semi-private novel types of acts has been a means to alleviate (if not to overcome) the lack of formal law-making capacity of private actors. It is crucial that those actors are not competent to create hard European norms that are binding on third parties, even if they observe the proper procedures and act with the intention to be legally bound. Because the option of hard law is foreclosed to these actors, they can only regulate and govern through soft policy instruments. So the creation of soft law is here not a deliberate choice between a hard and a soft instrument, but it is the strongest available form of norm-generation and commitment.

Integration of Non-state Actors into EU Law

The functions of private or 'hybrid' (public–private) soft law therefore differ from the functions of traditional public soft law, emanating from competent legal subjects. The former type of soft law integrates transnational non-state actors which are not (yet) formal subjects of law (such as transnational corporations (TNCs) and non-governmental organizations (NGOs)) into the fabric of EU law. In a soft way, those actors become co-lawmakers and co-enforcers. This devolution allows the formal legislators to concentrate on essential aspects and to benefit from the experience of the private entities.

Along these lines, the Commission praised co-regulation (by private actors with Union institutions) as follows:

> With a view to simplifying legislation, the Commission remains convinced that it is a method whose implementation – circumscribed by criteria laid down in a joint inter-institutional agreement – can prove to be a relevant option when it comes to adjusting legislation to the problems and sectors concerned, reducing the burden of legislative work by focusing on the essential aspects of legislation,

and drawing on the experience of interested parties, particularly operators and social partners. (European Commission, 2002b)

EVOLUTION

New and old modes of governance complement each other rather than acting as substitutes for each other. The tendency is probably from old modes towards new modes. The NMG 'soft law' involves a mix of new and old modes of governance. Soft law as an NMG is mixed with hard law ('old modes of governance') because political actors expect and desire specific indirect legal effects, which can be clustered as a triad of functions, depending on the relation of soft law to hard law (see Senden, 2004: 457–61 on the triad of functions in the European realm).

Pre-law Functions

Soft instruments fulfil a pre-law function when they are adopted with a view to the elaboration and preparation of future European legislation. In a situation where binding rules are unavailable or for other reasons are inopportune, soft instruments are expected to provide normative guidance, to build mutual confidence, and to concert political attitudes. Soft law may thereby give an impulse to further negotiation. The pre-law function of soft law arguably encompasses the following two indirect legal effects.

(a) 'Europeanization' of the subject matter?
In public international law, probably the most fundamental and uncontested effect of interstate soft law is the 'internationalization' of the subject matter it deals with. The adoption of a soft law instrument removes the subject involved from the *domaine réservé* of states.

However, the de-nationalizing effect via soft law functions differently within an international organization, such as the European Union. Here, the *domaine réservé* of the member states is defined by the founding treaties. It ends where competences have been transferred to the organization. Strictly legally speaking, organs and institutions cannot, by means of soft law in itself, increase the formal competences of the organization. The European Parliament (EP) stressed that reliance on soft law must not be misused to replace the Union's lack of legislative competence (European Parliament, 2007). Nevertheless, the production of soft law by organs and institutions, even if it is outside the competence of the organization, appears to be tolerated by member states and is normally not criticized (as would happen in the event of hard law-making) as being *ultra vires*.

So-called *ultra vires* soft law can therefore in practical terms pave the way to a formal extension of the competences of the organization which will be effected by a revision of the founding treaty. This has indeed happened in the European Union and former Community.

(b)   A promoting function

The second pre-law function, and probably the most important function generally attributed to soft law, is its promoting function. The promulgation of soft law declarations and the conclusion of soft agreements may indicate a growing *opinio iuris* in the direction of those instruments. Soft law thereby contributes to the development of hard law and is thus a pacemaker of legalization. In the EU, this happens notably in the field of private law (Robilant, 2006). Academic model codes, such as the most recent Common Frame of Reference (Bar et al., 2008), seek to promote legal harmonization.

However, issuing pre-legal soft law texts may also undermine the ordinary legislative process and create legal uncertainty. The new provision of Article 296(3) TFEU therefore makes it clear: 'When considering draft legislative acts, the European Parliament and the Council shall refrain from adopting acts not provided for by the relevant legislative procedure in the area in question' (Official Journal, 2008: 47–176).[17] In the same vein, the EP has pointed out that

> whereas it is legitimate for the Commission to make use of pre-legislative instruments, the pre-legislative process should not be abused nor unduly protracted; [the European Parliament] considers that, in areas such as the contract-law project, a point must come where the Commission decides whether or not to use its right of initiative and on what legal basis. (European Parliament, 2007)

Complementation ('Law-plus Functions')

Soft law and hard law increasingly intermesh and add up to more or less coherent normative regimes. In European social policy, for example, 'the proliferation of soft governance mechanisms does not crowd out more traditional hard governance. Although the open method of co-ordination very much dominates both public and academic discourse nowadays on EC-level social affairs, the number of binding legal instruments (Directives and Regulations) has not yet declined' (Falkner et al., 2005: 350). Within such 'mixed' regimes, soft law effectively complements hard law (Stefan, 2008).

Also, financial standards may be incorporated into (European) hard law. For instance, the IFRS mentioned above were incorporated into a Commission regulation of 2003, and their annexes, which contain the standards, are continually being amended (European Commission, 2003b: 1).

Moreover, it is generally accepted that soft law can make concrete and guide the interpretation of hard law. For instance, the ECJ found that a specific interpretation of a directive was confirmed by a joint declaration of the Commission and the Council, contained in the minutes of the session at which the directive was adopted (European Court of Justice, 1992: para. 12).

In another decision, the Court stressed that

> [a]ccording to the case-law of the Court, a declaration recorded in the minutes of the Council on the occasion of the adoption of a directive cannot be used for the purpose of interpreting a provision of that directive where no reference is made to the content of the declaration in the wording of the provision in question. . . . However, inasmuch as it serves to clarify a general concept such as that of an 'essentially similar medicinal product', as used in particular in Article 4.8(a)(iii) of directive 65/65 (as amended), a declaration of that kind may be taken into consideration when interpreting that provision. The definition of that concept adopted in the minutes of the Council is, moreover, used in the guidelines published by the Commission. (European Court of Justice, 1998a: paras 26–8)

In *Grimaldi*, the ECJ has held that national courts are obliged to take recommendations into account (in the sense of Article 288 TFEU [ex-Art. 249 EC Treaty]):

> [I]t must be stressed that the measures in question cannot therefore be regarded as having no legal effect. The national courts are bound to take recommendations into consideration in order to decide disputes submitted to them, in particular where they cast light on the interpretation of national measures adopted in order to implement them or where they are designed to supplement binding Community provisions. (European Court of Justice, 1989: para. 18)

It should be noted that the quality of a mandatory interpretation aid has been ascribed by the Court to recommendations – that is, formal soft law – but has not been ascribed to the instruments outside the TFEU which are analysed in this chapter. In practice, this constellation most often arises with regard to Commission recommendations and other soft law acts issued by the Commission, notably in the field of competition law.

Overall, the legal effects of complementing, supporting and interpreting primary and secondary Union law fulfil – in relation to hard law – a law-plus function.

Para-law Functions

Soft law instruments used as a substitute for legislation fulfil a para-law function. The EP criticizes this function and argues that soft law should not be used as a surrogate for legislation (European Parliament, 2007: para. L). But the para-law function normally does *not* mirror a regulatory choice between hard and soft law. In particular, those actors who do not possess legal capacity in the legal system concerned, for example, private persons, cannot enact hard law. Therefore they do not have any regulatory choice.

However, even among legally competent actors, the alternative to soft law is in most cases not hard law, but no regulation at all. Soft regulation is therefore often the means of escape from a no-go situation, not a deliberate 'alternative' to hard law. Soft law – especially in international law – may be an alternative to anarchy. A soft solution can overcome deadlocks in the relations between states when efforts at firmer solutions have failed. Powerful states may favour soft solutions which allow them to retain their liberty of action while at the same time displaying a cooperative attitude. Weak states might promote a soft law instrument on matters of concern to themselves as the best they can politically achieve. In the European realm, soft law is more often than not only the second-best solution.

EVALUATION

The Effectiveness of Soft Law as an NMG

European soft law is partly (in)effective or (in)efficient. Because soft law is not directly binding, non-compliance is not illegal in a traditional sense, but entails only soft legal consequences.

On the European level, case studies on compliance with soft legal instruments do not make it possible to draw general conclusions, but rather suggest that both sector- and country-specific differences exist. Gerda Falkner and associates studied compliance with selected recommendations which are in turn included in directives in the field of European social policy (Falkner et al., 2005: 178 ff.). They concluded that

> it depends on the preferences of domestic governments and/or social partners whether a specific recommendation is implemented as hard law, adopted in the form of a soft recommendation, or ignored completely. The country patterns also imply that cultural factors are at work when it comes to domestic reactions to EU soft law. (Ibid.: 189; Zürn and Joerges, 2005)

One explanation for compliance with European soft law might be the threat to enact hard law in the event of non-compliance with the former. This 'shadow of the law' is real in those areas where the Commission can take action. This is particularly relevant for European self- and co-regulation. Here the main sanction for non-compliance is the (potential) involvement of formal law-making institutions. Notably the Commission frequently indicates its intention to act in the area concerned if the social partners cannot reach agreement on their own. This threat to legislate is a highly effective stimulus for European self-regulation. In contrast, the OMC (as described above) is rather characterized by a low level of compliance.

Interestingly, there seem to be factors of compliance which do not depend on the theoretical hardness or softness of a given norm. These factors are:

1. the targets of the norm;
2. the content of the norm;
3. the perceived economic costs of compliance or non-compliance;
4. the relationship among the participants;
5. reputational concerns;
6. shared interests and values.

On (1), member states may find it easier to comply with norms that govern official behaviour than with obligations to regulate non-state behaviour.

On (2), the more precise the content of the obligation, the better compliance is likely to be. Ambiguity and open-endedness of European standards can limit efforts to secure compliance.

On (3), if it is costly to comply with soft law, because of economic costs or the lack of technical, administrative, or other capacity, compliance is less likely.

On (4), if there is a continuing long-term relationship among the participants in which they must interact, they are likely to comply.

On (5), within an international organization, therefore, concern about reputation may render binding contracts unnecessary. A shared desire to maximize welfare and minimize transaction costs may lead to compliance with informal norms without the need for legal enforcement.

On (6), finally, consensus about the norm positively affects compliance.

Because these factors work equally for hard and soft law, European soft law *may be as effective (or ineffective)* as European hard law.

The Legitimacy of Soft Law as an NMG

Participant actors and the broader public perceive soft law as an NMG as legitimate or illegitimate depending on circumstances. Resort to soft law may be the member states' attempt to gain (or feign) legitimacy and alleviate (or cover up) democratic deficiencies. It has been argued that, due to its indirect legal effects and the high level of compliance, soft law amounts to hard law 'in disguise' (Mörth, 2006: 129). The costume of 'softness' is used when it is politically convenient to avoid the term 'law' and to describe and present these programmes, action plans and memoranda as non-law. There are two reasons for this masquerade. One is that the term 'law' has unwanted connotations of coercion and hierarchy, which may in political terms be inopportune. Second, avoidance of the label 'law' avoids a discussion of the democratic deficiencies lying in the fact that important decisions are made outside the traditional government system (Ibid.: 130). This strategy might be called sneaking into (democratic) legitimacy.

Tension with European constitutional principles

The most important European constitutional principles *prima facie* discourage an excessive use of soft law. Among these are the rule of law (including the protection of legitimate expectations, legal certainty), transparency, democracy, the institutional balance, the external division of powers between member states and the Union, and the independence of the judiciary. Relying on these principles, the EP has severely criticized European soft law, stressing that

> whereas, where the Community has legislative competence but there seems to be a lack of political will to introduce legislation, the use of soft law is liable to circumvent the properly competent legislative bodies, may flout the principles of democracy and the rule of law under Article 6 of the EU Treaty [now Article 2 TEU], and also those of subsidiarity and proportionality under Article 5 of the EC Treaty [now Article 5 TEU], and may result in the Commission's acting ultra vires. (European Parliament, 2007: para. X)

1. Among the constitutional principles which are at stake, the principle of democracy is probably the most complicated. The use of soft law is liable to circumvent the properly competent legislative bodies, in particular the EP (Ibid.). In this context, we must distinguish between various phases: the choice between hard and soft law, the choice of the type of soft legal instrument, and finally the process of adopting soft law instruments. Depending on the phase, resort to soft law handicaps the Parliament. In order to strengthen the role of the EP in this context, the EP's proposal for an interinstitutional agreement between

the EP and the Commission on soft-law instruments in order to avoid a misuse of powers on the part of the executive (Ibid.: paras AA. 17) seems to make sense.

Additionally, it might be argued that other forms of democratic legitimacy may substitute for parliamentary involvement. From the point of view of deliberative democratic theory, the involvement of private actors makes the norm-setting process more democratic because some private parties are granted a voice in the democratic discourse. However, the facts that those speakers are seldom formally designated or elected, and that most of the private organizations do not possess any democratic internal structure, raise democratic concerns which cannot be silenced by merely invoking deliberation.

2. With regard to transparency, both the procedures and the modes of notification and publication of soft law matter. The plethora of forms and denominations of soft law also contributes to a lack of transparency. Soft law rather obscures regulation and thereby runs counter to the principle of transparency, which in turn serves both the rule of law and democracy. The use of soft law may generally create confusion and thus undermine the principle of legal security. In order to remedy this situation, publication and notification should be mandatory.

3. Another legitimacy problem is that European soft law affects the power structure and the allocation of competences across levels and between political actors. We have seen that it is so far unclear under what conditions an institution is competent to enact soft law. Must the competence be linked to the power to enact hard law or is it independent? With the latter hypothesis, there is the danger that soft law undermines the institutional balance of powers. Concretely, most European soft law is issued by the Commission. Thereby the Council and the Parliament are unduly marginalized. The Commission's excessive resort to soft law may disturb the institutional balance and may result in it acting *ultra vires* (Ibid.: paras AA. 1, L, X). The danger of circumventing the European Parliament by reliance on soft law also touches on the issue of the democratic justification or legitimacy of soft law.

4. The constitutional admissibility of soft law with a view to the external division of powers is doubtful. Under what conditions is member state sovereignty potentially infringed by reliance of soft law? In this context, the scope of the principle of conferral is crucial. We have seen that soft law instruments – notably action programmes – have been used in certain policy fields (notably the environment) to expand the competences of the Union. The legitimacy issue here is that this competence creep is apt to undermine the principle of conferred specific powers (*compétence d'attribution*). It might, however, be argued that

the concept of 'implied powers' may allow for resort to (some types) of soft law even if this power is not explicitly granted to the EU.

5. A further, probably competing, principle is the independence of the judiciary, which may be called into question by the imposition of strict interpretative guidelines in the form of soft law. In this sense, the EP deplored the use of soft law by the Commission where 'it extrapolates the case-law of the Court of Justice into uncharted territory' (Ibid.: para. AA. 5). This is an issue both for the Union courts and for the member states' courts.

6. The overall legitimacy question is in which instances the enactment of soft law is constitutionally inadmissible. There are instances in which institutions are obliged to enact hard law and thus do not limit themselves to the adoption of soft law only. There even might be a duty to transpose soft law into hard law at some point. Such an obligation may stem from the concrete enabling provisions in the treaty or from general European constitutional principles. The principles mentioned rather pull towards the enactment of hard legislation. In specific circumstances, these principles might give rise to an obligation to choose hard instead of soft regulation. Putting it differently, in specific circumstances they might even categorically prohibit the use of soft law.

Specific legitimacy problems of 'privatized' European soft law

'Private' or semi-private soft law, such as self- and co-regulation, and technical and financial standards, elaborated by European private organizations in collaboration with business and with the involvement of the Commission, raise particular problems of both effectiveness and legitimacy. First of all, excessive standardization may lead to over-regulation.[18] Second, the basis of legitimacy of this standard-setting activity is not, as is usually the case for private actors, their private autonomy and their consent. Standards have a general scope. They address and bind not only the norm-creators themselves (like a contract) but also third parties who are not the authors of these norms. The actors not only regulate themselves (their own future action) but intend to regulate other (mainly business) actors, who have not participated in the standard-setting themselves. Therefore consent alone cannot form the basis of legitimacy for the standards.

An additional basis of legitimacy could be delegation by governments or by the Union. If the member states had (permissibly) delegated the standard-setting authority to private actors, these standards would presumably be legitimate, because states have the overall legitimacy and authority to produce norms. However, is the extensive and highly dynamic and private standard-setting we are witnessing really merely a delegated exercise? The delegation perspective is just the beginning, not the end, of the question of the basis of legitimacy of non-state, especially genuinely private, standard-setting.

In a more practical perspective, it can be said that the involvement of business in standard-setting is apt to increase the effectiveness of the processes, and thus their output-legitimacy. Especially in the highly complex context of the global economy, national governments lack the information and the capacity to regulate issues which transcend the nation-state. The involvement of global business actors might compensate for this lack of regulatory capacity (Nowrot, 2006). Business actors bring in their expertise and their skills to design economically viable solutions. In fact, governmental standard-setting has arguably become dependent upon the economic data and technical solutions offered by firms. Further, the involvement of firms in the setting of standards creates a sense of ownership and therefore facilitates their later implementation. Finally, their more formalized inclusion could eliminate the informal attempts to influence European standard-setting and governance processes.

On the other hand, the involvement of business can also make standard-setting less effective, because it protracts or delays the development of standards, or distorts them, or may offset initiatives by others. However, the most obvious danger involved in the participation of TNCs in standard-setting is that it amounts to getting the fox to guard the henhouse. TNCs are primarily profit-driven, and their novel role as 'corporate citizens' is at best a secondary one. Firms do not per se pursue any (European) public interest (however it is defined), but first and foremost seek to make money. Business is interested in cooperating with international institutions in standard-setting not for the common good, but because global standards will minimize trade barriers resulting from national regulation, because they hope to influence global standards in their favour or gain prestige ('bluewash'), and finally because they can use the standard-setting forums to directly sponsor their own products. Firms also seek to embed 'best practices' in order to squeeze out competitors, which blurs the line between agreements on standards among firms and unfair anti-competitive understandings.

Nevertheless, even corporate profit-driven activity may have beneficial spillover effects for the public. It satisfies consumer needs, provides employment and increases wealth. It is therefore in the public interest not to subject business to standards that kill off its incentive to make profit. Also, the dangers of TNCs' involvement in standard-setting, notably the danger of capture by profit interests, are to some extent mitigated by the fact that global business is by no means a monolithic bloc with uniform objectives. For instance, during the negotiation of the Kyoto Protocol, which was quite intensively lobbied by business, the energy sector and the insurance sector had opposing interests (Nowrot, 2006: 235), which meant that their antagonistic inputs contributed to a more balanced solution.

Finally, there is the fact that standards are normally sold, and only in part offered to the public free of charge. This is an important difference between standards and the law made by states or international organizations. Moreover, this fact raises questions of legitimacy, because not all users are in an equal position to comply with the norms. All things considered, there is still the real danger of European standard-setting being unduly commercialized through business involvement. One remedy might be public/private–private standard-setting, in which NGO involvement might compensate for legitimacy deficits engendered by marketization.

CONCLUSION

The relationship between European soft law and the overall development of the integration process is ambiguous.

1. The softening of the European legal order might be an indicator of the strength and advanced stage of the integration process. In mature societies, not all relations need to be governed by law, but some may be left to social discourse and informal commitments. In fact, the existence of a strong and broad political, social and cultural consensus in a polity may (although it permits agreement on hard rules) paradoxically render hard regulation unnecessary in some domains, because the societal consensus facilitates the functioning of soft rules. This also means that stable polities that are built on a solid political and cultural consensus can afford soft law rather better than unstable ones. The European legal order is relatively 'mature' in terms of complexity and as far as the consensus on basic values is concerned. The proliferation of soft law on the European level can therefore be interpreted as a sign of strength. In this vein, the Commission, which in 2002 'examined the scope of soft law approaches at international level', was driven to 'assess the global environment and policy domains as less secure and less transparent than the EU environment, and in greater need of "hard law" providing the necessary security and transparency' (European Commission, 2002c: 26, para. 4).

2. On the other hand, European soft law may hamper the overall integration process. In particular, the adoption of non-binding acts with a dubious normative value may constitute window-dressing and present an excuse for not pursuing hard regulation. Moreover, the softening

of the law risks freezing the status quo of power constellations. Seen in that way, soft law is a fig leaf for power. Generally speaking, the softening of a legal order might be a sign of the weakness of its normative power. The softening is the consequence of a lack of consensus and of the reluctance to give up authority and control, which prevents the adoption of hard regulation.

3. The proliferation of soft European law is *both a symptom and a promoter of the intermeshing of international and European law*. This duality has been acknowledged with regard to the Union's international obligations. In this area, Advocate General Georges Cosmas found it

> clear that . . . the need for practical harmonisation . . . of a correct, effective and mutual approach to the Community's international obligations can only be based on procedures and obligations falling within an alternative legal framework often marked by a lack of strictness (soft law). That is neither paradoxical nor contradictory. It is justified by the variable geometry and the still incomplete institutionalisation of the coexistence of national, Community, and international legal orders. (European Court of Justice, 1998b: 76)

4. Arguably, the blurriness between international and EU law goes even further, and the increased reliance on soft law within the EU corresponds to the trend. EU law is in some fields evolving (or retrogressing) towards intergovernmentalism, away from supranationalism.[19] This renewed intergovernmentalism in some European policy areas borrows traditional instruments as used in international organizations (Schäfer, 2005). Moreover, EU enlargement has increased the political, economic, social and cultural diversity among the member states and has made substantial agreement in legal and political affairs more difficult, as happens within larger international organizations with global scope. Ardent supporters of supranationality, including the EP, criticize this trend which they perceive as a retrogression. The EP deplores that 'extensive recourse to "soft law" instruments would signify a shift from the unique Community model to that of a traditional international organisation' (European Parliament, 2007: para. E).

European soft law may be as effective or ineffective as EU legal acts. However, it raises serious legitimacy problems. These have become an issue within a political conflict between the European Parliament and the Commission, in which the EP suggests that the increased reliance on soft law signifies an illegitimate increase of the powers of the executive. To some extent, this conflict represents the tension between democracy and bureaucracy, in which democracy appears to risk marginalization.

Overall, therefore, the proliferation of European soft legal instruments appears to be a double-edged sword for the European integration process.

NOTES

1. I would like to thank Roland Bieber for valuable comments on an earlier version of this chapter, and Isabella Pagotto and Egle Svilpaite for research assistance.
2. Some articles date from the 1980s and 1990s (notably Wellens and Borchardt, 1989; see also Bothe, 1981; Snyder, 1993a, 1993b; Klabbers, 1994; Beveridge and Nott, 1998).
3. EP, Non-legislative Resolution of 4 Sept. 2007 on institutional and legal implications of the use of 'soft law' instruments (2007/2028 (INI)), paras A and AA. 19 (Doc. T6-0366/2007), available at http://www.europarl.europa.eu/oeil/file.jsp?id=5444052. This resolution sems to be especially directed against 'soft' Commission acts.
4. By norms, I understand prescriptions ('ought' phrases) as opposed to descriptions. Social norms seek to guide human behaviour.
5. *Legal* norms are a special type of social norm.
6. US S. Ct., *Jacobellis v Ohio*, 378 US 184 (1964), *Stewart*, Justice, concurring, on the indefinability of 'hard-core pornography': 'I shall not today attempt further to define the kinds of material I understand to be embraced within that shorthand description; and perhaps I could never succeed in intelligibly doing so. But I know it when I see it, and the motion picture involved in this case is not that'.
7. On the legal effects of European soft law, see Senden, 2004: 235–449; Wellens and Borchardt, 1989: 281–2. On the legal effects of international soft law, see Pellet, 2006: paras 105, 106, 108.
8. Referring to General Assembly Resolutions.
9. Arbitral Tribunal, Award on the merits in the dispute between Texaco Overseas Petroleum Company/California Asiatic Oil Company and the Government of the Libyan Arab Republic of 19 January 1977, para. 86 (ILM 17 (1978), 1, p. 29), with regard to UN resolutions.
10. Bürger, Gottfried August (2002: 64).
11. The same was true before the entry into force of the Lisbon Treaty with regard to Police and Judicial Cooperation in Criminal Matters under Title VI of the former TEU. The Council could adopt common positions, framework decisions, decisions, and conventions (ex-Art. 34 TEU).
12. This typology follows Senden (2004: 123ff.). For further (older) examples, see the table of institutional soft law acts in Senden (2004: xxxi).
13. Notice on exclusive dealing constructs with commercial agents, OJ 139, 24 December 1962, p. 2921; Notice on patent licensing agreement, OJ 139, 24 December 1962, p. 2922.
14. At the meeting of heads of government of the Community in Paris on 9/10 December 1974, the heads of state agreed to renounce the Luxembourg compromise (see para. 6 of the Communiqué of 10 December 1974). In 1982, decisions on agricultural prices were taken despite a British veto.
15. Available at http://www.easa-alliance.org/About-EASA/Who-What-Why-/page.aspx/110. The Charter was framed under the auspices of the EASA, a Brussels-based NGO (http://www.easa-alliance.org/) and signed in the presence of a Commission representative.
16. For (technical) standardization in the EU and EFTA, see 'General Guidelines for the Cooperation between CEN, CENELEC and ETSI and the European Commission and the European Free Trade Association' of 28 March 2003, OJ EC 2003/C 91/04, pp. 7–11.
17. Note that this provision only relates to 'legislative acts', not to other legal acts (cf. Art. 289(3) TFEU).
18. This is a criticism by the EP Resolution on soft law (European Parliament, 2007: para. A. 12).

19.   Studies on the European OMC suggest that reliance on soft instruments in the European economic, social and employment policy is a move towards intergovernmentalism (Schäfer, 2004a, 2004b).

REFERENCES

Ashiagbor, Diamond (2004), 'Soft harmonisation: the "Open Method of Coordination" in the European Employment Strategy', *European Public Law*, **10**, 305–32.
Bailey, Patricia M. (1999), 'The creation and enforcement of environmental agreements', *European Environmental Law Review*, **8**, 170–79.
Bar, Christian von, Eric Clive and Hans Schulte-Nölke (eds) (2008), *Principles, Definitions, and Model Rules of European Private Law: Draft Common Frame of Refererence (DFCR)*, prepared by the Study Group on a European Civil Code, Munich: Sellier European Law Publishers.
Beveridge, Fiona and Sue Nott (1998), 'A hard look at soft law', in P. Craig and C. Harlow (eds), *Lawmaking in the European Union*, The Hague: Kluwer Law International, pp. 285–309.
Bieber, Roland (1992), *Das Verfahrensrecht von Verfassungsorganen*, Baden-Baden: Nomos.
Borrás, Susana and Kerstin Jacobsson (2004), 'The open method of co-ordination and new governance patterns in the EU', *Journal of European Public Policy*, **11**, 185–208.
Börzel, Tanja A., Sonja Guttenbrunner and Simone Seper (2005), 'Conceptualizing new modes of governance in EU enlargement', 7 February, available at http://www.eu-newgov.org/database/DELIV/D12D01_Conceptualizing_NMG_in_EU-Enlargement.PDF.
Bothe, Michael (1981), '"Soft Law" in den Europäischen Gemeinschaften?', in Ingo von Münch (ed.), *Festschrift für Hansjürg Schlochauer*, Berlin: de Gruyter, pp. 761–75.
Bürger, Gottfried August (2002), *Wunderbare Reisen zu Wasser und Lande, Feldzüge und lustige Abenteuer des Freiherrn von Münchhausen*, based on the German edition (1788). [English original: Rudolph Erich Raspe, *The Surprising Adventures of Baron Munchhausen* (1785)].
Chinkin, Christine (2000), 'Normative development in the international legal system', in Dinah Shelton (ed.), *Commitment and Compliance: The Role of Non-Binding Norms in the International Legal System*, Oxford: Oxford University Press, pp. 21–42.
Council of the European Communities (1974), 'Council Resolution of 14 January 1974 on the participation of the European Communities in the European Science Foundation', Official Journal, C 7/2, 29 January.
Council of the European Communities (1983), 'Council Resolution of 25 July 1983 on framework programmes for Community research, development and demonstration activities and a first framework programme 1984 to 1987', Official Journal, C 208/1, 4 August.
Council of the European Communities (1985), 'Council Directive 85/337/EEC of 27 June 1985 on the assessment of the effects of certain public and private projects on the environment', Official Journal, L 175/40, 5 July.

Council of the European Communities (1991), 'Conclusions of the Council and the Ministers for Health of the Member States, meeting within the Council of 4 June 1991 on the monitoring of action to reduce drug demand', Official Journal, C 170/1, 29 June.

Council of the European Communities and Representatives of the Member States (1973), 'Declaration of the Council of the European Communities and of the representatives of the Governments of the Member States meeting in the Council of 22 November 1973 on the programme of action of the European Communities on the environment', Official Journal, C 112, 20 December.

Council of the European Communities and Representatives of the Member States (1977), 'Resolution of the Council of the European Communities and of the Representatives of the Governments of the Member States meeting within the Council of 17 May 1977 on the continuation and implementation of a European Community policy and action programme on the environment', Official Journal, C 139, 13 June.

Council of the European Communities and Representatives of the Member States (1983), 'Resolution of the Council of the European Communities and of the representatives of the Governments of the Member States, meeting within the Council of 7 February 1983 on the continuation and implementation of a European Community policy and action programme on the environment (1982 to 1986)', Official Journal, C 46, 17 February.

Council of the European Communities and Representatives of the Member States (1987), 'Resolution of the Council of the European Communities and of the representatives of the Governments of the Member States, meeting within the Council of 19 October 1987 on the continuation and implementation of a European Community policy and action programme on the environment (1987–1992)', Official Journal, C 328, 7 December.

Council of the European Union (1998a), 'Council conclusions on the future framework for Community action in the field of public health', Official Journal, C 390, 15 December.

Council of the European Union (1998b), 'Declaration by the Council (ECOFIN) and the Ministers meeting in that Council issued on 1 May 1998', Official Journal, L 139, 11 May.

Council of the European Union (1998c), 'European Code of Conduct on Arms Exports', 8 June, available at http://ue.eu.int/uedocs/cmsUpload/08675r2en8.pdf.

Council of the European Union and European Commission (1993), 'Code of Conduct concerning public access to Council and Commission documents', Official Journal, L 340, 31 December.

Council of the European Union and Representatives of the Governments of the Member States (1999), 'Resolution of the Council and the Representatives of the Governments of the Member States, meeting with the Council of 22 April 1999', Official Journal, C 125, 6 May.

Diedrichs, Udo (2005), 'Overview paper on classification and mapping of governing modes', 31 August, available at http://www.eu-newgov.org/database/DELIV/D01D08_Overview_classifying_NMGs.pdf.

European Commission (1962a), 'Communication from the Commission, Notice on exclusive dealing constructs with commercial agents', Official Journal, OJ 139, 24 December, Brussels.

European Commission (1962b), 'Communication from the Commission, Notice on patent licensing agreement', Official Journal, OJ 139, 24 December, Brussels.

European Commission (1996), 'Communication from the Commission to the Council and the European Parliament on Environmental Agreements', COM (1996) 561 final, 27 November, Brussels.
European Commission (1997), 'Communication from the Commission on Financial Services: Enhancing Consumer Confidence, Follow-up to the Green Paper on "Financial Services: Meeting Consumer Expectations"', COM (1997) 309 final, 26 June, Brussels.
European Commission (1998), 'Communication from the Commission, Notice of the expiry of certain anti-dumping measures', Official Journal, C 326, 24 October, Brussels.
European Commission (2001a), 'European governance: a white paper', COM (2001) 428 final, 25 July, Brussels.
European Commission (2001b), 'Communication from the Commission to the Council, the European Parliament, the Economic and Social Committee and the Committee of the Regions on the sixth environment action programme of the European Community Environment 2010: Our future, Our choice, – The Sixth Environment Action Programme', COM (2001) 31 final, 24 January, Brussels.
European Commission (2002a), 'Communication from the Commission, Action Plan Simplifying and Improving the Regulatory Environment', COM (2002) 278 final, 5 June, Brussels.
European Commission (2002b), 'Communication from the Commission to the European Parliament, the Council, the Economic and Social Committee and the Committee of the Regions, Environmental Agreements at Community Level, within the Framework of the Action Plan on the Simplification and Improvement of the Regulatory Environment', COM (2002) 412 final, 17 July, Brussels.
European Commission (2002c), 'Report from the Commission on European Governance', COM (2002) 705, 11 December, Brussels.
European Commission (2003a), 'General Guidelines for the Cooperation between CEN, CENELEC and ETSI and the European Commission and the European Free Trade Association', Official Journal, C 091, 8 March, Brussels.
European Commission (2003b), 'Commission Regulation (EC) No 1725/2003 of 29 September 2003 adopting certain international accounting standards in accordance with Regulation (EC) No 1606/2002 of the European Parliament and of the Council', Official Journal, L 261, 13 October, Brussels.
European Commission (2004a), 'Commission Interpretative Communication on certain aspects of the provisions on televised advertising in the "Television without frontiers" Directive', Official Journal, C 102, 28 April, Brussels.
European Commission (2004b), 'Communication from the Commission, Community Guidelines on State Aid for Rescuing and Restructuring firms in Difficulty', Official Journal, C 244, 1 October, Brussels.
European Commission (2005a), 'Green Paper Mortgage Credit in the EU', COM (2005) 327 final, 19 July, Brussels.
European Commission (2005b), 'White Paper on exchanges of information on convictions and the effect of such convictions in the European Union', COM (2005) 10 final, 25 January, Brussels.
European Court of Justice (1989), 'Judgment of the Court, Grimaldi v Fonds des maladies professionnelles', Case C-322/88, ECR I-4407, Luxembourg.
European Court of Justice (1992), 'Judgment of the Court, Nationale Raad van de Orde van Architecten v Egle', Case C-310/90, ECR I-177, 204, Luxembourg.

European Court of Justice (1998a), 'Judgment of the Court, The Queen v The Licensing Authority', Case C-368/96, ECR I-7967, Luxembourg.

European Court of Justice (1998b), 'Opinion of Advocate General Cosmos, Joint cases, Parfums Christian Dior SA v Tuk Consultancy BV, Assco Gerüste GmbH und Rob van Dijk v Wilhelm Layher GmbH & Co. KG and Layher BV', Case C-300/98 and C-392/98, Luxembourg.

European Parliament (2007), 'Non-legislative Resolution of 4 September on institutional and legal implications of the use of "soft law" instruments (2007/2028 (INI))', Doc. T6-0366/2007, available at http://www.europarl.europa.eu/oeil/file.jsp?id=5444052.

European Parliament and Council of the European Union (2005), 'Directive 2005/29/EC of the EP and of the Council ("Unfair Commercial Practice Directive")', Official Journal, L 149, 11 May.

European Parliament, Council of the European Union and European Commission (1999), 'Joint Declaration on practical arrangements for the new co-decision procedure (Art. 251 of the Treaty establishing the European Community)', Official Journal, C 148, 28 May.

European Parliament, Council of the European Union and European Commission (2000), 'Charter of fundamental rights of the European Union', Official Journal, C 364, 18 December.

European Parliament, Council of the European Union and European Commission (2003), 'Inter-institutional Agreement on Better law-making', Official Journal, C 321, 31 December.

Falkner, Gerda, Oliver Treib, Miriam Hartlapp and Simone Leiber (2005), *Complying with Europe: EU Harmonisation and Soft Law in the Member States*, Cambridge: Cambridge University Press.

Fuller, Lon L. (1969), *The Morality of Law*, rev. edn, New Haven and London: Yale University Press.

Hennebel, Ludovic and Gregory Lewkowicz (2007), 'Corégulation et responsabilité sociale des entreprises', in T. Berns, P.-F. Docquir, B. Frydman, L. Hennebel and G. Lewkowicz (eds), *Responsabilités des Entreprises et Corégulation*, Brussels: Bruylant, pp. 147–226.

Héritier, Adrienne (2003), 'New modes of governance in Europe: increasing political efficiency and policy effectiveness', in Tanja A. Börzel and Rachel Cichowski (eds), *The State of the European Union, Law, Politics and Society*, Oxford: Oxford University Press, pp. 199–243.

Hodson, Dermot (2001), 'The Open-Method as a new mode of governance: the case of soft economic policy coordination', *Journal of Common Market Studies*, **39**, 719–46.

Hummer, Waldemar (2004), 'Interinstitutionelle Vereinbarungen und "institutionelles Gleichgewicht"', in Waldemar Hummer (ed.), *Paradigmenwechsel im Europarecht zur Jahrtausendwende*, Vienna: Springer, pp. 111–80.

International Court of Justice (1996), 'Legality of the Threat or Use of Nuclear Weapons, Advisory Opinion of 8 July', ICJ Reports 1996, p. 226.

Jacobsson, Kerstin (2004), 'Between deliberation and discipline: soft governance in EU employment policy', in Ulrika Mörth (ed.), *Soft Law in Governance and Regulation: An Interdisciplinary Analysis*, Cheltenham, UK and Northampton, MA, USA: Edward Elgar, pp. 81–101.

Kirchner, Christian and Matthias Schmidt (2005), 'Private law-making: IFRS

– problems of hybrid standard setting', in Peter Nobel (ed.), *International Standards and the Law*, Bern: Staempfli Publishers Ltd., pp. 67–82.

Klabbers, Jan (1994), 'Informal instruments before the European Court of Justice', *Common Market Law Review*, **31**, 997–1023.

Klabbers, Jan (2006), 'Reflections on soft law in a privatized world', *Lakimies*, **7–8**, 1191–205.

Laffan, Brigid and Colin Shaw (2005), 'Classifying and mapping OMC in different policy areas', 29 July available at http://www.eu-newgov.org/database/DELIV/D02D09_Classifying_and_Mapping_OMC.pdf.

Mattli, Walter (2003), 'Public and private governance in setting international standards', in Miles Kahler and David A. Lake (eds), *Governance in a Global Economy*, Princeton, NJ/Oxford: Princeton University Press, pp. 199–225.

Mörth, Ulrika (2006), 'Soft regulation and global democracy', in Kerstin Sahlin-Andersson and Marie-Laure Djelic (eds), *Transnational Governance: Institutional Dynamics of Regulation*, Cambridge: Cambridge University Press, pp. 119–35.

Nasser, Salem Hikmat (2008), *Sources and Norms of International Law: A Study on Soft Law*, Glienecke/Nordbahn: Galda & Wilch.

Neuhold, Hanspeter (2005), 'The inadequacy of law-making by international treaties: "soft law" as an alternative?', in Rüdiger Wolfrum (ed.), *Developments of International Law in Treaty Making*, Berlin: Springer, pp. 39–52.

Nobel, Peter (ed.) (2005), *International Standards and the Law*, Bern: Staempfli Publishers Ltd.

Nowrot, Karsten (2006), *Normative Ordnungsstruktur und private Wirkungsmacht, Konsequenzen der Beteiligung transnationaler Unternehmen an den Rechtssetzungsprozessen im internationalen Wirtschaftssystem*, Berlin: Berliner Wissenschaftsverlag.

Official Journal of the European Union (2008), 'Consolidated Version of the Treaty on the Functioning of the European Union', C 115, 9 May, pp. 47–388.

Pellet, Alain (2006), 'Commentary on Art. 38', in Andreas Zimmermann, Christian Tomuschat and Karin Oellers-Frahm (eds), *The Statute of the International Court of Justice*, Oxford: Oxford University Press.

Peters, Anne, Lucy Koechlin, Till Förster and Gretta Fenner (eds) (2009), *Non-State Actors as Standard-Setters*, Cambridge: Cambridge University Press.

Regent, Sabrina (2003), 'The Open Method of Coordination: a new supranational form of governance', *European Law Journal*, **9**, 190–214.

Robilant, Anne (2006), 'Genealogies of soft law', *American Journal of Comparative Law*, **54**, 499–554.

Röthel, Anne (2007), 'Lex mercatoria, lex sportiva, lex technica', *Juristen Zeitung*, **62**, 755–63.

Schäfer, Armin (2004a), *Beyond the Community Method: Why the Open Method of Coordination was Introduced to EU Policy-making*, European Integration online Papers, **8**(13), available at http://eiop.or.at/eiop/texte/2004-013a.htm.

Schäfer, Armin (2004b), *A New Form of Governance? Comparing the Open Method of Coordination to Multilateral Surveillance by the IMF and the OECD*, Cologne: Max-Planck-Institute for the Study of Societies, MPIfG Working Paper 04/5.

Schäfer, Armin (2005), *Die neue Unverbindlichkeit. Wirtschaftspolitische Koordinierung in Europa*, Frankfurt am Main and New York: Campus Verlag.

Schepel, Harm (2005), *The Constitution of Private Governance: Product Standards in the Regulation of Integrating Markets*, Oxford/Portland: Hart Publishing.

Scott, Joanne and David M. Trubek (2002), 'Mind the gap: law and new approaches to governance in the European Union', *European Law Journal*, **8**, 1–18.

Senden, Linda (2004), *Soft Law in European Community Law*, Oxford: Hart Publishing.

Shelton, Dinah (2000), 'Introduction: law, non-law and the problem of "soft law"', in Dinah Shelton (ed.), *Commitment and Compliance: The Role of Non-Binding Norms in the International Legal System*, Oxford: Oxford University Press, pp. 1–42.

Shelton, Dinah (2006), 'International law and "relative normativity"', in Malcolm Evans (ed.), *International Law*, 2nd edn, Oxford: Oxford University Press.

Snyder, Francis (1993a), *Soft Law and Institutional Practice in the European Community*, EUI Working Paper Law No. 93/5, San Domenico di Fiesole: European University Institute.

Snyder, Francis (1993b), 'The effectiveness of European Community law: institutions, processes, tools and techniques', *Modern Law Review*, **56**, 19–54.

Snyder, Francis (1996), 'Interinstitutional agreements: forms and constitutional limitations', in Gerd Winter (ed.), *Sources and Categories of European Union Law: A Comparative and Reform Perspective*, Baden-Baden: Nomos, pp. 453–66.

Stefan, Oana Andreea (2008), 'European competition soft law in European courts: a matter of hard principles?', *European Law Journal*, **14**, 753–72.

Telò, Mario (2002), 'Governance and government in the European Union: the open method of coordination', in Maria Joao Rodrigues (ed.), *The New Knowledge Economy in Europe*, Cheltenham, UK and Northampton, MA, USA: Edward Elgar, pp. 242–71.

Treib, Oliver, Holger Bähr and Gerda Falkner (2005), *Modes of Governance: A Note Towards Conceptual Clarification*, European Governance Papers, no. N-05-02, Vienna: Department of Political Science, Institute for Advanced Studies available at http://www.connex-network.org/eurogov/pdf/egp-newgov-N-05-02.pdf.

Trubek, David M. and Louise G. Trubek (2005), 'Hard and soft law in the construction of Social Europe: the role of the Open Method of Coordination', *European Law Journal*, **11**, 343–64.

Trubek, David M., Patrick Cottrell and Mark Nance (2005), *'Soft Law', 'Hard Law', and European Integration: Toward a Theory of Hybridity*, Jean Monnet Working Paper 02/05, New York: New York University School of Law.

Van Calster, Geert and Kurt Deketelaere (2001), 'The use of voluntary agreements in the European Community's environmental policy', in Eric W. Orts and Kurt Deketelaere (eds), *Environmental Contracts, Comparative Approaches to Regulatory Innovation in the United States and Europe*, The Hague: Kluwer Law International, pp. 199–246.

Wellens, Karel and G. Borchardt (1989), 'Soft law in the European Community', *European Law Review*, **14**, 267–321.

Zeitlin, Jonathan and Philip Pochet (eds) (2005), *The Open Method of Coordination in Action: The European Employment and Social Inclusion Strategies*, Brussels: Peter Lang.

Zürn, Michael and Christian Joerges (eds) (2005), *Law and Governance in Postnational Europe: Compliance beyond the Nation-State*, Cambridge: Cambridge University Press.

3. Classifying and mapping the OMC in different policy areas

Colin Shaw

INTRODUCTION

Before assessing the impact of the Open Method of Coordination (OMC) on actual policies, it is worth noting its impact on the academic community, notably but not exclusively on those scholars who focus on European 'governance'. For these thinkers the OMC was, arguably, a 'godsend'. Two features guaranteed its importance to these researchers: first, it was 'new', that is a self-proclaimed and well-defined departure from existing practice that could be studied *in situ* and whose impact could be measured against the 'old' system. Second, it was clearly 'governance', that is a set of practices that worked outside the strictures of 'government' (in the case of the European Union, the legislative process) and whose methods were more open, experimental and potentially effective. The OMC was therefore seized upon by numerous researchers because of its promise of innovation in the field of European policy-making (new instruments) and because it seemed to extend the boundaries of policy-making to new areas traditionally beyond its realm (new policies). Changing and extending the scope of European integration seemed to be the early promise of the OMC. Hundreds of speculative papers immediately attempted to describe the potential importance of the method. Not only did the method itself seem to proliferate widely (as we shall see below), but interest in it grew as scholars sought to analyse the first findings of the many empirical studies that accompanied its launch. There was, and to a certain extent still is, an 'OMC bubble' – an over-emphasis on its impact by academics and policy-makers alike that has skewed expectations and made disappointment practically guaranteed.

MAPPING THE OPEN METHOD OF COORDINATION

This chapter addresses the issue of the OMC from the dual perspective of its mapping and its classification and will:

- map its use in different policy domains;
- analyse the form and function of OMC in different policy domains;
- explore the manner in which different EU institutions are engaged in or excluded from OMC processes.

To map is to chart; thus the bulk of this chapter will present empirical data on the development of the OMC and its institutionalization at EU level, and will try to shed some light on the OMC as a mode of governance. The main sections will present OMCs organized by policy areas and elements of institutional commitment to the OMC and the Lisbon strategy. Because OMC processes are, as a rule, both weakly constitutionalized and weakly institutionalized we have employed documentary analysis of (European) institutional communications (Presidency conclusions, Commission proposals, Council of Ministers press releases and so forth) to represent political energies surrounding the method. Given the variety and number of concurrent OMCs, our constant research question is how to account for the proliferation of certain processes and the demise of others by situating the method firmly within the Lisbon strategy. This final section will draw results and hypotheses together and look at them against the scientific objectives of the project.

The OMC and New Modes of Governance

A first analytical distinction is required to separate the OMC qua new mode of governance and OMC processes as iterations of this new mode. Whereas a general understanding of the features of the OMC would place it within the paradigm of 'new, soft modes', closer inspection of particular instances of the OMC show that the picture is more complex. As several authors (Radaelli, 2003; Rhodes, 2005) point out, the distinction between new and old, hard and soft modes of governance is one of degree rather than of category. OMC processes may all operate within weakly constitutionalized areas of Community competence (that is, after all, their *raison d'être*), they collectively display aspects of 'old' governance (the treaty basis of employment strategy) and 'new' governance (enterprise scoreboards), and can be both hard (financial penalties for fiscal surveillance) and soft (voluntary targets for research policy).

Rhodes (2005) provides a single explanatory variable (policy convergence potential) conjugated in several incremental stages (see Figure 3.1). Applying this template, all OMCs would appear all along the continuum of new modes of governance from simple benchmarking through voluntary objectives and structured coordination procedures. This approach can allow for the categorization of different OMCs along the continuum

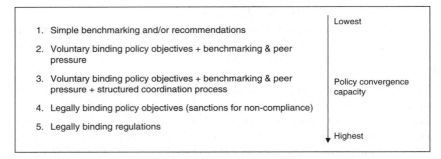

Figure 3.1   Policy convergence capacities

		Legal Instrument	
		Binding	Non-binding
Implementation	Rigid	I. Coercion	III. Targeting
	Flexible	II. Framework Regulation	IV. Voluntarism

Figure 3.2   Implementation frameworks of governance

but tells us little about the OMC itself qua governance. Similarly, the analytical framework of Falkner (2005) allows for the categorization of all modes of governance and for the distinction between different OMCs (with some appearing in boxes I, IIII or IV) but does not capture the specificity of the OMC as a distinct mode of governance (see Figure 3.2).

Methodological Approaches

A priori definitions of new modes of governance therefore provide a rough template for classifying OMCs but their usefulness breaks down when they are applied across all instances of the OMC. In the following section we present an a posteriori approach and search for structuring trajectories and patterns as they have appeared in the iteration of the OMC during a five-year period across 14 policy areas.

Empirical Observation

Mapping the open method across its multiple instances initially requires a purely inductive approach, for two reasons. Though the Lisbon Council

Conclusions provided a template for the method, different processes operationalize the method differently, sometimes introducing new elements while ignoring others. As a soft mode of governance par excellence, OMCs do not leave a distinct 'footprint'. Although traditional 'hard' modes of legislation have their dedicated monitoring bodies that track the advancement of procedures (for example Prelex for ongoing procedures), information on most OMCs has to be garnered by careful web searches on http://europa.eu/and other EU sites. This prima facie evidence can show patterns of execution but presents additional puzzles: why so many OMCs, why so few 'proper' OMCs?

Content Analysis

A second (related) methodological approach is that of content analysis of Community documents. Unlike hard legislation, OMCs rely mostly on discursive resonance within policy spheres in order to operate. Simply put, the OMC is about changing ideas in the absence of law. The method is given life through the selective political energies of institutional actors. We investigate this selectivity through an analysis of the occurrence of key terms in multiple Community documents. This mapping is conducted for the period from the launch of the Lisbon strategy (and the baptism of the open method) in March 2000. The data are presented with several important caveats but do allow for supplementary prima facie evidence as to how the OMC is used and by whom.

Critical Analysis

A third methodological tool is used to make sense of the empirical data and is suggested by Rhodes (2005), who reminds us that 'issues of power should be at the forefront of our quest to understand how and why new modes of governance emerge and to evaluate their consequences for governability, accountability, responsiveness and legitimacy' (Rhodes, 2005: 6). The shift from older to newer forms of governance 'raises questions of who sets the trajectory of change' (Ibid.: 6) which we hope will be central to our account of OMC processes. As mentioned above, the method operates at the level of ideas. Its toolbox of (among others) performance measurement, guidelines, benchmarking and peer reviews achieves policy change by shifting the rationality of policy goals. Jacobsson (2002) refers to discursive regulatory mechanisms to describe the building of new systems of governance. By analysing the OMC as a discursive regulatory mechanism and placing it firmly in the context of the Lisbon strategy, trajectories of change and their consequences appear.

Table 3.1   Pre-Lisbon non-binding coordination initiatives

Area	Title	Origin	Origin
Economic policy	Broad Economic Policy Guidelines	Maastricht Treaty	1992
Employment policy	European Employment Strategy	Luxembourg Summit	1997
Structural reform	Cardiff Process	Cardiff Summit	1998
Macroeconomic dialogue	Cologne Process	Cologne Summit	1999
Fiscal surveillance	Stability and Growth Pact	Protocol to Amsterdam Treaty	1999 (entry into force)

A veritable 'Lisbon dramaturgy' is created by the strategy. This 'policy narrative' (Radaelli, 1998) is constituted discursively by reference to common endogenous and exogenous pressures necessitating novel policy responses. The strategy can be likened to a one-act play (2000–2010) with ten scenes (the spring councils) and, whether the outcome is tragedy, farce or epic victory, the Lisbon strategy is discursively articulated as a form of political theatre, with its heroes and villains, friends and enemies, winners and losers where the EU is a fight against itself and its 'competitors'.

The Current Academic *Acquis* Regarding the OMC

The OMC Research Forum hosted by the European Union Centre at the University of Wisconsin-Madison currently (last consulted 20 July 2005) archives over 270 presentations and peer-reviewed articles on the OMC. As remarked earlier, the academic community's attention has been captured by the promise and challenges of the method. The coining of the expression 'Open Method of Coordination' by the Lisbon summit (2000) crystallized scholarly attention around emerging modes of governance that feature alternative steering modes to the established Community method. The Community's use of such modes (summarized in Table 3.1) is characterized by the reliance on non-legislative means of achieving its objectives. Accordingly, the coordination of economic policies between member states under the Broad Economic Policy Guidelines (BEPG) is tackled by non-binding country-specific recommendations from the Commission, adopted by the Council.

Dubbed 'soft modes' of governance, the rationale and appraisal of these processes have presented a puzzle for the academic community that seems to gravitate around two loci. First, an essentially legal *problématique* raises the question of how these new modes impact on existing modes of governance. Second, a more political analysis examines how they impact on existing policy trajectories.

The OMC qua New Mode

Although most authors situate the origin of new, soft modes of governance before the appearance of the OMC, if one is to judge by academic output, it has been anointed the new mode par excellence. The ideal-type of soft modes (cf. Héritier, 2001) involves the voluntary participation of private and public actors in intergovernmental target-setting and peer-reviewing under Community supervision. The ideal type of OMC procedure involves the consultative definition of common objectives followed by the identification of shared indicators and benchmarks, the elaboration of non-binding action plans, and periodic policy evaluation managed by the Commission. The discussion of the OMC as new governance highlights two potential impacts of the OMC on the traditional Community method.

The OMC as Substitutive of the Community Method

Those authors (see for example Radaelli, 2003; Maher, 2004; Syrpis, 2002; Kaiser and Prange, 2002) who analyse the impact of the OMC on the Community method weigh the advantages of the OMC against the danger it represents to the transparency, accountability and legitimacy of EU governance. As OMCs do not follow legally established procedures and are rather ad hoc in their execution, '[t]he democratic components of real-world OMC are weak in terms of participation, domestic salience of the process (as shown by media coverage and political interest), transparency of the discussions (only dedicated researchers have an idea of how indicators were chosen and agreed), communicative rationality, and democratic deliberation' (Radaelli, 2003).

The typical account of the OMC as substitutive of the Community method goes like this. Under the Community method, the presence of veto-players and ratchet decision-making can lead either to paralysis in the policy-making process or to the reluctance of member states to engage in further, irreversible supranationalization of domestic policies. If we add to this the implementation deficit of legislation approved under the Community method (cf. Falkner, 2005), this method can lead to policy failures and the search for alternative (better) governance modes. The

OMC has therefore emerged in the wake of the inadequacies of the older, traditional mode, and its application to new areas of European governance is seen as an attempt to avoid the inefficiencies associated with the latter. However, the hypothetical efficiency gains of the OMC are traded against the loss of democratic embeddedness of the Community method. Therefore, if the OMC is an alternative to the Community method, it has a flawed democratic pedigree and could represent a footloose, potentially corruptive mode of governance. This understanding of the OMC as a possible dilution of the Community method is indeed echoed in the provision in the Treaty of Lisbon for 'cooperation between the Member States and . . . the coordination of their action in all social policy fields (Article 156 TFEU)'. First, reference to the Open Method of Coordination as such is avoided outright (the 'constitutional effect' is circumvented). Second, the declaration in the Final Act annexed to the treaty qualifies the nature of such coordination, stating that any such action by member states is of a 'complementary nature' and 'shall serve to strengthen cooperation between Member States and not to harmonise national systems (Declaration on Article 156)'. The dual concern of preserving both the integrity of the Community method and the division of competence between member states and EU institutions is present in this final formulation.

This line of enquiry highlights the trade-off implicit in the recourse to an extra-treaty form of cooperation. Whereas these procedures may represent a gain in decision-making efficiency, they may deepen the perception of a democratic deficit in EU governance.

The OMC as Complementary to the Community Method

Another strand of academic literature (Hobbs and Njoya, 2005; Zeitlin, 2004; de la Porte and Nanz, 2004; Hartwig and Meyer, 2002; Jacobsson and Vifell, 2003) examines the potential of the OMC to enhance the quality of EU governance by gains in input legitimacy. The topic of the 'OMC as a deliberative mode of governance' examines the emergence of a third way in EU legislation that plots a course between hard modes (the Community method) and simple intergovernmental cooperation. The third way entails the solving of common problems by bringing together stakeholders, dipping into a 'marketplace of ideas' and drawing out ad hoc policy solutions that respond to the specificities of the problems.

The deliberative nature of the OMC, its openness, allows for the reflexive definition of objectives and thereby ensures better regulation as stakeholders are, by their very presence in the decision-making process, co-opted into policy goals. The iterative procedures of the OMC involve civil society at strategic moments in policy-making, allowing EU insti-tutions to dynamically review policy goals in a way that is beyond the Community method. This 'added value' of the OMC feeds into the debate on the democratic deficit separating citizens from EU institutions. An earlier attempt to introduce elements of reflexivity into the EU legislative procedures in the form of comitology was limited to hyper-selective addi-tion of policy 'experts' into the policy-making arena. And, while this mode might indeed have yielded better regulation, the democratic referential of comitology was so narrow as to make it, in terms of improving the percep-tion of democratic governance, a counter-productive effort. The OMC, it is argued, represents an improvement on comitology as it formally includes (at least in its ideal form) elements of civil society that would otherwise be voiceless.

Somewhat counter-intuitively, some authors argue that

> the only way to democratize the Community Method old or new from this per-spective is to demand of the technocrats, particularly in the Commission, that they disclose the ideological valence of their proposals, thus instigating the kind of partisan clashes in the Euro-polis typical of electoral debate in contemporary mass democracies. (Sabel and Zeitlin, 2003)

Thus the method opens a broadside to public opinion, presenting them with policy alternatives that can be debated and, ultimately, voted on.

Lastly, the open method is understood as complementary to the Community method as it adds a new instrument to the toolbox of the EU and can serve to prepare the ground for further integration. As the OMC operates beyond the formal limits of the sacrosanct 'Community com-petence', it initiates the process of policy coordination through a con-vergence of policy goals. While the OMC is portrayed elsewhere as a problem-solving instrument, this version sees it as a pathfinder for new areas of communitarization. The initial condition for integration is the political will to act together. As the OMC functions at the level of ideas, it can prime the pump of new Community action.

The OMC as Policy Response

A second broad strand of academic analysis focuses less on issues of democracy and efficiency and centres on the policy output imputable to OMC processes. The vast body of literature on the OMC is concerned with sectoral fields, with employment policy receiving most attention. The recurrent tension running through this line of investigation is whether the OMC is primarily a means of fostering competitiveness or a means of improving social welfare.

The OMC as a Competitiveness-fostering Exercise

Whereas criticisms of EU policy-making as 'constitutionalized neoliberalism' were actor-based, centring on the power of institutions such as the European Court of Justice and the Commission (Gill, 1998), a notable body of literature analyses the OMC as an essentially ideational mechanism delivering neoliberal reforms of social policies at a reduced political cost. Basing their understanding of governance on the Foucauldian concept of 'governmentality', these authors (Jacobsson, 2004; Savio and Palola, 2004; Haahr, 2004; Chalmers and Lodge, 2003) see the OMC as a 'discursive regulatory mechanism' (Jacobsson, 2004) that redefines social policy in the light of economic performance.

The governmentality of the OMC involves (a) the discursive construction of common economic and social challenges (global competition); (b) the removal of distributive politics from the political arena (problem-solving replacing contestation); (c) the creation of a new policy rationality (through statistical/technological remodelling, redefining policy choices in the light of challenges); and (d) the convergence of policy content towards a liberalizing agenda (workfarism, flexibility, employability, active ageing and so on). The dominant concept of competitiveness demands that social policy choices hitherto taken for granted – such as the pensionable age or an acceptable level of risk of unemployment – be rethought and (ultimately) redesigned with economic analysis of costs and benefit brought to the fore.

Whereas traditional Community methods imposed policy objectives 'from above', the OMC operates through the internalization of the exigencies of global challenges, thereby leading to a redefinition of what is politically possible and desirable. 'The most effective form of political control is to make one's conception of the world hegemonic, to set the political agenda in such a way that ideology becomes conceived of as natural or normal' (Jacobsson, 2002: 366). The focus on employability in the European Employment Strategy, it is argued (Jacobsson, 2002), imposes a supply-side perspective on labour markets, that is, markets are ill-served by the current supply of labour (price, quality), necessitating a new emphasis on adaptability, flexibility and so on.

The OMC introduces new techniques of governance (benchmarking, monitoring and so on) based on the comparative measurement of performance. Performance is understood as the proximity to 'best practice', itself identified as the most economically efficient player. This comparative exercise is accompanied by the subsumption of hitherto autonomous policy areas (for example education) into the master discourse of economic competition. The OMC is thereby used as an indirect means of regulation, of achieving performance in the form of efficiency measured in terms of productivity (see Haahr, 2004).

The OMC as a Welfare-fostering Exercise

A contending strand of literature argues that the OMC allows social goals to gain political purchase on economic policy-making. Without it the EU would pursue a uniquely market-making agenda to the exclusion of social objectives. The institutionalization of the Social inclusion OMC is pointed to as evidence of the OMC's role in promoting welfare-fostering policies at EU level. The systematic inclusion of civil society (for example anti-poverty associations) in the process, the use of common indicators and the establishment of concrete targets can serve to force uncooperative member states to act when before there was little incentive to do so. The strategic use of OMC performance techniques by non-institutional actors can displace traditional domestic policy choices in favour of new and better regulation. Similarly, the inclusion of welfare-enhancing objectives in the employment strategy (childcare provision, gender equity) paints a more complex picture of the social purpose of OMCs.

The impact of the OMC on European welfare states is examined by several authors and is seen by some (Jessop, 2002; Chalmers and Lodge, 2003) as being instrumental in the move away from a Keynesian 'welfarism' to Schumpterian 'workfarism'. The desirability of such a movement is the subject for debate, as is the ability of the OMC to operate such changes. However, the majority of academic commentators concur that the impact of the OMC on social policy in the EU is minimal (either because it is too early to measure an OMC effect, or because the OMC is incapable of transforming embedded systems).

Mapping the Open Method of Coordination

The OMC was specifically conceived within the political economy of the Lisbon strategy and designed to help achieve the strategic goal of making the Union 'the most competitive and dynamic knowledge-based economy in the world' (European Council, 2000). As such, it was to deliver change at national level without the need for implementing legislation at EU level. The means of achieving coordination are 'soft' in the sense that actors' behaviour will voluntarily change under similarly understood conditions. As noted above, the underlying rationale of the method is that member states face identical exogenous pressures to which they react according to differing endogenous capacities. The Lisbon presidency established a shopping list of instruments designed to achieve consensus on the way to solve common challenges. The method involves:

- fixing guidelines for the Union combined with specific timetables for achieving the goals which they set in the short, medium and long terms;
- establishing, where appropriate, quantitative and qualitative indicators and benchmarks against the best in the world and tailored to the needs of different member states and sectors as a means of comparing best practices;
- translating these European guidelines into national and regional policies by setting specific targets and adopting measures, taking into account national and regional differences;
- periodic monitoring, evaluation and peer review organized as mutual learning processes (European Council, 2000: para. 37).

Policy coordination under loose conditions of consistency (looser obviously than those required by a directive) has meant that each policy area has its own tailored OMC. This makes systematic mapping a delicate exercise. Two difficulties of classification present themselves immediately. When is an OMC an OMC and what distinguishes 'proper' OMCs from simple exercises in cooperation? As an extra-Community method, the right of initiative and implementation of the process is shared between a number of actors (the European Council, the Commission, the Council of Ministers). The 'ownership' of the process, significant for its future development but also for its classification, is therefore complex, as our analysis will show. Also, although the Lisbon presidency set out a description of what the method entailed, the set of policy instruments associated with each policy domain varies from the complete (Employment) to the more sparse (Immigration). Traditional forms of classification relying on CELEX and PreLex data are not very helpful, as the process, once launched by the European Council, is not tracked systematically by any European body.

Information on OMCs has been gathered from the institutional websites and databases and put together in an attempt to observe patterns or trends in OMC development. We have therefore resorted to a purely inductive effort at classification and use a working definition that the method as 'anything the Commission, European Council or Council of Ministers says it is'.

Policies: Analytical Table of OMC Policy Processes

The results of the inclusive approach are presented in Table 3.2. The OMC processes are organized by policy field and distinguished primarily by their operationalization of any of 13 'Lisbon instruments' associated with the method. A number of observations are necessary. First, a treaty basis, where applicable, is included in the table (row 1) even when it is extremely weak. As Community legislation in the field of education is not allowed, this has not been an obstacle to the development of, for example, OMC Education, as articles 149 and 150 of the Treaty on European Union (TEU) provide for measures 'encouraging cooperation between Member States' in education and 'support and supplement the action' in the field of vocational training. The treaty foothold, even though it precludes legislation, serves as a primary justification for fostering cooperation at an EU level of the type the OMC is designed to encourage. The origin of the OMC process is mapped in row 2. Since the term 'Open Method of Coordination' was coined during the Lisbon summit of March 2000, only processes initiated after this date can be systematically referred to as OMCs. Thus, we include other 'OMC-type' process (as several previous coordination procedures clearly inspired its design) but note the origin of the process in the respective European Council summits. Thus OMC Immigration was mooted during the Tampere European Council in October 1999 but was not given the 'OMC treatment' until 2001 (European Commission, 2001b).

Row 3 maps the existence of budgetary leverage in order to distinguish OMCs Research and Development (R&D), Sustainable Development Policy (SDP) and Fiscal Surveillance (Stability and Growth Pact, SGP). Only EU R&D policy has at its disposal a meaningful budget to promote coordination. Funds are distributed to individual member states that carry out research under strict conditions of cooperation with other member states. Framework Programmes 6 and 7 also require participants to institutionalize coordination in semi-permanent 'networks of excellence' and 'integrated projects'. The SGP can be said to have budgetary leverage as the protocol provides for fines levied on non-coordinating member states. Finally, the SDP has been conditionally associated with the granting of cohesion and structural funds. The European Court of Justice's leverage in a policy area is a convenient means of classifying traditional methods of policy-making and has only been included in the table (row 4) to identify two areas where the ECJ has clear-cut (SGP) or latent (Sustainable Development) influence. The provisions for the SGP under Article 104 TEU are justiciable, as recent case law involving the Commission against the Council has showed (ECJ, 2004). Also, in the areas of the environment and sustainable development the use of common targets for emissions may provide grounds for action against member states if they are shared with other processes such as the Kyoto Protocol. This dimension (the role of the ECJ in OMCs) is not explored here but could be an interesting line of enquiry for further research.

Table 3.2 *Analytical table of OMC processes by policy area*

Process	Macro-economic Policy	Employment	Fiscal Surveillance SGP	Immigration	Taxation	Better regulation	Training/ Education	Enterprise
Treaty basis	Strong Art. 99	Strong Art. 125-130	Strong 104 (Excessive Deficit Procedure)	Weak Art.61, 63	Weak Art. 91, 92, 93	None	Weak Art. 149, 150	Strong Art. 95, 157
Process announced	Treaty Provision Maastricht 1992	European Council Luxembourg 1997	Treaty Provisions Jan 99	European Council Tampere Oct 99	ECOFIN Nov 99 (Primarolo group) Feira Council 2000	European Council Lisbon Mar 2000	European Council Lisbon Mar 2000	European Council Lisbon Mar 2000
Community budgetary leverage	No	No	Yes	No	No	No	No	No
ECJ involvement	No	No	No	Yes/No	No	No	No	Yes/No
DG	ECFIN	EMPL	ECFIN	JAI	TAXUD	SG	EAC	ENTR MARKT
Council formation	EcoFin	EPSCO	European Council Ecofin	JHA	Ecofin	Ecofin	EYC	Competitive-ness
INSTRUMENTS								
Established common objectives	Yes	Yes	Yes	In preparation	Yes	No	Yes	Yes

Indicators	Yes	Yes	In preparation	No	No	Yes	Yes	*Yes (annual)*
EU targets	Yes	Yes	Certain areas	No	No	Yes	*Yes*	*Yes*
MS targets	Yes	No	Certain areas	No	No	Yes	*Certain MS*	*Certain MS*
Benchmarking	Yes	Yes	No	No	No	Yes	*Yes*	*Yes*
Best practice	Yes	Yes	Certain MS	Yes	Certain areas	No	*Yes*	*No*
Guidelines	Yes	Yes	Certain areas	Yes	Certain areas	Yes	*Yes*	*Yes*
Community Action Programme	Yes (Entrepreneurship Action Plan)	Yes (2010 programme)	Yes (Better lawmaking 2002–)	Yes (Fiscalis programme 2007)	In preparation (ARGO, Hague 2005–2010)	No	*Yes (Luxembourg Triennial)*	*Yes*
National action plans	No	No	Certain MS	No	In preparation	No	*Yes (annual)*	*Yes (annual)*
National strategies	No	No	Certain MS	No	Yes	No	*Yes*	*Yes*
Peer review process	No	No	In preparation for 2005	Yes (1999)	No	Yes	*Yes*	*No*
Scoreboards	Yes	Yes	No	No	Yes (Tampere biannual scoreboard)	No	*No*	*No*
Council recommendations	No	No	No	No	No	Yes	*Yes*	*Yes*
Commission recommendations	No	No	No	No	No	Yes	*Yes*	*Yes*

Note: Italics denote pre-Lisbon OMCs.

Each OMC is more or less associated with both a specific Commission Directorate-General (DG) and a Council formation. This leads to a connected observation – that there is a close correspondence between the organization of DGs and OMCs. Arguably, as OMC supervisor, the Commission will be systematically involved with all OMCs. However, the sectorial division of certain OMCs (Information society, Enterprise and, although it is not included in the table, Tourism) would seem to respond to a logic of 'One DG, One OMC'. As the method is easy to roll out in its initial stages, a degree of 'me too' might explain why some OMCs are organized as separate processes although there is clear overlap (and not simple synergies) with others. A Council formation is associated with each OMC process as they are involved with the definition of indicators, not to mention the management of the Lisbon strategy.

Prima facie observation of the development of the method can identify a set of 13 instruments ranging from guidelines to national action plans in the OMC toolbox. These instruments have been distilled from the list of measures set out by the Lisbon Council. In addition to the 'officially' prescribed (1) guidelines, (2) peer reviews, (3) indicators, (4) benchmarks, (5) best practices, and (6) targets, we include (7) Community action programmes, (8) national action plans, (9) national strategies, (10) scoreboards and (11) common objectives, plus (12) Commission and (13) Council recommendations (although these only apply to atypical OMCs) as elements allowing the classification of OMCs. The findings in Table 3.2 illustrate the disparity in use of instruments across policy fields. The OMCs have been organized by date, the earliest on the left (BEPGs), the newest to the right (Pensions).

Comparing and Classifying OMC Policy Processes

The 'ideal type' of OMC features key elements of these Lisbon instruments. Although there is no strict hierarchy among instruments, there is a sequential relationship between (1) common objectives, (2) indicators, (3) targets, (4) action plans and (5) periodic peer reviews. The other Lisbon instruments are essentially derivative of these key elements (benchmarks are derived from indicators, scoreboards from targets, best practice from peer reviews, guidelines from objectives). OMC development proceeds from common objectives establishing a field of common concern. Progress towards objectives can be measured once common indicators are established. Indicators allow comparison of the performance of member states which is, in turn, used to set targets. Once the targets are set, member states or the EU draw up action plans to meet the objectives. Peer reviewing allows badly performing member states to draw lessons from best practice. Without these key elements an OMC is, at best, 'cheap talk' (Borrás and Greve, 2004).

All OMCs have common objectives, usually adopted in the European Council conclusions. However, the absence of common indicators (and consequently, targets) in the Immigration, Taxation, Better regulation, Healthcare, Youth and pensions OMCs suggests that the elaboration of OMCs stalls at the definition of indicators. The absence of indicators has not meant that the action plans have not been put forward; however, these are exclusively Community action plans proposed by the Commission, and do not guarantee real-world coordination at the domestic level.

Furthermore, of those OMCs that benefit from indicators (Macroeconomic policy, Employment, Fiscal surveillance, Training and education, Enterprise, Information society, Research and Development, Social inclusion and Sustainable development), most have established EU targets. However, very few (Social inclusion, Employment, the SGP, Sustainable development, Enterprise) make use of national targets. There is an evident sliding scale of political commitment ranging from declarative objectives to national targets. If this filter is applied, only a select group of five OMCs can be said to even make mention of national targets 'Member States should set national targets for employment' (European Commission, 2005: 192).

Community action plans are a persistent feature of most OMCs but, as mentioned above, cannot be considered a reliable measure of political commitment to coordination. National action plans in the Employment, Macroeconomic policy and Social inclusion OMCs, and national strategy reports in Pensions, offer a better index of political will but would arguably exist anyway.

As for peer reviews, their periodization varies greatly, from ongoing reviews in OMC Social Inclusion (up to eight per year), annual rounds for Employment and triennial rounds for Pensions (the second round began in September 2005).

Certain OMCs are, by these standards, weak. Immigration, Youth, Tourism and Taxation present few of the elements necessary for establishing significant coordination procedures. Sustainable development, Better regulation, Healthcare and Pensions may lack essential elements but can be characterized as 'nascent'. OMCs Education, R&D, Information society, Enterprise, Social inclusion and Employment are, broadly speaking, well established. The strongest coordination procedures (Macroeconomic policy, Employment and Fiscal surveillance) are not OMCs in the strict sense as they preceded the baptism of the method in 2000 (see Table 3.3).

Table 3.3   Relative institutionalization of coordination processes (based on the use of Lisbon instruments)

Relative level of institutionalization	Policy area	Years since inception
VERY STRONG	Macroeconomic Policy	15
	Employment	10
	Fiscal Surveillance	8
STRONG	Training/Education	7
	Enterprise	7
	Information Society	7
	Research and Development	7
	Social inclusion	7
NASCENT	Sustainable Development	6
	Healthcare	6
	Pensions	6
	Better regulation	7
WEAK	Taxation	8
	Tourism	5
	Immigration	8
	Youth	5

Accounting for the Variety and Proliferation of OMCs

Several factors can be cited to account for the two particularities of the method. First, the OMC has developed beyond its original context of employment policy and is currently applied to very disparate areas such as immigration and tourism. Second, the method is rolled out in different ways, sometimes giving rise to strong coordination (Social inclusion), sometimes weak coordination (Youth policy). A first set of factors could explain the relative weakness of different OMCs.

The proliferation and variety of OMCs:

a. Time: OMCs become more embedded (institutionalized) over time, and the weaker OMCs are simply the latest instances of the process.
b. Treaty basis: OMCs require a treaty basis in order to develop fully.
c. Concurrent extra-Community coordination: OMCs benefiting from a parallel coordination process are strengthened by it.
d. Political experimentation: OMCs can be launched (and dropped) easily.

Temporal Factors

A first question in comparing and classifying OMCs is which are the 'strongest' and most elaborated instances. The most obvious approach would be to analyse the temporal factor. Table 3.3 presents coordination processes weighted by the relative level of institutionalization. If the length of time for which the process has been running is factored in, there is a correlation between weak and recent processes, strong and established ones. It might be concluded that, over time, other coordination procedures will also be increasingly institutionalized. This would support functional hypotheses of a 'fusion' or strengthening or coordination over time.

The Treaty Basis

The treaty provision for a coordination procedure, of course, guarantees its strength but is not, according to our analysis, a necessary condition for the vitality of all OMCs. Although education policy is the preserve of national legislatures, and its 'treaty purchase' is trivial, EU coordination in this field is growing in importance and impact.

The Lisbon Treaty could enhance the constitutional grounding of certain OMCs as it introduces a title (Art. 6 TFEU) that explicitly mentions Public health (Art. 168), Industry (Art. 173), Culture (Art. 167), Tourism (Art. 159), Education, Vocational training, Youth and Sport (Art. 165), Civil protection (Art. 196) and Administrative cooperation (Art. 197).

Extra-Community Initiatives, Domestic Influence and Counterfactual Evidence

Certain OMCs are mirrored and strengthened by concurrent coordination or cooperation initiatives (see Table 3.4). This makes evaluation of OMCs very difficult, as it is impossible to isolate an OMC effect from a concurrent coordination process. This is the case for both OMC Education (which is mirrored by a vigorous Bologna Process) and OMC Sustainable development (which is closely associated with the Kyoto Protocol). The Organisation for Economic Co-operation and Development (OECD) provides economic analysis services similar to the EU's BEPG and SGP in its annual economic surveys and country surveillance (see Heipertz and Verdun, 2004). The International Monetary Fund's (IMF) multilateral surveillance procedure called Article IV Consultations involves member state reporting of a similar type to that of the BEPG. The procedure concludes with the publication of recommendations on fiscal and economic

Table 3.4   Concurrent extra-Community coordination processes

Policy areas	Concurrent extra-Community initiatives
Macroeconomic Policy	OECD Economic Surveys
	IMF Article IV Consultations
Employment	OECD Jobs strategy (1994)
Fiscal Surveillance	OECD Country Surveillance
Training/Education	Bologna Process (1999)
Enterprise	–
Information Society	–
Research and Development	–
Social inclusion	–
Sustainable Development	Kyoto Protocol
Healthcare	–
Youth	–
Better Regulation	OECD Review of Regulatory Reform
Taxation	OECD forum against harmful tax practices (1988)
Tourism	–
Immigration	–
Pensions	–

policy. Therefore there is no 'null hypothesis', no clear benchmark from which the uncoordinated policy areas can be measured and their convergence mapped.

A second group of OMCs – Information society, R&D, and Enterprise – present difficulties for analysis as they present little or no counterfactual evidence of OMC coordination. Is member state investment in information technologies and innovation a result of EU 'added value' or national reactions to global challenges?

Political Experimentation at a Reduced Political Cost

Political experimentation (path-finding) by institutional actors (the Council, the Commission, or member states) could account for the proliferation of OMC processes. Under the existing Community method, initiatives can be bound by unwieldy rules of procedure and a surfeit of stakeholders during the elaboration stage. Often cited as an example in the domain, comitology was heralded as a forum for policy experimentation and expert decision-making. The process was open to institutional actors and non-institutional actors (mainly expert groups) invited to take part in discussions by the Commission. However, concerns about the democratic legitimacy of comitology prompted a review of working practices and what can be seen as either (1) greater participation by legitimated actors, or (2) its death by rigid institutionalization. It is argued that the tightening up of procedures and rules of participation strangled it of all innovation potential. The phenomenon is a familiar one in EU policy circles; all institutions jealously guard their own powers and closely observe those of others. New policy arenas are quickly populated by stakeholders, overcrowding ensues and paralysis can set in.

The OMC can serve as an alternative forum for policy experimentation that operates from without the 'shadow of institutionalization'. First, there are no established rules for actor participation. Second, political ownership (and therefore risk) is shared between participants. Third, it is iterative but not incremental, that is, progress is always voluntary and never locked in by legislation. Fourth, there is no direct budgetary impact and no arguing by participants over 'who gets what'. Lastly, it is 'new', that is it operates at the margin of Community competence and feels its way around obstacles, making up new procedures as it proceeds. In sum, it is a truly 'open' method. Consequently, its omission by name from the Constitutional Treaty, despite the favourable opinions of the four working groups mentioning it, was presumably prompted by concerns that its constitutionalization would rob it of its flexibility (de Búrca and Zeitlin, 2003).

The open method is, therefore, a risk-free method of path-finding in new policy areas. Illustrating this feature is OMC Immigration, which was initiated in 2000, leading to Commission proposals for a common policy in 2001. These were not adopted by the Council. The OMC served its purpose with little political cost to participants. As there is no voting procedure, those countries that were not ready to take part in a common immigration policy could simply opt out or persuade the others not to go any further with the process.

This 'try-it-for-size' approach to new policies could explain both its initial profusion and the relative weakness of certain OMCs. Political energy to coordinate at the EU level must be tested and the practice of 'kite flying' to test the prevailing wind is necessary in order to judge the feasibility of common measures. If this hypothesis is true, the method will rack up other policies and there could be an OMC Housing policy, an OMC Wage policy and so on.

The Open Method in Council Press Releases

The following series of graphs presents related data concerning the use of what can be called the 'Lisbon terminology', that is, references to elements associated with the method: indicators, peer review, social inclusion, common objectives, timetables, monitoring, action plans, guidelines, best practice and the knowledge-based economy. Again, the strong assumption is that the occurrence of these terms indicates some level of commitment to the Lisbon strategy. Obviously, some terms are general and are not specific to the strategy. Guidelines are a feature of many processes; however, the neutralizing effect of combining many terms for all Council meetings across several years can dampen any specific use of terms related to a single feature of policy-making.

Figure 3.3 presents the frequency with which the emblematic terms 'open method of coordination' or 'open coordination' are used by the different Council formations.

In contrast to the use of the term 'Lisbon strategy', the occurrence of the term 'open method of coordination' peaked in 2002 (at 38) and by 2004 had dropped steadily to the 2000 level (17). Recent references to the method have been largely due to the Education, Youth and Culture (EYC) Council (15 times in the two meetings taken together).

The 'discursive extinguishing' of reference to the OMC is unusual as one of the key features of the process is its iterative nature. One would expect that reference to the OMC, like the Lisbon strategy, would grow constantly. Once launched, an OMC procedure becomes subject to review, monitoring and reappraisal. Even though the Commission is given the role of process management by the European Council, it submits proposals and the findings of subcommittees on indicators and so on for the use of the OMC to the Council.

Figure 3.4 breaks down occurrences of references by Council formation and presents an institutional image of who is using the OMC, at least at the discursive level. The 'non-economic' formations (EYC and 'Employment, Social policy, Health and Consumer affairs', SOC) make more use of the term, suggesting that they see the method as more relevant to their work than the more purely economic formations (which do not refer to the OMC with as much intensity). The cases of the Economic and Financial Affairs (ECOFIN), Justice and Home Affairs (JHA), and surprisingly, Environment (ENV) councils are the most distinctive in that they refer to the OMC process only in passing.

Figure 3.5 compares references to the Lisbon strategy and the OMC in presidency conclusions. As mentioned above, many OMCs received presidency 'baptism' – such as Research and Development (R&D) (2003) – but no new process has been launched in recent years. However, the Lisbon strategy itself has remained a persistent topic. This may suggest that the OMC, especially after the criticisms of the mid-term review of 2004 (High Level Group), was no longer associated with the delivery of the strategy.

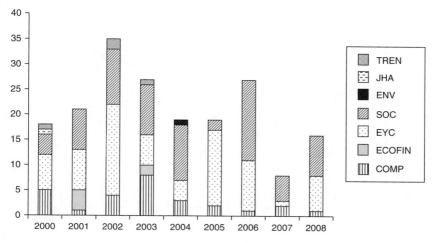

Source: Council website.

Figure 3.3 References to the OMC in Council press releases

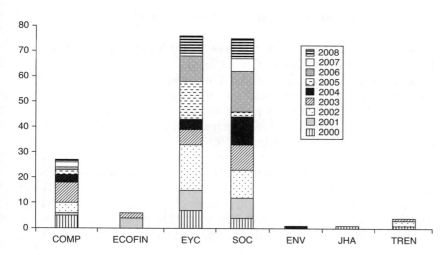

Source: Council website.

Figure 3.4 References to OMC in Council formations

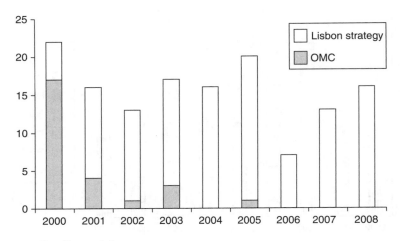

Source: Consilium website.

Figure 3.5   *References to the Lisbon strategy and the OMC in presidency conclusions, 2000–2008*

CONCLUSION AND DISCUSSION

Political Experimentation and the Proliferation of OMCs

As argued above, the OMC is, in one sense, the 'Community method lite'. Its weak institutionalization, limited legislative footprint and informal constitution make it a useful intergovernmental tool. The OMC is experimental, path-finding governance, a feature that is likely to be its saviour in spite of the more recent cooling of expectations surrounding it (Zeitlin and Pochet, 2005). In an era of enlargement, when the pressures for reform are great, the traditional methods of EU policy-making can seem a little pedestrian. National executives with an appetite for cooperating with each other need alternative avenues to full-blown supranational law-making. If the OMC only fulfils this role, it is likely to outlast its relationship with the Lisbon strategy. The OMC is still, however, an underexploited resource. The absence of commonly agreed indicators in key policy fields means that meaningful exchange is limited. Naming and shaming, one of the more vaunted aspects of the method, cannot bite if the shamed can retort that indicators do not capture the specificities of the situation.

However, the OMC as a permanent feature of European governance will live or die by its association with the Lisbon strategy. If our content analysis is correct, there has been a decoupling of the strategy from the

OMC which may indicate that it is simply not up to the task set: delivering economic growth. Any direct causal effect of the OMC in any policy area is of course difficult to isolate, and one can argue endlessly as to its real impact. As a 'discursive regulatory mechanism' it works at the level of ideas. However, it is not the only one. The national political sphere is still the arena where social policy is hammered out. An Europeanization of policy expectations (that is a common understanding of what, say, an employment policy is supposed to do) may be coherent at EU level but dissonant at the national one. And Lisbon is all about domestic change. Further research is necessary, and under way, to identify the Lisbon effect on national policies. Some of the other articles cited in the present chapter go a long way to answering this question. Inevitably, all distributive issues of the type the OMC ultimately deals with find their way to the doorstep, where candidates meet the electorate's demands.

The OMC's depoliticization of policy choices (its problem-solving mantle) is a useful stage in policy formulation. Its rationality of 'best and worst' plays out well in international forums where alternatives are numbered lists. When bureaucrats implement changes that remove income support from individuals (categories), alternatives reveal their social and political costs. Any depoliticization, one suspects, is temporary.

The Legacy of the Open Method of Coordination

With the Lisbon strategy's ten-year cycle coming to an end in 2010, is it possible to offer a verdict on the value of the OMC to EU governance? For many (see Zeitlin, 2009; EU Scientific and Technical Research Committee, 2004), it is simply too soon to tell, as the method has not been fully implemented. It could be argued that after ten years this is about as good as it is going to get for the OMC. At the very least, the initial enthusiasm for the method as such has waned (no new OMC processes have seen the light of day since 2005). Indeed, looking back on the programmes for change the method was intended to deliver (in the areas of R&D and eEurope especially), it is hard to see how it could be otherwise. It is as if the method gave licence to policy promoters (be they from the Commission or national arenas) to establish a wish list of 'good things' for Europe without the need for a clear rationale, a coherent plan or a concrete objective. Take, for example, the measures marshalled to promote the European Research Area (ERA). The project foresaw, among other things, an increase in R&D investment across Europe equivalent to the combined GDP of 11 of its (albeit) poorest members.[1] This is a major undertaking by any standards. OMC-style instruments of persuasion and policy-learning are inevitably incapable of affecting such transformation of research infrastructures and practices across Europe. The fault, arguably, lies more with the policy pro-nouncements rather than with the method itself. If a bad worker blames his tools, an over-optimistic policy-maker will blame the 'delivery'.

Good ideas do not easily translate into good policies. The OMC did not discover this rule of thumb but it does make it clearer. Look to any OMC and there are a plethora of excellent initiatives jostling for attention. Again an example: eEurope 2002 promised for 2003 that '(a)ll European citizens should have the possibility to have a health smart card to enable secure and confidential access to networked patient information' (Council of the European Union et al., 2000). The claim today seems almost fanciful; not only does such technology not exist in most member states, but its deploy-ment has been delayed, and not only because of purely technical issues: concerns about security and privacy, especially in the light of the many data-protection-related disasters, have stalled many projects.

The OMC is a child of the Lisbon summit, that is, a pre-dotcom bubble and pre-credit crunch world when ambitious, even fanciful plans to recre-ate the EU were in fashion. In today's straitened times, a more cautious approach built on the necessity of coordination rather than its favourabil-ity would seem more apposite.

Perhaps the lasting significance of the OMC will be in the inevitable disappointment it created. This disappointment points to a desire on the part of policy-makers and 'policy-takers' for a system of governance that is open, adaptive and accountable. These are noble and lofty goals for whom the relative impotence of the OMC to transform EU governance is a setback at most. It is also a lesson in the difficulty for the EU to exercise power and display legitimacy simultaneously.

NOTE

1. Three per cent of the EU27 GDP is €330052 million, or the combined GDP of Malta, Estonia, Latvia, Cyprus, Lithuania, Bulgaria, Slovenia, Luxembourg, Slovakia, Romania and Hungary. The shortfall of €130000 million is equal to the first eight of these 11 member states (source: own calculation based on Eurostat data for 2005).

REFERENCES

Apeldoorn, Bastiaan van (2002), *Transnational Capitalism and the Struggle over European Integration*, London: Routledge.
Borrás, S. and B. Greve (2004), 'Concluding remarks: new method or just cheap talk?', *Journal of European Public Policy*, **11**(2), 329–36.
Borrás, Susana and Kerstin Jacobsson (2004), 'The Open Method of Co-ordination

and new governance patterns in the EU', in *The Open Method of Co-ordination in the European Union*, Special issue of *Journal of European Public Policy*, **11**(2) (April), 185–208.

Chalmers, Damian and Martin Lodge (2003), 'The Open Method of Coordination and the European welfare state', European Union Studies Association (EUSA): Biennial Conference: 2003 (8th), 27–29 March, Nashville, TN.

Council of the European Union and European Commission (2000), 'eEurope 2002, An Information Society for all, Action Plan', Brussels.

de Búrca, Gráinne and Jonathan Zeitlin (2003), 'Constitutionalising the Open Method of Coordination: a note for the convention', CEPS Policy Brief No. 31, March 2003.

de la Porte, Caroline and Patrizia Nanz (2004), 'The OMC: a deliberative-democratic mode of governance? The cases of employment and pensions', *Journal of European Public Policy*, **11**(2), 267–88.

Diedrichs, Udo (2005), 'New modes of governance: preliminary remarks on an ambiguous concept', paper presented at cluster meeting 2, Florence, May 2005.

European Commission (2001a), 'European Commission white paper "a new impetus for European youth"', COM(2001) 681 final, Brussels.

European Commission (2001b), 'Communication from the Commission on an Open Method of Coordination for the Community Immigration Policy', COM(2001) 387 final, Brussels.

European Commission (2005), 'Working together for growth and jobs, next steps in implementing the revised Lisbon strategy', Commission Staff Working Paper, SEC (2005) 622/2, Brussels.

European Council (2000), 'Lisbon European Council 23 and 24 March 2000, presidency conclusions', Lisbon.

European Court of Justice (ECJ) (2004), 'Judgment of the Court (Full Court) of 13 July 2004 in Case C-27/04: Commission of the European Communities v Council of the European Union', Official Journal, C 228, 13 July.

European Union Scientific and Technical Research Committee (2004), 'CREST report on the application of the method of open coordination in favour of the Barcelona research investment objective', CREST 1206/04, 1 October, Brussels.

Falkner, Gerda (2005), *Complying with Europe: EU Harmonisation and Soft Law in the Member States*, Cambridge: Cambridge University Press.

Falkner, Gerda and Oliver Treib (2004), 'Explaining EU policy implementation across countries: three modes of adaptation', NEWGOV kick-off meeting, 10 December, Brussels.

Gill, Stephen (1998), 'European governance and new constitutionalism: economic and monetary union and alternatives to disciplinary neoliberalism in Europe', *New Political Economy*, **3**(1) (March), 5–26.

Haahr, Jens Henrik (2004), 'Open co-ordination as advanced liberal government', *Journal of European Public Policy*, **11**(2) (April), 209–30.

Hartwig, Ines and Christoph Meyer (2002), 'Towards deliberative network governance? Theorising socio-economic policy coordination in the European Union', GOVECOR working Paper, 12 December, University of Cologne.

Heipertz, Martin and Amy Verdun (2004) 'The dog that would never bite? On the origins of the Stability and Growth Pact', *Journal of European Public Policy*, **11**(5), 765–80.

Héritier, Adrienne (2001), 'New modes of governance in Europe: policy-making without legislating?', MPI Collective Goods Preprint no. 2001/14.

High Level Group (2004), *Facing the Challenge, The Lisbon Strategy for Growth and Employment*, Report from the High Level Group chaired by Wim Kok, available at http://europa.eu.int/comm/lisbon_strategy/index_en.html.

Hobbs, Richard and Wanjiru Njoya (2005), 'Regulating the European labour market: prospects and limitations of a reflexive governance approach', *British Journal of Industrial Relations*, **43** (June), 297–319.

Jacobsson, Kerstin (2002), 'Soft regulation and the subtle transformation of states: the case of EU employment policy', GOVECOR working paper, 16 July, University of Cologne.

Jacobsson, Kerstin (2004), 'Soft regulation and the subtle transformation of states: the case of EU employment policy', *Journal of European Social Policy*, no. 4.

Jacobsson, Kerstin and Åsa Vifell (2003), 'Integration by deliberation? On the role of committees in the Open Method of Coordination', paper prepared for the workshop 'The Forging of deliberative Supranationalism in the EU', Florence, 7–8 February.

Jessop, Bob (2002), 'The European Union and recent transformations in statehood', online paper available at http://www.lancs.ac.uk/fss/sociology/papers/jessop-eu-transformations-statehood.pdf.

Kaiser, Robert and Heiko Prange (2002), 'A new concept of deepening European integration? The European Research Area and the emerging role of policy coordination in a multi-level governance system', in European Integration online-Papers (EioP) **6**(18), available at http://eiop.or.at/eiop/texte/2002-018a.htm.

Maher, Imelda (2004), 'Law and the Open Method of Coordination', *Journal of Comparative Government and European Policy*, **2**(2), 248–63.

Radaelli, Claudio M. (1998), 'Policy narratives in the European Union: the case of harmful tax competition', EUI-RSCAS Working Papers 34, European University Institute (EUI), Robert Schuman Centre of Advanced Studies (RSCAS).

Radaelli, Claudio M. (2003), 'The Open Method of Coordination: a new governance architecture for the European Union?', SIEPS Report no. 1, Swedish Institute for European Policy Studies, Stockholm, March.

Radaelli, Claudio M. (2004), 'Who learns what? Policy learning and the Open Method of Coordination', paper prepared for ESRC seminar series, 24 November.

Rhodes, Martin (2005), 'The scientific objectives of the NEWGOV project: a revised framework', NEWGOV consortium conference, Florence, 30 May.

Sabel, Charles F. and Jonathan Zeitlin (2003), 'Active welfare, experimental governance, pragmatic constitutionalism: the new transformation of Europe', paper presented at 'The Modernisation of the European Social Model and EU Policies and Instruments Conference', Ioannina, Greece, 21–22 May.

Savio, Annikki and Elina Palola (2004), 'Post-Lisbon social policy: inventing the social in the confines of the European Union', paper presented at the ESPAnet annual conference, Oxford, 9–11 September.

Syrpis, Phil (2002), 'Legitimising European governance: taking subsidiarity seriously within the Open Method of Coordination', Department of Law Working Papers no. 2002/10, Florence: European University Institute.

Wessels, Wolfgang (2004a), 'Report of Cluster One workshop', NEWGOV kick-off meeting, Brussels, 10 December.

Wessels, Wolfgang (2004b), 'Emergence and evolution of modes of governance. Designing a treaty-based framework: towards an index of integration', paper presented at Cluster One meeting, Brussels.

Zeitlin, Jonathan (2004), 'Opening the OMC: a reflexive reform strategy', paper presented at the conference on 'The EES: Discussion and Institutionalisation', Brussels, 30–31 August, available at http://eucenter.wisc.edu/Opening_the_OMC_Brussels.htm.

Zeitlin, Jonathan (2009) 'Is the Open Method of Coordination an alternative to the community method?', in Renaud Dehousse (ed.), *The Community Method: Obstinate or Obsolete?*, London: Macmillan.

Zeitlin, Jonathan and Philippe Pochet with Lars Magnusson (eds) (2005), *The Open Method of Coordination in Action: The European Employment and Social Inclusion Strategies*, Brussels: Peter Lang.

4. The pensions OMC: why did it emerge and how has it evolved?

David Natali

INTRODUCTION

This chapter aims to shed light on the emergence within the European Union of the Open Method of Coordination (OMC) in the field of pensions. It does so by using the concept of *window of opportunity* (related to a revised 'garbage can' model). While that concept has usually been proposed for the analysis of agenda-setting and policy change (Keeler, 1993; Kingdon, 1995; Zahariadis, 2003), in this chapter it is used for the study of the introduction of new modes of governance[1] (NMGs) and to answer two more specific questions. First, why did the Pensions OMC emerge? And, second, how did it evolve?

The proposed model seems useful for at least three reasons. First, it allows for a multi-dimensional and multi-level analytical framework. From a descriptive perspective, it provides a wide map of multiple *socio-economic*, *institutional* and *political factors* (some of them related to elements of chance and human creativity) which affected the launch of the coordination process in the field. These forces, originating at both national and supranational level, led to a window of opportunity and then to an NMG. From a theoretical point of view, this allows for the combination of some of the traditional theories of European integration (neo-functionalism, new institutionalism and intergovernmentalism). As Peterson and Bomberg (1999: 9) have argued, the EU is 'heavily nuanced, constantly changing and even kaleidoscopic' and thus resists simple characterizations and/or a general theory. Consistently, the following framework draws on the interaction of different theories.[2]

Second, the model helps to specify the mechanisms that translate critical junctures into lasting political legacies. The role of key *political entrepreneurs* in particular proves important when it comes to defining problems, envisaging solutions, and collecting consensus for a renewed EU intervention. In the following, we make reference to the Director General of the DG Employment and Social Affairs of the Commission, the then Belgian

Minister Frank Vandenbroucke (one of the architects of the OMC), and the Italian administrative elite.

Finally, the use of a multi-dimensional and multi-level framework helps us to identify the main peculiarities of the Pensions OMC, its emergence and first evolution (before the broader process of 'streamlining' with other social protection and inclusion OMCs). While some of the factors mentioned above were determinants of the broader Lisbon strategy, others are typical of pensions policy. Their combination helps explain the peculiar 'weakness' of the process of coordinating national pension reforms (in terms of its convergence capacity).

The first section briefly summarizes the key steps for the launch and first implementation of the Pensions OMC in the period 1999–2003 and its peculiar traits. Section 2 introduces the multi-dimensional and multi-level framework based on the concept of *window of opportunity*. Sections 3 to 5 present the main socioeconomic, institutional and political factors that led to the launch of the new method. Their interaction rather than their independence explain the launch of the OMC in the field. Section 6 presents conclusions.

THE OPEN METHOD OF COORDINATION ON PENSIONS: A 'WEAK' AND 'LIGHT' PROCESS

According to the conclusions of the Lisbon summit of 2000, the OMC aims to organize a learning process about how to cope with the common challenges of the global economy in a coordinated way, while also respecting national diversity. It consists of defining common strategic guidelines at European level for coping with structural change and then organizing a process whereby member states emulate each other in applying them, stimulating the exchange of best practices, while taking account of national characteristics. Its main procedures are common guidelines to be implemented at national level, periodic monitoring, and evaluation and peer review accompanied by indicators and benchmarks.

Forms of European coordination have developed over time. Already envisaged for budget policy under the Maastricht Treaty, they were then introduced for employment policy through the Amsterdam Treaty and for social inclusion and social protection (Scharpf, 2002). In 1999, the Commission issued the communication, 'A concerted strategy for modernising social protection' (Commission of the European Community, 1999). In terms of policy goals, the report stressed that social protection institutions are at the core of the European social model. It proposed their modernization in order to contribute to the economic competitiveness of Europe. In terms of procedures, the document indicated a number of instruments to improve the exchange of national expertise, promote stricter cooperation between EU institutions, and involve key stakeholders at different levels of governance (supranational, national and local). The key components of the OMC, in terms of both goals and procedures, were de facto already defined (de la Porte, 2003).

Still in 1999, under the Finnish presidency, the decision was taken to set up the High-level Working Group to tackle social protection issues common to all member states. This working group was then integrated and mentioned in the Nice Treaty as the Social Protection Committee (SPC). As requested by the Lisbon summit, the European Commission published a communication on Safe and Sustainable Pensions at the end of 2000. The Stockholm European Council of February 2001 made reference for the first time to the Open Method of Coordination to be introduced in this domain, while the Gothenburg Council of June 2001 endorsed the three broad objectives (or pillars) of the process (SPC, 2001). They were defined in terms of the need to guarantee the social adequacy, the financial sustainability and the modernization of pension programmes according to the changing social and economic conditions. In December, the Laeken summit (under the Belgian presidency) adopted the Joint Report on Objectives and Working Methods prepared by the SPC and the Economic Policy Committee (EPC) with 11 sub-objectives (under the three objectives of social adequacy, financial sustainability and modernization), working methods and the timetable for the first 'round' of the process. Member states were invited to prepare national strategy reports (NSRs) about their national pension programmes for September 2002. Then in March 2003 the Commission and the Council were to present the Joint Report to summarize common trends in pensions policy across the EU (see Vanhercke, 2006b for a more precise historical account). The following sections will seek to answer the question regarding why the Pensions OMC emerged.

Compared to other OMCs (for example the European Employment Strategy), the Pensions OMC (at least for its first years of implementation) has been defined as a 'partial' (Vanhercke, 2006b: 13) and 'closed' method of coordination (Natali, 2006), in that:

- it lacks an explicit reference in the treaty;
- common voluntary objectives are mainly qualitative;
- there are no explicit recommendations to member states, and thus neither formal nor moral sanctions;
- it lacks common indicators agreed on by member states (at least as for the first cycle of its implementation);

- the participation of stakeholders (both social partners and social NGOs) has proved particularly limited in that there is no formal requirement for them to participate or to be consulted in the process;
- national strategy reports represent a 'state of the art' of pension programmes rather than an action plan for the future;
- benchmarking is very limited and the peer review process is weak (see Schludi 2003).

As Citi and Rhodes (2007) put it, the coordination of pension programmes is thus characterized by a low 'convergence capacity'. The two authors establish a single variable for locating different policy instruments in terms of five discrete steps and calibrate the convergence capacity accordingly. The Pensions OMC is included in step 2 (low convergence effects) in that it is based on voluntary objectives plus weak forms of benchmarking and peer pressure. In other words, there is little room for learning and no fundamental alteration of the incentive structure of the national policy-making process (Eckardt, 2004). Moreover, as de la Porte and Nanz (2004) show, it is characterized by low participation of social partners and civil society organizations and restricted room for public debate.

The following sections will also seek to answer a second question: why is the Pensions OMC such a 'light' process of coordination (much weaker than those on employment and other social policies)?

THE EMERGENCE OF NEW MODES OF GOVERNANCE: A MULTI-DIMENSIONAL AND MULTI-LEVEL APPROACH

The literature on the launch of new modes of governance in the social policy domain has mainly focused on *neo-functional, intergovernmental* and *new institutionalist* theories. For *neo-functionalists* the emergence of social OMCs is largely dependent on economic integration and the consequent loss of national capacity to promote social rights. Decisions related to economic integration (that is the Single Market and Economic and Monetary Union, EMU) 'spillover' and stimulate further acts of integration in the employment and social domains. Scharpf (2002) and Ioannou and Niemann (2003) have followed that approach and stressed the importance of social and political demands for the advancement of social Europe and the technocratic process led by national governments and experts for the introduction of NMGs. Neo-functionalism has been criticized for ignoring the political rationality of EU decision-making, and for underestimating the potential for inefficiency and for stagnation in European integration (Schäfer, 2004).

Neo-institutionalists have suggested supranational institutions enjoy much autonomy (from national governments) in defining and pursuing their own set of preferences, and in increasing their control over the policy-making process. Gaps between national governments' preferences and the functioning of supranational institutions are thus determined by the autonomy of supranational institutions, the unintended consequences of integration, the multiplicity of interests of the actors taking office, and the restricted time horizon of decision-makers. Institutional obstacles and costs limit the capacity of national institutions to react to 'agency losses', while they increase the power and competences of supranational actors (see Pierson, 1996a; Pollack, 1997; de la Porte, 2007). As Vanhercke (2006a; 2006b) argues, the introduction of the OMC on social protection seems to be related to the earlier emergence of new governing modes on employment and then on social inclusion. On the one hand, the first OMCs represented a set of instruments that were easily adaptable to further policy domains. On the other, the Commission (on the basis of the role it played and the capabilities matured in other policies), acted as a broker to aggregate consensus. New institutionalism has been criticized (a) because it is unable to shed light on the persistent ability of national governments to choose different modes of integration with different degrees of delegation, and tends to overestimate the impact of unintended consequences and costs (related to previous steps) on future decisions, and (b) because it underestimates the role of actor constellations (see Schäfer, 2004).

For *intergovernmentalists*, EU integration is mainly related to the interaction of member states. Governments are rational self-interested actors who define their interests, aggregate social demands and negotiate with each other. The leftward electoral swing in the second part of the 1990s, the action of some members (that is Portugal and Belgium) and of newcomers in the EU (for example Sweden), and a broad intergovernmental approach contributed to the launch of OMCs (Goetschy, 1999; Jenson and Pochet, 2002). Critics of this approach are mainly concerned about a more open interaction between governments, supranational institutions and interest groups, as well as the influence of international organizations on the definition of members' interests and preferences (Vanhercke, 2006a).

Moreover, the theories mentioned above have been the object of some broader and common critical remarks. First, as Peterson and Bomberg (1999) argue, their individual application to EU integration shows some limitations. Not a single one of them can represent by itself 'the' general theory for the understanding of EU decision-making. This decision-making is a complex and deep form of regionalism that resists simple generalizations (Sandholtz, 1996). Second, as to applying them to the emergence of new governing modes on social issues, these theories seem too generic and unable to capture the peculiar traits of each process and its independent variables. The complexity of European integration has a 'policy-based' dimension too. In line with the seminal work by Lowi (1964), key features of a particular policy have an influence on the political process (for example the logic of interaction, the nature of interests and preferences, and so on). To add a further complication, decision-making is typically multi-level: supranational and national levels interact. Here I refer to the seminal work of Putnam (1988) on 'two-level games' based on the interaction of diplomacy (at supranational level) and domestic politics (see also Scharpf, 1986).

In line with these broad remarks, this section proposes a multi-dimensional and multi-level framework. This explains the emergence of an NMG in terms of the interaction of different variables leading to a window of opportunity and then innovation. I understand the introduction of new modes of governance as the result of a number of factors rather than a single independent variable. Some of them are identifiable and rationally explainable; some are imponderable (Kingdon, 1995; Zahariadis, 2003). Moreover, some operate at national level and some others at supranational level.

Opportunities for innovation are usually very few. Lock-in effects, the generally conservative features of democratic political institutions and the risky nature of innovation all represent decisive constraints on change. By contrast, other phenomena may open windows representing an opportunity for advocates of proposals to direct attention to problems and consequently to adopt solutions. Despite their rarity, it is precisely these windows that make possible major changes. Authors such as Kingdon (1995) have used the 'garbage can' model to study the fluidity of policy-making and the role played by elements of chance and human creativity. This model recognizes that political phenomena are irregular and heavily influenced by very broad determinants. Fortuitous factors can play a decisive role in putting a certain issue at the core of the political debate. In a previous work, I have proposed a revised and more deterministic interpretation of the 'policy change' model (based on the concept of window of opportunity) that is designed to cope with its main shortcomings (Natali, 2004).[3]

The framework in Figure 4.1 is based on some key elements: *socio-economic, political and institutional factors*. The first two are related to the problem and political 'streams' defined by Kingdon (1995). *Political* and *socioeconomic factors* capture the attention of decision-makers by means of different elements as Kingdon describes them. Indicators (such

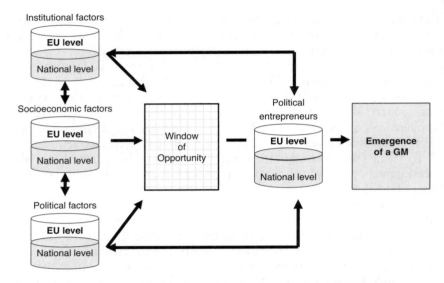

Figure 4.1   Window of opportunity for the emergence of governing modes

as economic stagnation, or a growing budget deficit) as well as focusing events (symbolic events and so on) call attention to problems. Moreover, other political events such as a new climate of public opinion or a turnover of key political and administrative personnel can enlarge or restrict the room to manoeuvre for innovation.

Institutional factors seem particularly important in the analysis of European integration. The emergence of forms of coordination of economic and budget policies has represented an important example to be replicated in other areas through the dynamics of learning and mimicking (Pochet, 2001; Moreno and Palier, 2004). What is more, these institutional dynamics in a certain field can produce effects on other policy areas (functional spillover effect). This is particularly true in the case of pensions. Fiscal and monetary policy decisions have affected welfare problems directly (see Featherstone, 2004). Moreover, innovations are assumed to be the result of a process that includes more than a single episode. Actors' behaviour and factors at time t influence events at time $t + 1$. To sum up, socioeconomic, political and institutional factors interact with each other and thus lead to a window of opportunity for the emergence of new governing modes.

To explain the logic of such a process clearly, the model needs further elaboration. Here, I claim that *political entrepreneurs* have an important role. These are energetic and talented individuals who are capable of producing unexpected changes (see Zerbinati and Souitaris, 2002 for a review of the literature on policy entrepreneurship). They couple solutions, problems and political momentum (Kingdon, 1995). As in a previous work (Natali, 2004), I assume that they have a proactive role. As the analysis of the emergence of the OMC confirms, not only do they make use of a given policy window, but they also contribute to its opening. The following sections will focus on a few of their capabilities: the elaboration of *strategic orientations* (which are the definition of problems and proposals), and the *commitment and control of resources* (in particular the maximization of consensus for changes through diplomatic alliances) (Riker, 1986; Zahariadis, 2003).[4]

SOCIOECONOMIC FACTORS: COMMON CHALLENGES TO PENSION SYSTEMS IN EUROPE

By the end of the 1970s a number of economic and social pressures had placed social policies in general, and pensions policies in particular, under stress. Changes in the labour market, new family patterns, demographic strains and globalization were seen as severe constraints on social provision (Anderson, 2002; Taylor-Gooby, 2004). In line with the EU jargon, these challenges affected both the 'financial sustainability' and the 'social adequacy' of pensions (Commission of the European Community and European Council, 2003). In the 1980s, some publications (especially those from international organizations, such as OECD, 1988 and World Bank, 1994) started a major debate at the level of both public opinion and political elites. The following summarizes some key aspects of the 'pension problem' at the end of the twentieth century.

Population ageing has been the first main source of increased tensions. It consists of three different but interrelated issues: the increase in life expectancy, the exit from the labour market of the so-called baby-boom generation (born between 1945 and 1965), and the huge reduction in birth rates (EPC, 1997, 2003). Old-age pension schemes, introduced between the late nineteenth century and the early twentieth century, were directed to a minority of the population and benefits were paid only for a short period, but demographic changes have impacted adversely on their financial viability. As early as in the 1980s, international organizations projected a dramatic increase of public pension outlays as a result of demographic trends. As proposed by Schludi (2005), calculations by the Organisation for Economic Co-operation and Development (OECD) published in 1988 proved that there were growing financial strains on old-age programmes. Public spending in the EU countries was expected to reach dramatic high levels unless reforms were carried out: pensions commitments would account for 35 per cent of gross domestic product (GDP) in Italy, 30 per cent in Germany and about 27 per cent in France. These indicators contributed greatly to pensions cutbacks being put at the top of the (national and European) political agenda[5] (Bonoli and Shinkawa, 2005).

Growing general financial strains have presented a second challenge. They are only partly to be explained in terms of population ageing. Other dynamics have also played a role. In some countries, in fact, pension schemes started to show financial instability well before the concrete impact of demographic change was felt. Pressures have arisen because the economic development of European countries has been more limited compared to the rapid growth in the first three decades after World War II. The maturation of the pension system contributed to put it under financial strain as well: a growing number of older workers left the labour market just when the more generous rules introduced earlier were being implemented. The existence of large state budget deficits (and debts) represented a further short-term pressure as pensions were partly financed out of the public budget (Schludi, 2003).

The evolution of labour markets and societal institutions (for example the family) put old-age programmes under siege too. Pension systems were mainly directed to protect long-term contract jobs and sustain stable and long careers, and were based on the assumption of full employment (Esping-Andersen, 1996). Stable family structures that provided care for the elderly and other dependent groups were the norm in the social structure (in particular in continental and southern Europe). In the second part of the twentieth century, however, families started to change their profile and thus weaken the functional link between social policy *in action* and social needs. Meanwhile the development of the labour markets has been characterized by the increased importance of flexible contracts (for example temporary and part-time jobs). Subsequent 'new' social risks have necessitated the revision of 'old' programmes (Taylor-Gooby, 2004).

In this socioeconomic context, European integration has represented a double threat for the national welfare state, and especially for pension systems. On the one hand, the widening of the internal market has led to more open financial markets and capital mobility and thus reduced the capacity of national governments to increase taxation (Bonoli, 2003). If investors perceive the level of taxes as too high, they may decide to move their activities elsewhere. This pressure is assumed to be particularly acute for countries where pensions are financed through contributions and general taxation. On the other hand, and consistently, monetary union and the coordination of budgetary policies have greatly reduced the capacity of member states to control exchange rates and budget deficits. This leads us to the institutional factors that contributed to open the window of opportunity. To sum up, both socioeconomic pressures at national level and European integration were consistent with the strength of the EU's steering capacity in the field.

INSTITUTIONAL FACTORS: EUROPEAN INTEGRATION VS NATIONAL WELFARE STATES

While socioeconomic strains affected all western countries, EU members faced reinforced pressures. As Scharpf (2002) and then Ferrera (2005) put it, the EU has been based on a political and constitutional asymmetry between economic and social policy functions. The latter is designed at national level in the shadow of the 'constitutionalized' European law on market integration and liberalization. In line with neo-functionalism, economic integration is assumed to 'spillover' and stimulate a demand for further integration in the social policy domains through societal and technocratic processes (see Ioannou and Niemann, 2003). In line with a functionalist perspective, common challenges to the 'golden age' pension programmes forced member states to react, but European integration limited their capacity to find solutions. Both elements were consistent with some more active form of EU intervention.

At the end of the twentieth century, at the European level the 'pension issue' was not new. Since its emergence, the EU has dealt with it according to different (but complementary) dimensions.

The first axis of intervention concerns the development of integrated, transparent and efficient financial markets by eliminating obstacles to investments in supplementary pension funds. Here, the EU has acted through the legislative or Community method.[6] As Borrás and Jacobsson (2004) put it, that attempt to harmonize individual and collective rights has reached its limits. More specific aspects of the functioning of national programmes might be partly addressed by introducing new European legislation, but more effective broader measures could not be imposed on individual member states.

The second action aims to address population ageing through the coordination of macroeconomic policy (and especially of budget policies). In that sense, the Maastricht Treaty and then the Stability and Growth Pact (SGP) and the Broad Economic Policy Guidelines (BEPG) have been the main instruments of action. As mentioned above, during the 1990s national governments were forced to leave the budget-spending paradigm in favour of a more restricted financial policy. Limits to public expenditure on pensions arising from the Maastricht Treaty and then the SGP largely contributed to cutbacks (Pakaslahti and Pochet, 2003). That coordination of macroeconomic policy represented a twofold stimulus for more explicit EU action on social policies. On the one hand, it led to the acceleration of the European debate on social issues (where socially-oriented actors were initially excluded). As Hemerijck and Ferrera (2004: 251) stressed, by the 1990s employment and social policies had begun to find their way onto the European agenda. On the other hand, according to the proposal by Jacques Delors, it represented a template for similar soft governance on social issues (see Ross, 1995; Pochet, 2001). Empirical evidence shows the active role of EU institutions (that is the Commission) in pressing member states to use the OMC to tackle the coordination of national pension reforms (see Vanhercke, 2006b). This confirms that the new-institutionalist perspective can help in assessing the complex intergovernmental but also interinstitutional dynamic of the EU.

While these supranational dynamics were all favourable to the coordination of pensions, there were opposing strong pressures at member state level. Despite the demands for 'more social Europe', national governments have traditionally been reluctant to transfer their responsibility to the EU. Tackling pensions problems means engaging with what Pierson (1996b: 2001) has called an 'immovable object': welfare (and in particular pension) programmes are still sticky entities. First, electoral incentives are huge. Virtually every citizen (current pensioners and future beneficiaries as well) has a stake in public (and to a lesser extent in non-public) pensions. Support for current pension programmes thus remains intense and creates potentially strong opposition to reforms, as well as to the EU challenge to national autonomy. As shown by Ferrera (2005: 105), national institutions represent the main source of solidarity throughout the social structure and of strong political bonds between citizens and policy-makers, through the mediation of political parties and interest groups. This is true for welfare schemes in general, but pensions are the most expensive and thus most popular programme by far; in 2003, pension outlays (for old age, disability and survivors) represented more than 50 per cent of total social spending in the EU 25 (Natali, 2006; 2008).

Moreover, lock-in effects further reinforce the stability of existing national pensions institutions: multiple vetoes and mechanisms of path dependence make certain courses of action hard to reverse once they are initiated. Again, this is particularly true for pension arrangements which are mature and thus consistent with increasing returns (Pierson, 2001). I argue that these impediments to innovation have worked against the uploading of responsibilities to the EU. For instance, the degree of institutional diversity with respect to pension systems is somewhat higher than it is in the case of other social policies (Schludi, 2003: 42). In fact, if the diversity of national welfare states is a traditional trait of the European social dimension, it is particularly huge in the field under scrutiny here. Normative assumptions about what a pension system is and what it is expected to perform differ, with consequences for the definition of common objectives and indicators.[7]

Third, pension programmes mainly developed at national level. Key actors (political institutions and actors, and social partners) in the field are mainly national, while supra- and sub-national players are traditionally weak. National and European NGOs which exert so much influence in other OMCs (for example on social inclusion) are absent from the domain of pensions (see Vanhercke, 2006a; 2006b). Thus, the number of stakeholders interested in the field is much smaller and the room for an EU-level network (of organized interests) is reduced as well.

The combination of these three factors seems to limit the room for an effective European intervention in the domain and thus to reduce the dimension of the window for an NMG. It is not surprising that member states have not accepted transfers of sovereignty to the EU level.

POLITICAL FACTORS AND THE ROLE OF NATIONAL AND EUROPEAN ENTREPRENEURS

Common challenges to national pension programmes and the progress of European integration contributed to put pensions at the core of a major European debate. Other factors should, however, be addressed in order to improve our understanding of how those pressures led to the emergence of the OMC (see Figure 4.1). This section focuses on the *political events* which at the end of the 1990s favoured the launch of new modes of governance on pensions. Then, we focus on the role of *political entrepreneurs*, both within the EU institutions and in single member states. For the former, we refer to the key role of actors in the DG Employment and Social Affairs. On the latter, we refer to national political decision-makers and administrative elites in two countries. We consider Belgium and Italy as part of the coalition that favoured the launch of the Pensions OMC.

As far as *political events* are concerned, the existence of left-of-centre governments in the majority of the EU countries at the end of the 1990s (for example in the biggest countries, like France, Germany, Italy and the UK) was a real stimulus that contributed to open a window of opportunity (Jenson and Pochet, 2002). According to the intergovernmental approach briefly summarized in section 1, this represented a major political event consistent with the turnover of the key political personnel in Europe. Mass protest movements in some countries (for example France and Italy) did show that there was mounting criticism of the proposed reforms of welfare programmes and a fear of new attacks (in the shadow of EMU) on social rights 'as we know them'. High spending on pensions and the (electoral and political) costs of reforms were at the top of the political debate in many countries as well. The rise of centre–left governments was largely interpreted as the effort to put employment and social policies at the top of both national and European agendas (Palier, 2003). As the actors who worked on this dossier at the time confirmed, the shared understanding on the need for innovation was decisive for the launch of the OMC in social protection:

> All the governments were conscious of the need for reforming pensions across Europe. At the same time, the fact that in a majority of countries left-of-centre governments ruled, favoured a common position to define a new 'compromise' between pressures for changes and the re-statement of key principles of the European social model. (Interview with a member of the Cabinet of the Belgian Minister of Social Affairs 2000, Brussels, 8 February 2005)

In the words of Hemerijck and Ferrera (2004: 274), 'the social democratic moment' of the 1990s defined social protection as a productive factor and helped to reinforce the social dimension of the Union. Yet the social democratic leadership was much more ambivalent about the concrete uploading of competences on social protection (as well as employment) policy. As Schäfer (2004: 12) argued, 'there has never been as strong a coalition in favour of internationalizing employment (and social) policy as there was in Maastricht for monetary union'. This is even more true for pensions (see the previous section). On the other hand, new modes of governance were accepted in that they represented neo-voluntarist soft methods, combining EU action with subsidiarity and flexibility. Here again, multiple forces 'clashed' with each other and pushed in different, if not opposite, directions.

The Role of the Commission

Thus, the 'conflict' between opposite forces, some favourable to EU coordination and some others against it, did limit the opportunity for concrete action. Political entrepreneurs contributed greatly to creating the window of opportunity and then used it to launch the coordination of national pension reforms. Between the Lisbon Summit of 2000 and the European Council of Stockholm in 2001, the interaction of some of these actors was decisive. The Director General for Employment and Social Affairs of the Commission was particularly active in addressing the pensions issue and envisaging the introduction of the OMC process in this field too.

The role of the DGV was decisive to put the interest on pensions and introduce the OMC method on this issue as well. In 2000, governments shared the idea to put two issues at the core of the Social Agenda: [the] fight against social exclusion (through the OMC process) and the modernization of social protection schemes through the reform of the Rule 1408/71. Odile Quintin (High-level servant of DGV) in a meeting with the Belgian Minister Vandenbroucke, before the Belgian Presidency of the EU, stressed the need to implement an autonomous OMC for pensions policy. (Interview, member of the Cabinet of the Belgian Minister of Social Affairs 2000, Brussels, 8 February 2005; see also Vanhercke, 2006b)

As introduced above, the first European reports on old-age programmes came from the economic actors such as the Ecofin Council and its technical bodies. What is more, after the Maastricht Treaty, economic ministers were particularly active in promoting cutbacks to social protection programmes in order to guarantee the present and future viability of the public budget. As Pochet (2003) put it, socially-oriented institutions (the DG on Social Affairs and its Director General in particular) reacted to the risk of being isolated and only playing a residual role in the process.

The contribution by Mrs Quintin at the occasion of the Conference 'Towards a New Welfare Architecture for Europe?', organized under the Belgian Presidency in 2001, clearly exemplified her approach to the pension problem and the role the EU should play. She stressed two lessons to be drawn from the debate on reforms across Europe, both implicitly related to the launch of a European coordination:

- policy-makers should have to learn from each other, in that they share the same objectives (building solid pension schemes), face the same problems (the imbalance between active and inactive part of the population), and comply with the same rules (sound public finances and high-level social protection);
- policy-makers should talk to other 'professionals' who also play a role in making (pensions) building safe. That means the need for cross-interaction between different policy areas (for example employment and public finances) (see also Quintin, 2002).

Hence, the Director General did influence the *strategic orientations* of key actors in the European political game (first of all national leaders) for the definition of the (pensions) problem and the solution.

The Role of Single Member States: The Case of Belgium and Italy

The Belgian Minister for Social Affairs and Pensions, Frank Vandenbroucke, also favoured the introduction of a form of coordination on pensions (Vanhercke, 2006b; Natali, 2008). He was particularly active in influencing the *strategic orientations* of other actors. The beginning of this section has shown that the political leaders of left-of-centre national governments had a twofold aim. They proved particularly sensitive to both the reinforcement of the social dimension of Europe and its modernization. At the same time, the EU could provide an exogenous constraint as a convenient excuse to justify innovations that were consistent with these goals (see Featherstone, 2004). In Belgium, for instance, pensions was a much-debated issue at the end of the 1990s:

> The (Belgian) Minister took into consideration a new legislative intervention at the national level. To do it, a new rhetoric able to enlarge the social consensus for reforms was needed. To do that, it was important to mobilise social actors (especially trade unions) and the public opinion in general on some key issues: for instance, on early retirement, and the low level of employment rates (especially between the older part of the population) in Belgium. The goal was to stress the opportunity to combine traditional objectives of the socialist party (in terms of adequacy of social protection) and the need for its financial sustainability. In that context, the efforts from the DGV were warmly welcome. (Interview with the then member of the Cabinet of the Belgian Minister of Social Affairs in 2000; Brussels, 8 February 2005)

The Belgian minister had been engaged in European social advancements since 1999 when in a speech at the University of Amsterdam he proposed his own interpretation of the concept of the *active welfare state*, consistent with New Labour's project for *positive welfare*. That label was related to the redefinition of both national welfare policies and the European project in a broader sense (see Cassiers et al., 2005). Given his personal mixed background (as both political leader and an academic), he was able to play a crucial role in advancing both the scholarly debate and EU politics on social policy as well (and the strategic orientation of the other actors).

In 2001, he took the initiative to enlarge support for and the room for implementation of the OMC. While a complex diplomatic game was going on in the attempt to enlarge the opportunity for the rapid introduction of the method for social protection, the Belgian Presidency of the EU organized three different conferences: the first in September in Antwerp on social inclusion, the second in November in Leuven on social protection, and the third in December in Ghent on health care (Berghman and Okma, 2002; Natali, 2008). In particular, the competent minister prepared the conference on social protection through the launch in 2000 of the proposals made in four scientific reports (from noted academics).[8] These contributions should allow a 'new architecture' of social protection systems to be defined. The preparation of these scientific works contributed to the more precise understanding of pension policy challenges and led to European procedures concerning pensions to be introduced. At that time, the role of the Belgian presidency was particularly important given that the concrete implementation of the decisions of Lisbon on pensions was still a work in progress.

In the closing note of that conference, Vandenbroucke (2001 and 2002: 534–5) stressed that the OMC represented an effective instrument for social progress and a credible commitment to a social Europe. On the basis of the experts' reports, the minister then summarized some of the key aspects of pensions policy (and politics) to be considered through the new form of coordination. First, the demographic problem was defined as one of 'an increasing share of spending'. From this perspective, it makes no difference whether these expenditures are accounted for within the public budget or not. Consequently, the issue was not limited to the adequacy and viability of the First Pillar, but was related to the adequacy and viability of the non-public pillars too. A new emphasis was thus placed on the potential inter-generational conflict and the need to consider present and future spending in terms of social justice (and not only of financial sustainability). The OMC could help to address all these challenges through the exchange of reliable information, the implementation of dynamics of learning and mimicking, and the definition of common objectives that would be able to define the European social model clearly (Vandenbroucke, 2002: 535). Thus, the minister helped to disseminate orientations to solutions, not only problems.

Other countries worked for the emergence of the Pensions OMC. As the former *attaché social* of the Permanent Representation of Italy to the European Union has argued (and civil servants of DG Employment have confirmed), the Italian bureaucracy acted as a promoter of a coalition of countries favourable to the introduction of the OMC on pensions:

> We (the Italian representatives) used a typical diplomatic strategy to build alliances, in particular with France and Belgium. Belgium was represented by the Minister Vandenbroucke, while France had a strong bureaucratic structure, represented by Raoul Briet who then became the first president of the Social Protection Committee. (Interview with the then Italian *attaché social* in 2000, Berlin, 9 May 2005)

The bilateral contacts between the Jospin government in France (and the Minister for Social Affairs, Martine Aubry, in particular) and the Italian Government (and the Minister for Employment and Social Affairs there, Antonio Bassolino) prepared the ground for the respective bureaucracies. Yet the active role of the administrative elite was not the result of a specific impetus provided by the Italian politicians. Again, the former *attaché social* of the Permanent Representation of Italy to the EU clarifies that point: 'Political leaders did follow our activism there was not a real strategy, also because the (Italian) legislature ended in 2001 and politicians had other interests at that time' (Interview with the then Italian *attaché social* in 2000, Berlin, 9 May 2005).

The Italian administrative elite acted to play a role in the emerging process well beyond the political mandate given by their political counter-parts. Why did Italy work for the launch of the Pensions OMC? A member of the Indicators sub-group of the Social Protection Committee clearly indicates the reason for this activism:

> For Italy, the OMC represented the opportunity to put pensions on the EU agenda with a twofold aim: on the one hand, that of presenting progresses implemented through reforms in the 1990s; on the other, to develop a debate on present and future problems still to deal with. (Interview with a member of the SPC Indicators sub-group, Brussels, 5 April 2005)

At that time the Italian reform of 1995 could be considered a good practice to 'promote' at the European level. It consisted of a progressive containment of total public spending through the revision of some of the pensions system rules (for example the benefit structure). Then, the reform was implemented in parallel with a process of monitoring of total spending and of the func-tioning of the system through a new administrative body (the Unit for the Evaluation of Pension Spending). The objective of that unit was to produce projections and technical expertise (for example definition of indicators) in order to develop an in-depth exchange of information for the analysis and the assessment of the long-term evolution of public pensions. Such an approach (consistent with the method of coordination in progress) was lacking in the other member states. What is more, the new legislation was concerted by the government and trade union representatives (Natali and Rhodes, 2004). As confirmed by the then representative of Italy to the EU on social issues, 'we were convinced to have a pension reform that could be a model for the other members . . . and in fact at the Stockholm Council the Italian and Swedish reforms both represented the benchmark for the other members' (Interview with the then Italian *attaché social* in 2000, Berlin, 9 May 2005).

In other social policy sectors Italy was a latecomer more than a model (see Ferrera, 1997; Ferrera and Sacchi, 2005). This further explains Italy's interest in working for the launch of the Pensions OMC.

CONCLUSION

The study of the events between the end of the 1990s and the beginning of the twenty-first century has helped us to assess the interaction of a number of variables. These produced the right conditions for the emergence of a (not-so-large) *window of opportunity* that some political entrepreneurs used to launch a new mode of governance in the pension field.

The multi-dimensional and multi-level framework we have proposed has allowed us to map the multiple socioeconomic, political and institutional factors that favoured the appearance of that window. While socioeconomic pressures (reinforced by European integration) were consistent with more direct EU intervention, institutional and political factors were more inconsistent with direct EU intervention.

From an institutional point of view, European integration represented a source of strains on national pensions, a limit to member states' capacity to find solutions, and a source of parallel pressure for more demands for supranational coordination. New modes of governance in the economic and employment field represented a template for the development of similar forms of coordination on social issues as well. But the persistent strength and diversity of national pension institutions led to the opposite – the strict respect of the principle of subsidiarity.

The influence of political events at the time was ambiguous. The vast majority of left-of-centre governments at the end of the 1990s did favour and use the resurgent interest in the social dimension of Europe. Yet they were not enthusiastic about more advanced forms of coordination. In this author's own view, moreover, electoral incentives related to national pension programmes help to explain the reason for this.

In such a political context, some political entrepreneurs were able to create and disseminate some key strategic orientations on the 'pensions problem' and its solution. The Director General of the DG on Employment and Social Affairs and the Belgian minister competent in these matters both contributed to defining a problem (financial strains on pension systems and their inability to deal with new risks), proposing a solution (a 'new' mode of governance at the EU level), and arranging the political consensus for the emergence of a new institution. The Italian administrative elite contributed to commit and organize key resources in terms of consensus and technical expertise (as a consequence of its reforms of the early 1990s).

Finally, this chapter has shed some light on the peculiarities of the emergence of the OMC in pensions policy through the combination of different theoretical approaches.

NOTES

1. I refer here to the definition of governance proposed by Peterson and Bomberg (1999): the imposition of overall direction or control on the allocation of valued resources.

2. Vanhercke (2006a) talks of the need for theoretical 'eclecticism' in the analysis of European integration.
3. A vast debate has developed on the vices and virtues of such an approach (see Mucciaroni, 1992: 461–7; Bendor et al., 2001: 184–7; Olsen, 2001: 191–4; Zahariadis, 2003). Some authors have pointed out the vagueness of the independent variables within the 'policy change' model (in particular in the seminal work by Kingdon, 1995) as its first limit (Mucciaroni, 1992; Bendor et al., 2001).
4. This chapter will focus on different types of entrepreneurs: political leaders, national and European high-level bureaucrats, and experts. I refer to interviews with key actors who participated in the first elaboration of the EU strategies on social policy.
5. The former EU Commissioner Fritz Bolkenstein used the label 'pension time bomb' to describe the foreseeable problems regarding the financial viability of pension programmes (Bolkenstein, 2001). This can be interpreted as a *focusing event* that contributed to the dramatization of pension problems.
6. Some directives and rules traced the European discipline of public and private pension programmes. Of these, rule 1612/68 and rule 1408/71 related to rights for transborder workers' rights in social security programmes (Pochet, 2003).
7. On the problems dealt with by EU technical bodies concerning the definition of common objectives and indicators for pensions, see Cornilleau et al. (2003).
8. Four issues were at the centre of that scientific effort: (a) pensions, (b) employment, (c) intergenerational solidarity, family and care policies, and (d) procedural aspects of the renewed European framework. Oxford University Press published a book edited by G. Esping-Andersen in 2002 (Esping-Andersen et al., 2002).

REFERENCES

Anderson, Karen M. (2002), 'The Europeanization of pension arrangements: convergence or divergence?', in Caroline de la Porte and Philippe Pochet (eds), *Building Social Europe through the Open Method of Co-ordination*, Brussels: Peter Lang, pp. 251–84.

Bendor, Jonathan, Terry M. Moe and Kenneth W. Shotts (2001), 'Recycling the garbage can: an assessment of the research program', *American Political Science Review*, **95**(1), 169–90.

Berghman, Jos and Kieke G. Okma (2002), 'Vers une nouvelle architecture de la protection sociale en Europe: Une contribution de la présidence belge', *Revue Belge de Sécurité Sociale*, **3**, September, 419–26.

Bolkenstein, Frits (2001), 'Defusing Europe's pensions timebomb', Speech to the European Commission, 6 February, available at http://europa.eu/rapid/press-ReleasesAction.do?reference=SPEECH/01/52&format=HTML&aged=1&language=EN&guiLanguage=en.

Bonoli, Giuliano (2003), 'Two worlds of pension reform in Western Europe', *Comparative Politics*, **35**(4), 399–416.

Bonoli, Giuliano and Toshimitsu Shinkawa (2005), 'Population ageing and the logics of pension reform in Western Europe, East Asia and North America', in G. Bonoli and T. Shinkawa (eds), *Ageing and Pension Reform Around the World*, Cheltenham, UK and Northampton, MA, USA: Edward Elgar, pp. 1–23.

Borrás, Susana and Kerstin Jacobsson (2004), 'The open method of coordination and new governance patters in the EU', *Journal of European Public Policy*, **11**(2), 185–208.

Cassiers, Isabelle, Philippe Pochet and Pascale Vielle (2005), 'Introduction. L'Etat social actif. Vers un changement de paradigme?', in P. Vielle, P. Pochet and I. Cassiers (eds), *L'Etat Social Actif. Vers un Changement de Paradigme?*, Brussels: P.I.E. Peter Lang, pp. 13–32.

Citi, Manuele and Martin Rhodes (2007), 'New modes of governance in the EU: common objectives versus national preferences', European Governance papers (EUROGOV), no. N-07-01, available at http://www.connex-network. org/eurogov/pdf/egp-newgov-N-07-01.pdf.

Commission of the European Community (1999), 'Communication from the Commission, "A concerted strategy for the modernisation of social protection"', COM (1999) 347, 14 July, Brussels.

Commission of the European Community and European Council (2003), 'Joint report by the Commission and the Council on adequate and sustainable pensions', March, available at http://ec.europa.eu/employment_social/news/2002/ dec/joint_pensions_report_en.pdf.

Cornilleau, Gerard, Alexis Dantec, Antoine Math and Henri Sterdyniak (2003), 'La méthode ouverte de coordination et le rapport conjoint sur les retraites, une analyse critique', Working Paper no. 12/6, Paris: Conseil d'orientations de Retraites.

de la Porte, Caroline (2003), 'How relevant is the pensions OMC to the reform of pension systems in EU member states?', in Cristophe Degryse and Philippe Pochet, (eds), *Social Developments in the European Union 2002*, Brussels: European Trade Union Institute, Observatoire Social Européen and Saltsa, pp. 253–77.

de la Porte, Caroline (2007), 'Institutional emergence, development and influence of new modes of governance: the open method in employment and social inclusion', Ph.D. thesis, EUI, European University Institute of Florence, forthcoming.

de la Porte, Caroline and Patrizia Nanz (2004), 'OMC – A deliberative–democratic mode of governance? The cases of employment and pensions', *Journal of European Public Policy*, **11**(2), 267–88.

Eckardt, Martina (2004), 'The Open Method of Coordination on pensions: an economic analysis of its effects on pension reforms', *Journal of European Social Policy*, **15**(3), 247–67.

EPC (1997), 'The reform of European pension systems', opinion addressed to the Council and the Commission, II/220/97, 6 October, Brussels.

EPC (2003), 'The impact of ageing populations on public finances: overview of analysis carried out at EU level and proposals for a future work programme', Report by the EPC working Group on Ageing Population adopted by the Ecofin Council on 4 November, EPC/ECFIN/453/03, 22 October, Brussels, available at http://europa.eu.int/comm/economy_finance/epc/documents/2003/ pensionmaster_en.pdf.

Esping-Andersen, Gøsta (1996), 'Welfare states without work: the impasse of labour shedding and familialism in Continental European social policy', in Gøsta Esping-Andersen (ed.), *Welfare States in Transition*, London: Sage Publications, pp. 66–87.

Esping-Andersen, Gøsta, Duncan Gallie, Anton Hemerijck and John Myles (eds) (2002), *Why we Need a New Welfare State*, Oxford: Oxford University Press.

European Council (2000), 'Presidency Conclusions', Lisbon European Council, 23–24 March, Lisbon.

Featherstone, Kevin (2004), 'The political dynamics of external empowerment:

the emergence of EMU and the challenge to the European social model', in Andrew Martin and George Ross (eds), *Euros and Europeans: Monetary Integration and the European Model of Society*, Cambridge: Cambridge University Press, pp. 226–47.

Ferrera, Maurizio (1997), 'The uncertain future of the Italian welfare state', *West European Politics*, **20**(1), 231–49.

Ferrera, Maurizio (2005), *The Boundaries of Welfare: European Integration and the New Spatial Politics of Social Protection*, Oxford: Oxford University Press.

Ferrera, Maurizio and Stefano Sacchi (2005), 'The Open Method of Co-ordination and national institutional capabilities: the Italian experience', in Jonathan Zeitlin and Philippe Pochet (eds), *The Open Method of Co-ordination in Action*, Brussels: Peter Lang, pp. 137–72.

Goetschy, Janine (1999), 'The European Employment Strategy: genesis and development', *European Journal of Industrial Relations*, **5**, 117–37.

Hemerijck, Anton and Maurizio Ferrera (2004), 'Welfare reform in the shadow of EMU', in Andrew Martin and George Ross (eds), *Euros and Europeans: Monetary Integration and the European Model of Society*, Cambridge: Cambridge University Press, pp. 248–77.

Ioannou, Demosthenes and Arne Niemann (2003), 'Taking stock of the open method of coordination: nature, modus operandi and theoretical perspectives', Dresdner Arbeitspapiere Internationale Beziehungen (DAP) no. 8, Dresden: Dresdner AIB, Technische Universität Dresden.

Jenson, Jane and Philippe Pochet (2002), 'Employment and social policy since Maastricht: standing up to the European Monetary Union', paper prepared for the Year of the Euro, Nanovic Institute for European Studies, University of Notre Dame, 5–8 December, Canada research chair in citizenship and governance.

Keeler, John T.S. (1993), *Réformer. Les Conditions du Changement Politique*, Paris: Presses Universitaires de France.

Kingdon, John W. (1995), *Agendas, Alternatives and Public Policies*, New York: HarperCollins.

Lowi, Theodore J. (1964), 'American business, public policy, case studies and political theory', *World Politics*, **4**, 677–715.

Moreno, Luis and Bruno Palier (2004), 'The Europeanization of welfare: paradigmatic shifts and social policy reforms', Working Paper no. 04/05, Unidad de Politicas Comparadas (CSIC), University of Madrid.

Mucciaroni, Gary (1992), 'The garbage can model & the study of policy making: a critique', *Polity*, **XXIV**(3), 459–82.

Natali, David (2004), 'Europeanization, policy arenas, and creative opportunism: the politics of welfare state reforms in Italy', *Journal of European Public Policy*, **11**(6), 1077–95.

Natali, David (2006), 'Le Pensioni nell'Europa a 25: il coordinamento delle strategie di riforma', Working Paper for URGE (Research Unit on European Governance) no. 01/06, Moncalieri, Italy.

Natali, David (2008), *Pensions in Europe, European Pensions*, Brussels: PIE-Peter Lang.

Natali, David and Martin Rhodes (2004), 'Trade-offs and veto players: reforming pensions in France and Italy', *French Politics*, **2**(1), 1–23.

OECD (1988), *Reforming Public Pensions*, Paris: OECD.

Olsen, Johan P. (2001), 'Garbage cans, new institutionalism, and the study of politics', *American Political Science Review*, **95**(1), 191–8.

Pakaslahti, Johannes and Philippe Pochet (2003), 'The social dimension of the changing European Union', Sitra publication no. 256, Brussels and Helsinki: SITRA and Observatoire Social Européen.

Palier, Bruno (2003), *La Réforme de Retraite*, Paris: Presses Universitaires de France.

Peterson, John and Elizabeth Bomberg (1999), 'Making sense of EU-decision making', in John Peterson and Elizabeth Bomberg, *Decision-Making in the European Union*, London: Macmillan, pp. 4–30.

Pierson, Paul (1996a), 'The path to European integration: a historical institutionalist analysis', *Comparative Political Studies*, **29**, 123–63.

Pierson, Paul (1996b), 'The new politics of the welfare state', *World Politics*, **48**, 143–79.

Pierson, Paul (2001), 'Coping with permanent austerity: welfare state restructuring in affluent democracies', in P. Pierson (ed.), *The New Politics of the Welfare State*, Oxford: Oxford University Press, pp. 410–56.

Pochet, Philippe (2001), 'Méthode ouverte de coordination et modèle social européen', Working Paper no. 03/01, Montreal: Institute for European Studies, University of Montreal and McGill University.

Pochet, Philippe (2003), 'Pensions: the European debate', in G.L. Clark and N. Witheside (eds), *Pension Security in the 21st Century: Redrawing the Public–Private Debate*, Oxford: Oxford University Press, pp. 44–63.

Pollack, Mark A. (1997), 'Delegation, agency and agenda setting in the European Community', *International Organisation*, **51**, 99–134.

Putnam, Robert D. (1988), 'Diplomacy and domestic politics: the logic of two-level games', *International Organization*, no. 42/3, 427–60.

Quintin, Odile (2002), 'Towards a new architecture for social protection in Europe? A broader perspective on pension policies', *Revue Belge de Sécurité Sociale*, **3**, September, 483–8.

Riker, William H. (1986), *The Art of Political Manipulation*, New Haven and London: Yale University Press.

Ross, George (1995), *Jacques Delors and European Integration*, Oxford: Polity Press.

Sandholtz, Wayne (1996), 'Membership matters: limits of functional approach to European institutions', *Journal of Common Market Studies*, **34**(3), 403–29.

Schäfer, Armin (2004), 'Beyond the Community method: why the Open Method of Coordination was introduced to EU policy-making', European Integration Online Papers (EIOP), no. 8/13, available at http://eiop.or.at/eiop/texte/2004-013a.htm.

Scharpf, Fritz W. (1986), 'The joint-decision trap: lessons from German federalism and European integration', *Public Administration Review*, **66**, 239–78.

Scharpf, Fritz W. (2002), 'The European Social Model: coping with the challenges of diversity', *Journal of Common Market Studies*, **40**(4), 645–70.

Schludi, Martin (2003), 'Chances and limitations of benchmarking in the reform of welfare state structures: the case of pension policy', Amsterdam Institute for Advanced Labour Studies, Working Paper no. 10/03.

Schludi, Martin (2005), *The Reform of Bismarckian Pension Systems*, Amsterdam: Amsterdam University Press.

SPC (2001), 'Adequate and sustainable pensions', Report by the Social Protection Committee to the Göteborg European Council on the Future Evolution of

Social Protection, June, available at http://ec.europa.eu/employment_social/spsi/docs/social_protection/goteborg_en.pdf.

Taylor-Gooby, Peter (2004), 'New social risks in postindustrial society: some evidence on responses to active labour market policies from Eurobarometer', *International Social Security Review*, **57**(3), July, 45–64.

Vandenbroucke, Frank (2001), 'Safeguarding Europe's pension systems: the challenge of social justice', paper presented at the Conference on Safe and Sustainable Pensions in Europe organized by the Swedish Presidency and European Commission, Stockholm, 4 April, available at http://oud.frankvandenbroucke.be/html/soc/T-010404.htm.

Vandenbroucke, Frank (2002), 'The Open Co-ordination on Pensions and the future of Europe's Social Model', *Revue Belge de Sécurité Sociale*, **3**, September, 533–42.

Vanhercke, Bart (2006a), 'Political spill-over, changing advocacy coalition, path-dependency or domestic politics? Theorizing the emergence of the social protection OMCs', paper presented at the Conference on Governing Work and Welfare in an Enlarged Europe, University of Wisconsin, Madison, 19–20 May 2006.

Vanhercke, Bart (2006b), 'Variations in institutionalization of hybrid social protection OMCs: the choice for non-constitutionalisation and the emergence of hard soft law', paper presented at the annual ESPAnet conference, Bremen, 21–23 September 2006.

World Bank (1994), *Averting the Old Age Crisis*, Washington, DC: World Bank.

Zahariadis, Nikolaos (2003), *Ambiguity and Choice in Public Policy*, Washington, DC: Georgetown University Press.

Zerbinati, Stefania and Vangelis Souitaris (2002), 'Entrepreneurship in the public sector: a framework of analysis in European local governments', paper presented at the Babson Kauffman Entrepreneurship Research Conference, University of Colorado.

5. Social policy and environmental policy: comparing modes of governance

Oliver Treib, Holger Bähr and Gerda Falkner

1 INTRODUCTION

The European Union (EU) is a highly sectorized polity. The different policy areas are marked by a wide variety of legislative procedures, constellations of actors and policy instruments. To grasp the logic of policy-making in the EU, we thus need a toolkit to understand the differences and similarities between policy areas. The concepts of governance and modes of governance are useful instruments for arriving at this understanding. In this chapter, we use these conceptual tools to analyse the emergence and evolution of modes of governance in EU social policy and EU environmental policy. We use the term 'governance' in a broad sense as structures of societal coordination and control in order to encompass both developments in the policy areas concerned and differences between the two policy areas within one concept. However, a broad conception of governance covering the structures of the whole process of policy-making adds to the complexity and easily loses the organizing and structuring function of the concept. We therefore disentangle the concept into three dimensions: (1) the way in which societal interests are incorporated into the initiation, formulation and adoption of policies (interest intermediation); (2) the institutional rules determining who is entitled to take part in decision-making and how decisions are taken (modes of interaction); and (3) the way in which agreed policy objectives are implemented (policy instruments).

The two policy areas have been chosen for analytical reasons. EU social policy and EU environmental policy are suitable for a comparative analysis because they constitute similar cases. First, both policy areas are primarily characterized by regulatory policy, which seeks to promote the public interest by constraining private activities (Francis, 1993: 1–2). Second, the dominant mode of integration in both policy areas is market-correcting positive integration. In other words, the goal is not to remove obstacles to trade and economic competition, but to reconstruct economic regulation at a higher level of governance (Hix, 2005: 251–60). The fact that the two policy areas are thus broadly similar in terms of their basic rationales makes it easier to identify causal conditions that might account for differences in the modes of governance prevalent in the two fields.

The chapter proceeds as follows. Section 2 draws up an analytical scheme to show the three dimensions of governance: interest intermediation, modes of interaction, and policy instruments. Section 3 addresses the emergence and evolution of governance modes in EU social policy, while section 4 deals with EU environmental policy. The final section gives a comparative overview of the emergence and evolution of modes of governance in the two policy areas and discusses which factors account for the different dynamics, and the differences in resulting governing modes, in both policy areas.

2 MODES OF GOVERNANCE

The term 'governance' means many things to many people. In a recent article which formed the introduction to a symposium on European governance in the *Journal of European Public Policy*, Caporaso and Wittenbrinck (2006: 471) stated that '[i]ronically, to understand the new modes of governance, the term "governance" is not a good place to start, since it has meant too many things'. This statement echoes a similar assessment R.A.W. Rhodes (1997: 15) made a decade ago: '[governance] has too many meanings to be useful'. Despite this conceptual ambiguity, or maybe even as a result of it, the term enjoys great popularity in the literature and the authors just mentioned do not abandon it either. At a general level, governance can be conceived as societal steering and coordination or, in the words of Pierre and Peters (2005: 6), it refers to 'the nature of state–society relationships in the pursuit of collective interests'. Beyond this basic understanding, however, the multivalent universe of governance begins. Some authors conceive governance primarily in terms of the relationship between public and private actors in the process of policy formation (Rhodes, 1997; Eising and Kohler-Koch, 1999). Others argue that governance refers to systems of rules that shape the interactions of social actors in policy-making (Rosenau, 1992; Mayntz, 2004). A further strand of the literature conceptualizes governance as a 'mode of political steering' (Héritier, 2002: 185; see also Knill and Lenschow, 2003), referring to the way in which policy goals, once they have been agreed, are put into practice.

In our view, governance encompasses all these understandings. To avoid conceptual confusion, however, the different dimensions of governance need to be disentangled and treated separately. Our conceptualization of governance and modes of governance thus rests on the following three dimensions: (1) governance as forms of interest intermediation; (2) governance as institutional modes of interaction; and (3) governance as different types of policy instruments.

Forms of *interest intermediation* describe the way in which societal interests are incorporated into the process of policy-making. They account for the relationship between public and private actors, including power relations and mutual dependence on resources. In democratic countries the political process consists of the interaction both between political elites and between citizens and those elites. The actors involved in this process have particular interests, preferences, opinions and beliefs, as well as different resources in order to participate in the formation of public policies. Citizens and groups of citizens participate in the political process in various ways by feeding their interests into the political system. Citizens take part in democratic elections, political parties recruit members of parliament and governments, and associations represent the interests of sections of society such as employers and employees, as well as diffuse societal interests such as environmental or consumer protection. In different political systems and different sectors, different styles of interest intermediation have developed.

The literature usually distinguishes two main types of interest intermediation: pluralism and corporatism. In *pluralism* societal groups interact in a non-hierarchical competition in order to get their interests reflected in public policies. These groups are founded on a voluntary basis. State authorities do not intervene in the organization of societal groups and they also do not guarantee privileges for certain groups (Truman, 1951; Dahl, 1961). In *corporatism*, the state grants privileged access to a limited number of – typically strong, hierarchically organized – associations. As a reciprocal gesture, associations support agreements with the government and other associations vis-à-vis their members (Schmitter, 1974). A further form of interest intermediation is represented by *policy networks*. Policy networks denote a horizontal constellation of interdependent actors. Actors in policy networks are systematically interlinked but there is no hierarchical subordination. Corporatist arrangements can be considered as a specific type of policy network. However, policy networks are also represented by loose issue networks, which have more similarities with pluralist interest intermediation (Kenis and Schneider, 1991).

When policy proposals are discussed during the stage of policy formation and adopted or rejected at the end of that stage, the *mode of interaction* affects the scope and content of the resulting policy outputs. Modes of interaction are institutional arrangements that shape the constellation of actors and specify the decision rules under which policy outputs are adopted. They determine the degree of autonomy of individual actors on the one hand and the capability of collective action on the other. Mayntz and Scharpf (1995: 60–62; see also Scharpf, 1997: 46–7) identify four modes of interaction: unilateral action, negotiated agreement, majority vote, and hierarchical direction. In unilateral action, actors choose among political alternatives without coordinating their actions with other actors. In negotiated agreement, actors unanimously agree on common courses of action. The agreements may be of different degrees of permanence and may be obligatory upon actors to different degrees. In majority vote, the majority of the actors adopt decisions that also apply to those actors who have voted against them. In hierarchical direction, finally, a single actor possesses the power to make collectively binding decisions and to employ collective resources.

As far as the EU is concerned, modes of interaction specify the inter-action between the member states and between the member states and the political institutions of the EU. When policy outputs are adopted at the European level, three modes of interaction are relevant: negotiated agreement, majority vote and hierarchical direction. (Unilateral action describes the situation of member state competition in the absence of EU-wide regulation, as in the field of tax policy.) In the EU context, these modes of interaction have been dubbed, respectively, intergovernmen-tal negotiation, joint decision-making and supranational centralization (Scharpf, 2001, 2006a: 847–54; Bulmer and Padgett, 2005). The modes of interaction prevalent in a particular policy area mainly depend on the provisions made in the treaties. If the treaties give member state govern-ments exclusive competence to determine, unanimously, the direction of common action, without the Commission or the European Parliament playing a decisive role in decision-making, the interaction mode is *inter-governmental negotiation*. The same mode prevails in the First Pillar in all those areas where decisions in the Council have to be taken by unanimous agreement. Although the supranational institutions have a more prominent role to play here, the member state governments still form the centre of decision-making. If one of them objects to common action, no European policy can be adopted. *Joint decision-making* applies if policies depend on the Commission's exclusive right of initiative, the Council's agreement by majority and, increasingly, an affirmative vote by the European Parliament.[1] Finally, *supranational centralization* occurs if the competence to make collectively binding decisions is delegated to an autonomous agency or the EC Treaty sets down policy goals which are directly applicable in the member states, and may thus be enforced directly by the Commission and the European Court of Justice (ECJ).

After European policy outputs are adopted, they have to be implemented in the member states in order to be effective. *Policy instruments* are means at the disposal of the political actors in order to implement policy goals contained in policy outputs (Howlett, 1991: 2). In the multi-level governance system of the EU, the legal form of policy instruments crucially affects the relationship between the political institutions of the EU and the member states. In this chapter, therefore, we concentrate on the *legal form* of policy instruments. The available legal instruments in the EU are regulations, directives, recommendations, resolutions, declarations and conclusions. Regulations exert a direct legal effect in the member states. Directives have to be transposed into national law. Both regulations and directives are *hard law*, which legally obliges member states to do what is laid down in a given piece of legislation. Recommendations, resolutions, declarations and conclusions, in contrast, represent *soft law*. Soft law consists of rules of conduct that may have a certain legal effect but do not have any legally binding force. There are, however, further legal forms of European policy outputs which do not have a general regulatory intention. Decisions are hard law but refer only to single member states or citizens and are not relevant to the policy of the entire EU. Communications are soft law but set out the policy position of the Commission on a particular problem. They appear under different headings, as green papers, white papers, reports, strategies or communications, and play a mere declaratory role (Senden, 2004; Bogdandy et al., 2004).

The following two sections deal with the emergence and evolution of modes of governance in EU social policy and EU environmental policy, respectively. Modes of governance in the two policy areas are analysed in the dimensions of interest intermediation, modes of interaction, and policy instruments. Interest intermediation and modes of interaction are described on the basis of the secondary literature and primary sources. Our analysis of the evolution of legal acts is based on data from the Celex and Eur-Lex databases.

To be sure, conducting such a quantitative analysis involves a number of methodological problems. In particular, the substantive importance of different legal acts cannot be taken into account. Laws with a broad field of application and far-reaching regulatory implications in many member states, such as the directives on working time or drinking water, are given the same weight as narrowly circumscribed measures with only minor impact at the domestic level, such as directives on individual types of machines or measures that merely update or slightly revise prior directives. An analysis that compares two policy areas and covers several decades cannot avoid distortions of this type. At any rate, analysing the regulatory contents, and the domestic policy impacts, of several hundred legal acts would have exceeded the resources available to us. To reduce the problem, our analysis distinguishes 'original' pieces of legislation from directives and regulations that merely amend existing legal acts, extend their scope or provide application rules. Furthermore, we are confident that the remaining distortions do not invalidate our analysis. After all, we are primarily interested in comparing policy outputs in two policy areas. There is little reason to believe that the bias resulting from the varying importance of different legal acts differs systematically between our two policy areas. Only such a systematic bias would imply serious problems for our analysis here.

3   MODES OF GOVERNANCE IN EU SOCIAL POLICY

Interest Intermediation in EU Social Policy

Interest intermediation in EU social policy evolved from a type of network governance into a mixture of network governance and a quasi-corporatist governing mode (Falkner, 1999). While the ultimate power to adopt social policy proposals traditionally lay firmly in the hands of member state governments, in the early 1970s trade unions and employers' associations had already been given the opportunity to participate actively in the process of policy formation. In 1974, the first of a series of tripartite conferences brought together representatives of the Council, the Commission, and labour and capital on both the national and the European level. Due to employer opposition, however, these conferences remained talking shops, and there were no tangible results, which is why the unions finally pulled out of the talks (Gorges, 1996: 130). In the mid-1980s, Jacques Delors as President of the Commission started a new initiative to institutionalize corporatist governing modes in EU social policy by launching the so-called 'Val-Duchesse social dialogue' between the European umbrella organizations of labour and capital.

However, it was only the Social Protocol of the 1992 Maastricht Treaty that finally paved the way for the creation of a corporatist mode of interest intermediation in EU social policy. According to the new procedures laid down in the Protocol, the Commission has a legal obligation to consult both sides of industry twice before submitting proposals in the social policy field. Management and labour may, on the occasion of such consultation, inform the Commission of their wish to initiate negotiations in order to reach a collective agreement on the matter in question. This would bring conventional decision-making to a standstill for at least nine months. Such agreements can, at the joint request of their signatories, be incorporated in a directive, which transforms the social partner text into binding EU legislation to be implemented by the member states. Alternatively, the signatory parties may also take care of the implementation of their agreements through their own member organizations. Since Maastricht, the EU-level social partners have thus become formal participants in the making of social policy legislation. In fact, the new procedure fits the classic formula for corporatist concertation, that is, 'a mode of policy formation in which formally designated interest associations are incorporated within the process of authoritative decision-making and implementation' (Schmitter, 1981: 295). Since the Amsterdam Treaty revisions of 1997, this corporatist 'bargained legislation' procedure has formed part of the EC Treaty (Falkner, 1998, 1999; Treib and Falkner, 2009).

Although the new bargaining track has been used successfully several times, traditional policy formation through the Council, the Commission and the European Parliament was not replaced by this new social partner procedure. Instead, policy networks in the legislative arena and corporatism in the social partner arena coexist and even influence each other (for an overview, see Falkner, 2000; Treib and Falkner, 2009). Given the general scepticism of employers' organizations towards Europe-wide social standards, the most important factor determining whether the Europe-wide umbrella associations of management and labour choose the bargaining track is the likelihood of legislation if negotiations do not take place. There is no doubt that, so far, social partner negotiations on social policy measures at the EU level have taken place 'in the shadow of the law' (Bercusson, 1992: 185). There are many indicators that a high probability of Council action on a matter represents a spur for employers' associations to look actively for a compromise with trade unions. If governments and the Commission put pressure on management by expressing their readiness to otherwise adopt social regulation themselves, the employers are visibly and admittedly more ready for compromise. Just as at the national level, corporatist negotiations thus need some backing from public authorities. Moreover, the possible scope of collective bargaining at the European level is limited as not all issues are considered suitable for collective bargaining by the social partner organizations. If a proposal does not belong to the issue areas that are frequently subject to collective bargaining at the domestic level, the EU-level social partners are unlikely to enter into negotiations on that issue. This has been demonstrated by several cases where both sides of industry refused to enter into negotiations for exactly these reasons.

Despite the availability of a corporatist bargaining track, network governance is thus still the dominant mode of interest intermediation in EU social policy. Since the Maastricht Treaty, only three social partner agreements have actually been transformed into legally binding directives. Recently, the social partners reached two further agreements, on telework (2002) and on work-related stress (2004). However, they did not request the incorporation of these accords into binding legislation, but decided to implement them through their own member organizations. However, given the heterogeneity of interests among both sides of industry in many countries and the lack of hierarchical oversight of the European associations, it is questionable whether the two agreements will have much of an impact at the domestic level. The remaining social policy initiatives were adopted on the basis of the traditional law-making procedure. In quantitative terms, therefore, network governance is much more important than the corporatist mode of interest intermediation in EU social policy.

Modes of Interaction in EU Social Policy

Whether political and societal actors succeed in influencing the adoption of policy outputs in accordance with their interest depends to a great extent on the mode of interaction. The treaty provides legal competences for EU regulation and decision rules for adopting such regulation. Both treaty-based competences and decision rules determine the mode of interaction and affect actors' opportunity to shape a policy output. The mode of interaction in EU social policy, operationalized by the treaty-based competences and the decision rules, has been subject to changes since the European Economic Community (EEC) was established. The original EEC Treaty provided for legislative competence with regard to the free movement of workers and social security coordination. Only policy measures relating to the free movement of workers could be passed by qualified majority voting (QMV). Moreover, policy measures could only be adopted if they were related to the Common Market.[2] Those measures were subject to intergovernmental negotiations and required unanimity in the Council in order to be adopted. However, further treaty amendments extended joint decision-making to further issue areas allowing the adoption of policy outputs by QMV. The changes are shown in Table 5.1.

Traditionally, most decisions in the area of EU social policy had to be taken on the basis of unanimity in the Council. As a result of successive treaty amendments, the areas characterized by the interaction mode 'intergovernmental negotiation' are nowadays restricted to anti-discrimination,

Table 5.1   *Treaty-based competences and decision rules in EU social policy*

Explicit Community competence for:	EEC Treaty 1957	Single European Act 1986	Maastricht Social Agreement 1992	Amsterdam Treaty 1997	Nice Treaty 2001
'measures' to improve transnational cooperation under Art. 137	–	–	–	–	++
'incentive measures' to combat discrimination as defined by Art. 13	–	–	–	–	++
action against discrimination on grounds of sex, race, ethnic origin, belief, disability, age, sexual orientation (new Art. 13)	–	–	–	+	+
'measures' combating social exclusion	–	–	–	++	++
'measures' assuring equal opportunities and treatment of both women and men	–	–	–	++	++
employment policy coordination	–	–	–	++	++
funding for employment policy	–	–	+	+	–
social security and protection of workers	–	–	+	+	+
protection of workers where employment contract is terminated	–	–	+	+	+
collective interest representation, co-determination	–	–	+	+	+
employment of third-country nationals	–	–	+	+	+
working conditions (general)	–	–	++	++	++
worker information and consultation	–	–	++	++	++
gender equality for labour force	–	–	++	++	++
integration in labour market	–	–	++	++	++
working environment (health and safety)	–	++	++	++	++
social security coordination	+	+	no impact	+	+
free movement of workers	++	++	no impact	++	++

Notes:
– Not mentioned.
+ Decision by unanimity.
++ Decision by qualified majority.

Source: Falkner (2006: 81).

collective interest representation and co-determination, social security and protection of workers, and funding for employment policy (Falkner, 2006: 80–82). In contrast, many social policy measures may now be adopted on the basis of the co-decision procedure, with QMV in the Council and the European Parliament acting as co-legislator. The fields covered by the joint-decision mode in EU social policy include health and safety in the workplace and working conditions in general, information for and consultation of workers, the integration of persons excluded from the labour market, and equal treatment of women and men with regard to labour market opportunities and treatment at work. The joint-decision mode also applies to those social policy measures that contribute to the completion of the Common Market and are passed on the basis of Article 94 of the EC Treaty.

Further areas where decision-making is based on the joint-decision mode, with the Council deciding on the basis of QMV, include employment policy, social exclusion, the modernization of social protection systems and incentives to combat discrimination. In these issue areas, however, the Community may not adopt binding legislation but may act only on the basis of soft law, for example, in the European Employment Strategy or in the open method of coordination (OMC) on pensions or on social inclusion. Thus, the core of national welfare states, which consists of social security systems set up to tackle the risks related to ageing, illness, invalidity, unemployment and poverty, is only affected by soft, non-binding EU policies. Furthermore, a number of particularly contentious areas of industrial relations are explicitly excluded from any European intervention. These include the right to strike or to impose lockouts, the right of association and the determination of wages and salaries.

There is no agency to which regulatory powers are delegated in the area of EU social policy. There are three European agencies that broadly belong to the field of social policy: the European Foundation for the Improvement of Living and Working Conditions, in Dublin, the European Agency for Safety and Health at Work, in Bilbao, and the European Agency for Fundamental Rights, in Vienna. These agencies do not, however, possess any 'real' decision-making powers. Rather than making binding decisions, the primary aim of these agencies is to collect and disseminate information and to foster cooperation between stakeholders in their particular fields of activity (Griller and Orator, 2006).

In contrast to these agencies, elements of supranational centralization are to be discerned in the independent interpretation of Community law by the European Court of Justice. The Court has proved to be rather active in interpreting (and often expanding) the social policy principles enshrined in the treaties as well as in secondary Community legislation. Judicial activism has been particularly pronounced in the field of gender equality. On the basis of expansive interpretations of the principle of equal pay for women and men, which was laid down in the 1957 Treaty of Rome, and of a number of gender equality directives adopted in the 1970s and 1980s, the Court has thus actively contributed to the EU's gender equality policy (for an overview, see Shaw 2001).

Legal Instruments in EU Social Policy

The modes of interaction described in the previous section determine which legal instruments may be adopted at the European level and how their adoption takes place. In overall terms, 284 policy outputs were passed in EU social policy between 1958 and 2006. The first legal act of EU social policy was a regulation adopted in 1958. It referred to the social security of migrant workers and was amended several times in the years that followed. The first non-binding policy output was passed in 1963. Between 1958 and 2006 the amount of both hard law and soft law increased steadily. The evolution of legal instruments in EU social policy is shown in Figure 5.1. At no point in this period did the number of newly adopted directives and regulations exceed the number of non-binding policy outputs. Moreover, the number of amendments, application rules and extensions was always larger than the number of new regulations and directives. Hard law exceeds soft law only if directives and regulations and their amendments, applications rules and extensions are added together. In this case, hard law and soft law show a quantitative evolution that runs in parallel. The increase in the volume of soft law accelerated in the early 1980s and slowed down at the beginning of the twenty-first century. Soft law thus plays a considerable role in EU social policy, although it does not supersede hard law.

The observation that EU social policy is marked by both hard and soft law is also confirmed when we consider the comparative shares of the different types of legal instruments in EU social policy year by year, which is shown in Figure 5.2. In the 1970s and the early 1980s hard law prevailed, accounting for the largest share of policy outputs adopted each year. However, in the following years the share of soft law increased. In several years, more than half of the policy outputs were adopted in the form of soft law. Directives and regulations accounted for more than half of the policy outputs only in 2004 and 2006, when the adoption of soft law stagnated. Amendments, application rules and extensions of existing hard law make up a considerable proportion of hard law during the whole period.

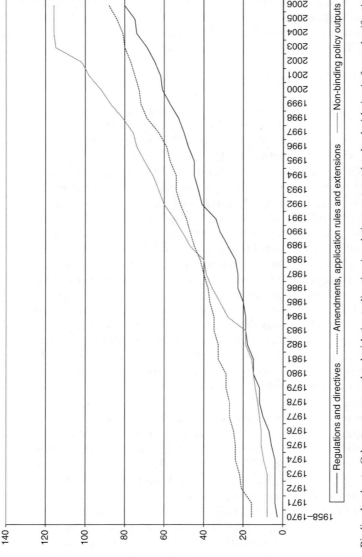

Source: Binding legal acts: Celex > menu search > legislation > directives/regulations, not restricted to legislation in force, classification headings > 5 freedom of movement for workers and social policy > 5.10 freedom of movement for workers / 5.20 social policy, without wrong classifications; non-binding legal acts: Eur-Lex > simple search > legislation > other acts, not restricted to acts in force, classification headings > 5 freedom of movement for workers and social policy > 5.10 freedom of movement for workers / 5.20 social policy, counted are declarations, conclusions, resolutions, and recommendations, without wrong classifications. The non-binding legal acts were collected on the basis of Eur-Lex because it is not possible to search for other legal acts than decisions, directives or regulations via the Celex menu search. Celex and Eur-Lex use the same database and classification.

Figure 5.1   Evolution of legal instruments in EU social policy, 1970–2006

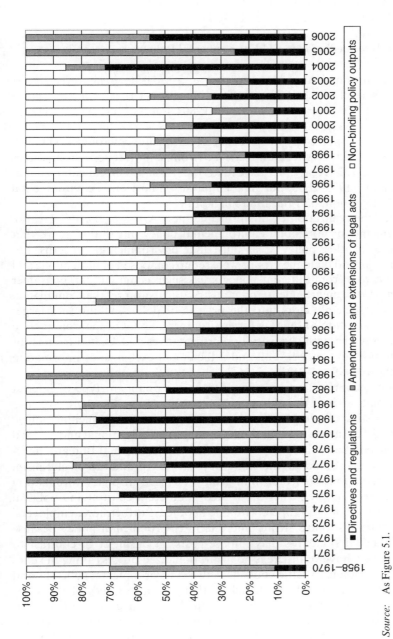

Source: As Figure 5.1.

Figure 5.2 Comparative shares of different legal instruments in EU social policy, 1970–2006

4   MODES OF GOVERNANCE IN EU ENVIRONMENTAL POLICY

Interest Intermediation in EU Environmental Policy

When environmental policy emerged as a separate policy area at the European level in the 1970s, it offered no distinct type of interest intermediation. However, since the mid-1980s interest intermediation has increasingly taken the form of policy networks. The emergence of policy networks was spurred by the principle of horizontal environmental policy integration laid down in different Environmental Action Programmes and in the EC Treaty. In particular the Fifth Environmental Action Programme (1993–2000) put great emphasis on horizontal environmental policy integration, and the 1986 Single European Act established a legal basis for the realization of this principle (new Art. 6 of the EC Treaty). The principle of horizontal environmental policy integration states that measures in other policy areas must take environmental concerns into account. Several dialogue groups were set up composed of both public and private actors from different policy areas such as agriculture, consumer protection, the environment and industry. Furthermore, the Commission integrated societal actors into the process of policy-making to a larger extent. In addition to funding for environmental NGOs, the Commission increasingly met with civil society representatives and created forums for consultation and cooperation and a facilitated exchange of information (Lenschow, 1999: 44–48).

Policy networks have thus come to be the dominant type of interest intermediation in EU environmental policy. However, there are also characteristics of pluralism and corporatism in environmental policy. Despite the existence of an umbrella organization of national and sectoral environmental associations (the European Environmental Bureau), interactions of environmental interest groups display properties of pluralism. There are various environmental groups engaged in policy formulation at the European level. They are rooted in different cultural and political traditions and often compete with one another. Furthermore, employers' associations also have strong interests in environmental policy because environmental standards may impose costs on business. In contrast to social policy, however, there is no institutionalized process along the lines of social dialogue to settle conflicts between environmental concerns and the interests of capital. Nevertheless, there are also traces of corporatism in EU environmental policy. When the directive on the conservation of natural habitats and of wild fauna and flora was formulated, for example, the Commission gave privileged access to two environmental organizations, the Royal Society for the Protection of Birds and the World Wildlife Fund, in order to cope with the wide variety of input by environmental interest associations. The two organizations coordinated and 'bundled up' the interests of environmental groups throughout Europe (Eichener, 2000: 285–6).

Modes of Interaction in EU Environmental Policy

In EU environmental policy, political and societal actors thus struggle for political power and aim to solve policy problems mostly within policy networks. Whether decisions are taken and which policy goals are adopted, however, depend on the mode of interaction. Both EU competences and decision rules are specified by the treaties. The evolution of treaty-based competences and decision rules in EU environmental policy is presented in Table 5.2. The original EEC Treaty did not provide explicitly for competences in environmental policy. European environmental measures could only be taken on the basis of the subsidiary competence provisions of the treaties, which allowed for Community action that was necessary in order to complete the internal market or that seemed necessary to attain the general goals of the Community. Those measures had to be decided by unanimity.

In 1986, the Single European Act introduced the legal basis for the adoption of legislation that seeks to protect the natural environment, and it changed the decision rules. Thereafter, policy outputs that affect the Common Market could be passed by QMV whereas policy outputs which were adopted solely to protect the environment required unanimity. The Maastricht Treaty, which came into force in 1992, extended QMV to almost all environmental measures, regardless of whether they affect the Common Market or not. Hence, joint decision-making became the predominant governing mode in EU environmental policy. There are only a few exceptions that are still subject to unanimous decision-making. Policies are formulated in the mode of intergovernmental negotiation if measures concern fiscal provisions or affect town and country planning, the quantitative management of water resources, or land use not related to waste management. Finally, those measures which affect the mix of energy supply from different sources in the member states remain subject to unanimous decisions (Krämer, 2003: 72–84; Knill, 2003: 28–36).

Supranational centralization is of minor relevance in EU environmental policies. In 1994, the European Environmental Agency was founded. However, in contrast to the Environmental Protection Agency in the USA, which has legislative and executive powers, the European Environmental Agency's functions are restricted to collecting and analysing information.

Table 5.2   Treaty-based competences and decision rules in EU environmental policy

Explicit Community competence for:	EEC Treaty 1957	Single European Act 1986	Maastricht Treaty 1992	Amsterdam Treaty 1997	Nice Treaty 2001
environmental measures which contribute to the completion of the internal market	–	++	++	++	++
environmental measures which are exclusively directed to protect the environment	–	+	++ (five exceptions, see below)	++ (five exceptions, see below)	++ (five exceptions, see below)
provisions primarily of a fiscal nature	–	+	+	+	+
measures affecting town and country planning	–	+	+	+	+
measures affecting quantitative management of water resources or affecting, directly or indirectly, the availability of those resources	–	+	+	+	+
measures affecting land use, with exception of waste management	–	+	+	+	+
measures significantly affecting a member state's choice between different energy sources and the general structure of its energy supply	–	+	+	+	+

Notes:
– Not mentioned.
+ Decision by unanimity.
++ Decision by qualified majority.

It does not have any regulative competences. The European Court of Justice is not directly involved in adopting environmental policy outputs but its interpretations of the treaty's competence clauses had a certain impact on policy formation in environmental policy. This was particularly important before the Single European Act, when there was no explicit legal competence to adopt EU environmental legislation. The ECJ repeatedly confirmed that environmental legislation could be passed on the basis of two clauses that allowed Community action deemed necessary for the effective functioning of the Common Market or for the achievement of the Community's general objectives (now enshrined in Arts 94 and 308 of the EC Treaty; see Knill, 2003: 98–101). Albeit not directly involved in policy formulation, rulings of the ECJ also affected the relative weight of economic and environmental principles in the EU's activities. In cases based on Article 28 of the EC Treaty, which prohibits quantitative restrictions on imports, the Court, under certain conditions, considered environmental aims to be relevant to justifying restrictions on trade (Notaro and Poli, 2002: 503–509).

Legal Instruments in EU Environmental Policy

As in EU social policy, the legal instruments in EU environmental policy consist of both hard law and soft law. However, hard law measures outnumber soft law by far in the environmental field. Figure 5.3 shows the evolution of legal instruments in EU environmental policy. Between 1970 and 2006, 168 directives and regulations were adopted. In addition, 111 amendments, extensions and application rules, which also have the form of hard law, were passed. During the same period, recommendations, resolutions, declarations and conclusions add up to a total of 75. Only in 1975 did the number of non-binding policy outputs exceed the number of directives and regulations in force. While the volume of both hard law and soft law has increased since the emergence of the policy area, directives and regulations increased to a far greater extent than non-binding policy outputs. This result also holds if amendments, extensions and application rules of legal acts are neglected. If they are taken into account the gap between hard law and soft law widens further.

The dominance of hard law in EU environmental policy is also confirmed by the shares of the different types of legal instruments, which are shown in Figure 5.4. At the beginning of the 1970s, directives and regulations prevailed. In the following years, amendments, extensions and application rules as well as non-binding policy outputs became a firm component of EU environmental policy. However, newly adopted directives and regulations remained salient in quantitative terms. In several years

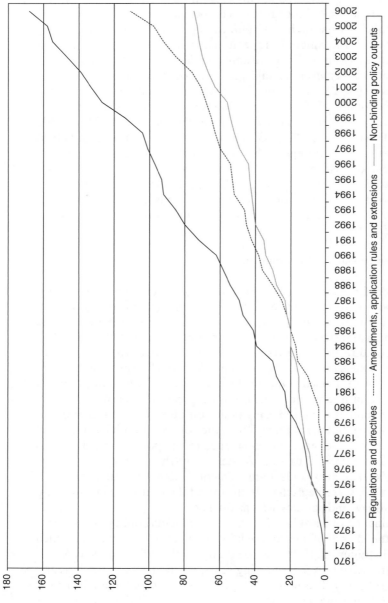

Source: Binding legal acts: Celex > menu search > legislation > directives/regulations, not restricted to legislation in force, classification headings > 15 environment, consumers and health protection > 15.10 environment, without wrong classifications; non-binding legal acts: Eur-Lex > simple search > legislation > other acts, not restricted to acts in force, classification headings > 15 environment, consumers and health protection > 15.10 environment. The items that have been counted are declarations, conclusions, resolutions and recommendations that are not wrongly classified.

Figure 5.3   Evolution of legal instruments in EU environmental policy, 1970–2006

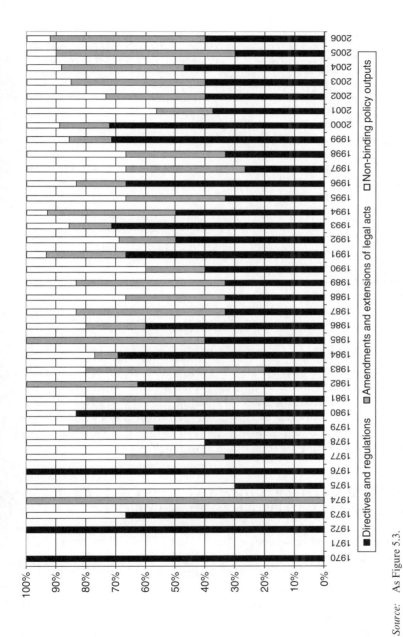

Source: As Figure 5.3.

Figure 5.4 Comparative shares of different legal instruments in EU environmental policy, 1970–2006

Table 5.3   Modes of governance in EU social policy and EU environmental policy

	Interest intermediation	Modes of interaction	Policy instruments
EU social policy	Policy networks +++ Corporatism ++	Joint decision-making ++ Intergovernmental negotiation ++ Supranational centralization ++	Hard law ++ Soft law ++
EU environmental policy	Policy networks +++ Pluralism + Corporatism +	Joint decision-making +++ Intergovernmental negotiation + Supranational centralization +	Hard law +++ Soft law +

Notes:
Role of respective mode of governance is:
+ Weak.
++ Significant.
+++ Dominant.

they accounted for more than half of all policy outputs, while they never made up less than one-fifth of the policy outputs adopted each year. If the total amount of hard law, including amendments, extensions and application rules, is considered, the share of binding legal acts is overwhelming. During the period, soft law usually accounted for less than one-third of the policy outputs adopted each year. Only in 1975 and in 1978 were more non-binding policy outputs than binding legal acts passed.

5   PATTERNS OF GOVERNANCE IN TWO POLICY AREAS: TOWARDS AN EXPLANATION

The previous sections have demonstrated that EU social policy and EU environmental policy are characterized by different mixes of governance modes. The governance modes of each dimension identified in the two policy areas are summarized in Table 5.3. The dominant form of governance in EU environmental policy may be described by the Community method, which combines interest intermediation in policy networks, joint decision-making between the Commission, the European Parliament and the Council of Ministers on the basis of QMV, and goal attainment through hard law. In EU social policy, the modes of governance are more diverse. In addition to the Community method, policy-making also takes place in the context of the OMC, which combines interest intermediation through policy networks, intergovernmental negotiation and the adoption of soft law. A number of important issue areas in EU social policy thus still require unanimity in the Council, while the largest part of issues in environmental policy may be adopted on the basis of QMV. Soft law is more important in social policy than in environmental policy, and corporatist forms of interest intermediation play a more significant role in social policy than in environmental policy.

How can we explain these patterns and the way they emerged? The fact that corporatist forms of interest intermediation are more important in EU social policy than in EU environmental policy seems to mirror domestic traditions in both policy areas. In all countries that have traditions of corporatism, social policy is the prime policy area where this mode of tripartite concertation has come to fruition. Trade union and employers' organizations thus also belong to the oldest and best-organized interest associations at the European level (Eising, 2001). Interest intermediation in environmental policy, by contrast, has seldom been marked by corporatist structures, although countries such as Germany have a certain tradition of regulation through voluntary agreements concluded by industrial associations (Töller, 2004: 11).

Explaining why integration has gone further in the environmental policy field in terms of both decision-making rules and binding policy outputs, reveals a more fundamental variation between the two policy areas. At first sight, the competences and decision-making procedures in both policy areas developed in remarkably similar ways. Originally, Community action in both areas had to rely mostly on the subsidiary competence provisions of the treaties, which required unanimous agreement among member state governments. Explicit legislative competences and decision-making by qualified majority voting were expanded in the context of the internal market programme. Environmental policy was largely communitarized in the Single European Act, while the major reforms of the treaty provisions in social policy were effectuated through the Maastricht Treaty. Functional arguments in favour of more effective European cooperation met with less resistance in environmental policy, where proponents could argue that European action was necessary to combat transborder pollution and that the replacement of the multitude of national regulative schemes by a Europe-wide regulatory framework would provide a 'level playing field' for companies and would thus be beneficial for completing the internal market.

In social policy, the internal market programme also induced a pro-integrative dynamic. However, those who argued that the internal market needed to be accompanied by an effective social dimension in order to avoid social dumping – mostly trade unionists, left-wing politicians from countries with a high standard of living and the Commission under Jacques Delors – met with fierce resistance, especially by the Conservative British government, who rejected European social policy both on ideological grounds and because of the expected costs for the UK. Moreover, almost all member state governments have been defending their autonomy with regard to regulating core areas of the welfare state, such as pensions, healthcare, unemployment benefits or other social security programmes. In EU social policy, therefore, the functional spillover from the internal market got stuck halfway owing to the political resistance by member state governments.

This variation in the integration dynamics reveals three major differences between the two policy areas. These differences account for the fact that the overall level of political conflict is higher in EU social policy than in EU environmental policy, and that environmental policy is thus further integrated both in terms of decision-making modes and in terms of binding legislative output.

1. *Domestic policy legacies are more diverse and institutionally more deeply rooted in social policy than in environmental policy.* The historical evolution of welfare states in Europe is closely connected to the process of nation-building, and welfare programmes are thus deeply entrenched in member state institutions (Alber, 1982; Esping-Andersen, 1990). This process has given rise to a diverse set of welfare-state regimes. These regimes vary significantly with regard to the organization of the respective social security systems (Flora, 1986–1987; Esping-Andersen, 1990, 1999; Castles, 1995; Ostner and Lewis, 1995; Ferrera, 1996) and in the shape of the respective domestic industrial relations models and employment rights regimes (Crouch, 1993; Ebbinghaus and Visser, 1997; Ferner and Hyman, 1999; Gold, 1993).

    Environmental policy is also marked by different domestic regulatory models. As Héritier and her collaborators (1996) have shown, European environmental policy-making has long been characterized by the conflict between the British model of immission control based on flexible standards and the German model of emission control through hierarchical command-and-control instruments. In overall terms, however, the diversity of domestic regulatory models is not as high as it is in social policy, and domestic environmental policy legacies are considerably younger and less deeply institutionalized than social policy traditions. Environmental policy is a relatively young policy area at the domestic level as well: it did not begin to become institutionalized in European countries until the 1970s. At that time most member states, except the UK and Ireland, adhered to the German model of command-and-control instruments and emission-based standards. The differences have been further reduced since then. The UK and Ireland have gone a long way towards emission-based standards, while Germany and many other countries have increasingly complemented their tradition of command-and-control regulation with flexible instruments along the lines of the British model (Liefferink and Jordan, 2004; Jordan and Liefferink, 2004; Weale et al., 2000).

Given the relatively late institutionalization of environmental policy, moreover, many environmental policy issues put on the agenda at the European level concern phenomena for which many member states have not yet adopted any domestic regulations. All these factors suggest that the problem of domestic 'policy pre-emption' (Pierson and Leibfried, 1995: 22) by member states' regulatory traditions is significantly less severe in EU environmental policy than in EU social policy.

2. *In EU environmental policy, less conflict-prone types of regulation are more frequent than they are in EU social policy.* This argument refers to the distinction between product standards and process standards (Scharpf, 1999: 106–113). Product standards, regulating things such as machine safety, noise emission standards or the ergonomics of workplace equipment, may imply significant costs for industry. At the same time, however, both producers and member states have an interest in common product standards because they facilitate the marketing of the products concerned throughout the internal market, which would be hampered if a producer had to comply with a patchwork of diverse national standards. In this sense, product standards are less conflict-prone and thus easier to adopt than process standards such as provisions on maximum working hours or information rights for trade unions, which impose costs on companies without creating market benefits. Our data suggest that product standards are more frequent in environmental policy than they are in social policy. If we break down the field of environmental policy into individual issue areas and look at those where most product-related laws are to be expected, we see that the issue areas of noise pollution, chemical safety, industrial safety and biodiversity make up one-third of all binding policy outputs. Further product standards are to be expected in other issue areas such as the monitoring of atmospheric pollution and waste management. In the field of social policy, in contrast, the

only issue area where we should find product standards is occupational safety and health, which accounts for about a quarter of all binding legislation in EU social policy.

3. *Domestic electorates are significantly more favourable towards regulating environmental issues at the European level than towards transferring social policy competences to the European level.* As Eurobarometer data shows, the vast majority of EU citizens want environmental issues to be tackled at the European level, while an equally vast majority deem welfare issues to be a domestic domain (Kritzinger, 2005: 58–63). Against this background, member state governments have little reason to support EU-level regulation of social policy issues, whereas expanding EU environmental policy is fully legitimated by domestic constituencies. Although everyday policy-making at the EU level usually does not enter into domestic election campaigns, these results underline that governments will have little problem defending EU environmental standards at home, while they will have a hard time convincing their domestic electorates of common European action in social policy.

These three factors are the reason why member states were willing to transfer a wide range of environmental competences to the European level and why they also accepted majority voting in almost all issue areas of environmental policy, while member state resistance has ensured that important issues in social policy still remain in the exclusive hands of domestic governments, are subject to unanimity or may only be tackled through soft, non-binding modes of governance. Similarly, these factors explain why EU law-making in environmental policy proceeded more smoothly than it did in social policy. The overall lower level of conflict in environmental policy facilitated the adoption of a higher number of binding policy outputs even before QMV was introduced. Social policy, in contrast, is marked by a lower number of overall policy outputs, and in the absence of sufficient political will among member state governments, it has seen a more frequent recourse to more autonomy-protecting soft-law instruments.

In the end, our explanation is an intergovernmental one. This does not mean, however, that we reject the pro-integrative role of the European Commission and the European Court of Justice or the growing impact of the European Parliament. Instead, we argue that these influences are relatively similar in our two policy areas, which means that they cannot account for the differences in the evolution of modes of governance. What remains as an explanation is the different integration preferences of member state governments. Again, the differences in government preferences in the two policy areas cannot be explained by factors such as party political ideologies, since these either should be relatively similar (if we think about general stances towards European integration) or should not be stable enough over time (if we think about left–right politics). Instead, we argue that the differences between EU social policy and EU environmental policy may be put down to relatively stable structural features of both policy areas: differences in the level of long-term institutional entrenchment of domestic policy legacies, in the types of standardization problems dealt with and in popular support for further European integration at the domestic level.

NOTES

1. The distinction between intergovernmental negotiation and the joint-decision mode is based on our own (re)interpretation of Scharpf's writings, as the line he draws between the two modes is not quite as sharp as it could be. In our view, it is unclear whether Scharpf sees the type of decision rule that is applicable in the Council as the decisive criterion, as we suggest above, or whether the role of the Commission, the Court and the European Parliament is more important. At any rate, he is unclear about whether those areas within the First Pillar where the Council decides by unanimity belong to the mode of intergovernmental negotiation, as the decision rule is the same as in the Second and Third Pillars (Scharpf, 2001: 9; 2006a: 847–9), or whether these areas have to be subsumed under the joint-decision mode, as the role of the Commission and the European Parliament is much more important here than outside the First Pillar (Scharpf, 2006b: 12). We have opted for the first alternative as we think the actual negotiation dynamics are determined much more by the decision rule in the Council than by the formal role of the supranational institutions.
2. This was laid down in the so-called subsidiary competence provisions. Laws in the member states which 'directly affect the establishment or functioning of the common market' could be approximated by a unanimous Council decision on the basis of a Commission proposal (Art. 100 EEC Treaty). The Treaty also stipulated that in so far as 'action by the Community should prove necessary to attain, in the course of the operation of the common market, one of the objectives of the Community, and this Treaty has not provided the necessary powers, the Council shall, acting unanimously on a proposal from the Commission and after consulting the European Parliament, take the appropriate measures' (Art. 235 EEC Treaty).

REFERENCES

Alber, Jens (1982), *Vom Armenhaus zum Wohlfahrtsstaat: Analysen zur Entwicklung der Sozialversicherung in Westeuropa*, Frankfurt: Campus.
Bercusson, Brian (1992), 'Maastricht: a fundamental change in European labour law', *Industrial Relations Journal*, **23**(2), 177–90.
Bogdandy, Armin von, Felix Arndt and Jürgen Bast (2004), 'Legal instruments in European Union law and their reform: a systematic approach on an empirical basis', *Yearbook of European Law*, **23**, 91–136.

Bulmer, Simon and Stephen Padgett (2005), 'Policy transfer in the European Union: an institutionalist perspective', *British Journal of Political Science*, **35**(1), 103–26.

Caporaso, James and Joerg Wittenbrinck (2006), 'The new modes of governance and political authority in Europe', *Journal of European Public Policy*, **13**(4), 471–80.

Castles, Francis G. (1995), 'Welfare state development in Southern Europe', *West European Politics*, **18**(2), 291–313.

Council of the European Union (1992), 'Council Directive 92/43/EEC on the conservation of natural habitats and of wild fauna and flora', Official Journal, L 206, 21 May.

Crouch, Colin (1993), *Industrial Relations and European State Traditions*, Oxford: Clarendon Press.

Dahl, Robert A. (1961), *Who Governs? Democracy and Power in the American City*, New Haven and London: Yale University Press.

Ebbinghaus, Bernhard and Jelle Visser (1997), 'Der Wandel der Arbeitsbeziehungen im westeuropäischen Vergleich', in Stefan Hradil and Stefan Immerfall (eds), *Die westeuropäischen Gesellschaften im Vergleich*, Opladen: Leske & Budrich, pp. 333–76.

Eichener, Volker (2000), *Das Entscheidungssystem der Europäischen Union: Institutionelle Analyse und demokratietheoretische Bewertung*, Opladen: Leske & Budrich.

Eising, Rainer (2001), 'Interessenvermittlung in der Europäischen Union', in Werner Reutter and Peter Rütters (eds), *Verbände und Verbandssysteme in Westeuropa*, Opladen: Leske & Budrich, pp. 453–76.

Eising, Rainer and Beate Kohler-Koch (1999), 'Introduction: network governance in the European Union', in Beate Kohler-Koch and Rainer Eising (eds), *The Transformation of Governance in the European Union*, London: Routledge, pp. 3–13.

Esping-Andersen, Gøsta (1990), *The Three Worlds of Welfare Capitalism*, Cambridge: Polity Press.

Esping-Andersen, Gøsta (1999), *Social Foundations of Postindustrial Economies*, Oxford: Oxford University Press.

European Commission (1999), 'Communication from the Commission: Europe's Environment: What directions for the future? The Global Assessment of the European Community Programme of Policy and Action in relation to the environment and sustainable development, "Towards Sustainability"', COM(1999) 543 final, 24 November, Brussels.

European Commission (2002), 'Communication from the Commission: The European social dialogue, a force for innovation and change, Proposal for a Council Decision establishing a Tripartite Social Summit for Growth and Employment', COM(2002) 341 final, 26 June, Brussels.

Falkner, Gerda (1998), *EU Social Policy in the 1990s: Towards a Corporatist Policy Community*, London: Routledge.

Falkner, Gerda (1999), 'European social policy: towards multi-level and multi-actor governance', in Beate Kohler-Koch and Rainer Eising (eds), *The Transformation of Governance in the European Union*, London: Routledge, pp. 83–97.

Falkner, Gerda (2000), 'The Council or the social partners? EC social policy between diplomacy and collective bargaining', *Journal of European Public Policy*, **7**(5), 705–24.

Falkner, Gerda (2006), 'Forms of governance in European Union social policy: continuity and/or change', *International Social Security Review*, **59**(2), 77–103.

Ferner, Anthony and Richard Hyman (eds) (1999), *Changing Industrial Relations in Europe*, 2nd edn, Oxford: Blackwell.

Ferrera, Maurizio (1996), 'The "Southern model" of welfare in social Europe', *Journal of European Social Policy*, **6**(1), 17–37.

Flora, Peter (ed.) (1986–1987), *Growth to Limits: The Western European Welfare States Since World War II, Vols 1–3*, Berlin: De Gruyter.

Francis, John G. (1993), *The Politics of Regulation: A Comparative Perspective*, Cambridge: Blackwell.

Gold, Michael (ed.) (1993), *The Social Dimension: Employment Policy in the European Community*, London: Macmillan.

Gorges, Michael J. (1996), *Euro-Corporatism? Interest Intermediation in the European Community*, Lanham, MD: University Press of America.

Griller, Stefan and Andreas Orator (2006), '"Mapping the jungle": a legal attempt to classify European agencies', NEWGOV Deliverable 04/32, Florence: European University Institute, available at http://www.eu-newgov.org/pro tected_pages/DELIV/D04%20D32_Working_Paper_Mapping_the_Jungle.pdf.

Héritier, Adrienne (2002), 'New modes of governance in Europe: policy-making without legislating?', in Adrienne Héritier (ed.), *Common Goods: Reinventing European and International Governance*, Lanham, MD: Rowman & Littlefield, pp. 185–206.

Héritier, Adrienne, Christoph Knill and Susanne Mingers (1996), *Ringing the Changes in Europe: Regulatory Competition and the Transformation of the State: Britain, France, Germany*, Berlin: de Gruyter.

Hix, Simon (2005), *The Political System of the European Union*, 2nd edn, Basingstoke and New York: Palgrave.

Howlett, Michael (1991), 'Policy instruments, policy styles, and policy implementation: national approaches to theories of instrument choice', *Policy Studies Journal*, **19**(2), pp. 1–21.

Jordan, Andrew and Duncan Liefferink (2004), 'Europeanization and convergence: comparative conclusions', in Andrew Jordan and Duncan Liefferink (eds), *Environmental Policy in Europe: The Europeanization of National Environmental Policy*, London: Routledge, pp. 224–5.

Kenis, Patrick and Volker Schneider (1991), 'Policy networks and policy analysis: scrutinizing a new analytical toolbox', in Bernd Marin and Renate Mayntz (eds), *Policy Networks: Empirical Evidence and Theoretical Considerations*, Frankfurt am Main: Campus, pp. 25–59.

Knill, Christoph (2003), *Europäische Umweltpolitik: Steuerungsprobleme und Regulierungsmuster im Mehrebenensystem*, Opladen: Leske & Budrich.

Knill, Christoph and Andrea Lenschow (2003), *Modes of Regulation in the Governance of the European Union: Towards a Comprehensive Evaluation*, European Integration Online Papers 7, available at http://eiop.or.at/eiop/texte/2003-001a.htm.

Krämer, Ludwig (2003), *EC Environmental Law*, London: Sweet & Maxwell.

Kritzinger, Sylvia (2005), 'European identity building from the perspective of efficiency', *Comparative European Politics*, **3**(1), 50–75.

Lenschow, Andrea (1999), 'Transformation in European environmental governance', in Beate Kohler-Koch and Rainer Eising (eds), *The Transformation of Governance in the European Union*, London: Routledge, pp. 39–60.

Liefferink, Duncan and Andrew Jordan (2004), 'Measuring Europeanization and policy convergence: national baseline conditions', in Andrew Jordan and Duncan Liefferink (eds), *The Europeanization of National Environmental Policy*, London: Routledge, pp. 32–46.

Mayntz, Renate (2004), 'Governance Theory als fortentwickelte Steuerungstheorie?', MPIfG Working Paper 04/1, Cologne: Max-Planck-Institut für Gesellschaftsforschung, available at http://www.mpi-fg-koeln.mpg.de/pu/workpap/wp04-1/wp04-1.html.

Mayntz, Renate and Fritz W. Scharpf (1995), 'Der Ansatz des akteurzentrierten Institutionalismus', in Renate Mayntz and Fritz W. Scharpf (eds), *Gesellschaftliche Selbstregelung und politische Steuerung*, Frankfurt: Campus, pp. 39–72.

Notaro, Nicola and Sara Poli (2002), 'Environmental law 2000–2001', *Yearbook of European Law*, **21**, 489–534.

Ostner, Ilona and Jane Lewis (1995), 'Gender and the evolution of European social policies', in Stephan Leibfried and Paul Pierson (eds), *European Social Policy: Between Fragmentation and Integration*, Washington, DC: Brookings Institution, pp. 159–94.

Pierre, Jon and B. Guy Peters (2005), *Governing Complex Societies: Trajectories and Scenarios*, Basingstoke and New York: Palgrave.

Pierson, Paul and Stephan Leibfried (1995), 'Multitiered institutions and the making of social policy', in Stephan Leibfried and Paul Pierson (eds), *European Social Policy: Between Fragmentation and Integration*, Washington, DC: Brookings Institution, pp. 1–40.

Rhodes, R.A.W. (1997), *Understanding Governance: Policy Networks, Governance, Reflexivity and Accountability*, Buckingham: Open University Press.

Rosenau, James N. (1992), 'Governance, order, and change in world politics', in James N. Rosenau and Ernst-Otto Czempiel (eds), *Governance without Government: Order and Change in World Politics*, Cambridge: Cambridge University Press, pp. 1–29.

Scharpf, Fritz W. (1997), *Games Real Actors Play: Actor Centered Institutionalism in Policy Research*, Boulder, CO: Westview Press.

Scharpf, Fritz W. (1999), *Governing in Europe: Effective and Democratic?*, Oxford: Oxford University Press.

Scharpf, Fritz W. (2001), 'Notes toward a theory of multilevel governing in Europe', *Scandinavian Political Studies*, **24**(1), 1–26.

Scharpf, Fritz W. (2006a), 'The joint-decision trap revisited', *Journal of Common Market Studies*, **44**(4), 845–64.

Scharpf, Fritz W. (2006b), *Problem Solving Effectiveness and Democratic Accountability in the EU*, IHS Working Paper Political Science Series 107, Vienna: Institut für Höhere Studien.

Schmitter, Philippe C. (1974), 'Still the century of corporatism?', *Review of Politics*, **35**, 85–131.

Schmitter, Philippe C. (1981), 'Interest intermediation and regime governability in contemporary Western Europe and North America', in Suzanne Berger (ed.), *Organising Interests in Western Europe: Pluralism, Corporatism, and the Transformation of Politics*, Cambridge: Cambridge University Press, pp. 287–327.

Senden, Linda (2004), *Soft Law in European Community Law*, Oxford: Hart.

Shaw, Jo (2001), 'Gender and the Court of Justice', in Gráinne De Burca and

J.H.H. Weiler (eds), *The European Court of Justice*, Oxford: Oxford University Press, pp. 87–142.

Töller, Annette E. (2004), 'The Europeanization of public policies: understanding idiosyncratic mechanisms and contingent results', European Integration Online Papers **8**(9), available at http://eiop.or.at/eiop/texte/2004-009a.htm.

Treib, Oliver and Gerda Falkner (2009), 'Bargaining and lobbying in EU social policy', in David Coen and Jeremy J. Richardson (eds), *Lobbying the European Union: Institutions, Actors and Issues*, Oxford: Oxford University Press, pp. 247–67.

Truman, David B. (1951), *The Governmental Process: Political Interests and Public Opinion*, New York: David A. Knopf.

Weale, Albert, Geoffrey Pridham, Michelle Cini, Dimitrios Konstadakopulos, Martin Porter and Brendan Flynn (2000), *Environmental Governance in Europe: An Ever Closer Ecological Union?*, Oxford: Oxford University Press.

6. Cohesion policy in the new member states: unfolding new modes of governance?

Kálmán Dezséri and Krisztina Vida

INTRODUCTION

This chapter analyses briefly the governance modes of cohesion policy at the European Union level and, in more detail, its implementation in eight new member states, putting special emphasis on the existence of new modes of governance in this policy field.[1]

At the European level the elements of 'new' (or rather alternative) modes of governance complement the classical modes by providing for a 'learning path' before sovereignty is ceded to the EU level, and for more efficiency, democracy and legitimacy after sovereignty has been ceded. Thus it seems justifiable to speak of 'mixed modes' of governance, pointing to the combination of old, or classical, and new methods, showing the signs of continuous evolution in both the horizontal (EU institutions' interactions) and the vertical (involvement of regional and local partners) dimensions.

As regards national implementation of cohesion policy, the EU has created a framework of legal, procedural and financial conditions that actually initiate a kind of decentralization and involvement of the regional and local governments, civil society and other stakeholders in policy formulation, implementation and monitoring processes, with a view to enabling EU structural assistance to be efficiently absorbed. Although there are no EU rules binding member states to decentralize and maximize participation, effective utilization of the different funds does call for compliance with these principles (Lakatos, 2007: 178). Thus, through the design and implementation of cohesion policy, new, multi-level and multi-actor types of governance modes can be identified. This chapter sheds light on the emergence and evolution of these phenomena in eight new member states, and finally attempts to evaluate them from a theoretical point of view.

THE EVOLUTION OF COHESION POLICY MODES OF GOVERNANCE AT THE EUROPEAN LEVEL

The issue of regional disparities in the Community – which was only marginally mentioned in the founding treaties – attracted more attention with the Northern enlargement of 1973. As a response to the entry of new, problematic regions (for example the declining industrial zones of the UK, and a whole country with a low level of development, Ireland) in 1975 a new financial instrument, the European Regional Development Fund (ERDF), was created. Though this was a very important step forward, the creation of the new fund did not amount to a Community-level regional policy as such because it only contributed (up to 50 per cent) to certain regional development projects of member states (under the categories of industrial and infrastructural investment), according to their applicable financial quota. This stage only served as a learning path before the shift was made from such an intergovernmentally managed 'mechanism of paying' to a genuine treaty-based policy, managed by means of the 'classical' Community method (Vida, 2007: 90–94).

There was then a comprehensive renewal of European regional development policy in 1987–88 after the Southern enlargements and the re-launching of market liberalization. The 1986 Single European Act was a package deal containing not only the establishment of the Single Market but also several other measures, including a thoroughgoing revision of the Community approach to regional policy. Based on the Single European Act, the 1988 reform entailed a considerable increase in financial commitments and substantial changes in the objectives and implementation of the Structural Funds. Thus European regional policy went through a process of major supranational upgrading and became a fully-fledged treaty-based policy. This implied that the decision-making mechanism and the roles of all relevant institutions (the Commission, the Council, the European Parliament) were defined and the instruments of legally binding secondary legislation were introduced. Moreover, the legislation on and implementation of regional policy became subject to the judgement of the European Court of Justice and to investigation and reporting by the Court of Auditors. The new provisions and principles provided possibilities for a coherent Community policy in the classical sense ('old mode') to be developed (Treib et al., 2005), while guaranteeing a more autonomous role for the Commission and challenging the positions of the central governments of member states by involving sub-national partners under the newly introduced partnership principle. This meant that the elements of new modes of governance also gained ground and penetrated further (Vida, 2007: 94–7).

The emerging governance of structural policy had a dual nature, consisting of the old mode of governance (one of its main features being initial intergovernmental agreement, and gradual evolution towards a Community policy) and the new mode (involvement of sub-national actors on the basis of partnership). This expanding involvement of regional/local, social, civil and economic partners in the process of preparing, implementing, monitoring and evaluating development programmes gradually brought about the emergence of multi-level and multi-actor governance systems. At the same time it became the sole right of member states to designate or authorize competent regional, local and professional bodies as well as social and economic partners to participate in the whole process of this policy. Because of the flexibility of the provisions, a wide variety of institutional set-ups and degrees of partner involvement emerged (Dezséri, 2007).

The next important step in the evolution of structural policy was the Maastricht Treaty of 1992 (entering into force in 1993), which defined economic and social cohesion within the Union as one of the priority objectives, alongside Economic and Monetary Union and the Internal Market. The treaty provisions and successive regulations of the Council redefined and reinforced the roles, tasks and responsibilities of EU institutions and the modes of governance of regional policy-making. The Maastricht Treaty also created the Committee of the Regions and set up the Cohesion Fund to provide financial assistance for less-developed member states to modernize their infrastructure and implement environmental protection projects and investments. All in all, the rules on the Cohesion Fund reflected a clear step back from the new/innovative governance type of the Structural Funds towards a more conservative and member state-based policy implementation, reminiscent of the pre-1987 functioning of the ERDF (Bache, 1998; Vida, 2007: 97–101).

The Amsterdam Treaty of 1997 and the Nice Treaty of 2001 (coming into force in 1999 and 2003, respectively) confirmed the strategic importance of the economic and social cohesion of member states as a Community policy aim, without essentially altering the institutional set-up. At the same time, the Treaty of Nice brought about a further step towards communitarization of this policy by transforming unanimity into qualified majority voting after 1 January 2007.

Originating from the solid and continuously reinforced legal basis, there is by now a very rich body of secondary legislation (made up overwhelmingly of Commission decisions regulating in detail the implementation of the funds by member states). The key regulations of 1988, 1992, 1999 and 2006 laid down the main rules of cohesion policy governance, containing a range of innovative modes as well. Among others, the key provisions of Council Regulation 1083/2006 made explicit reference to cooperation with the 'competent regional, local, urban and other public authorities', with the 'economic and social partners' and also with 'any other appropriate body representing civil society, environmental partners, nongovernmental organisations, and bodies responsible for promoting equality between men and women' during the whole process of development projects receiving financial assistance from the Structural Funds. This is very much in line with the European Commission's advocacy in its 2001 White Paper on European Governance of more active communication with stakeholders and their political representatives, to initiate 'a circle, based on feedback, networks and involvement from policy creation to implementation at all levels' (European Commission, 2001: 11).

As an interim conclusion, we agree with Liesbet Hooghe that at least four kinds of justification for partnership can be identified (Hooghe, 1998: 469): first, it increases efficiency; second, it strengthens the cooperation and mobilization of indigenous resources by the relevant actors in a nonhierarchical fashion; third, it gives weaker sub-national actors a stronger voice, highlighting the need for greater solidarity; and, finally, partnership can be a good vehicle for greater democratization in general. Despite all these potentially positive impacts, partnership has been applied in very different ways and to very different extents in the different member states. According to the regulations mentioned above, national 'varieties' are of course allowed; nevertheless, the overall picture shows that the application of partnership 'has fallen short of expectations' (Hooghe, 1998: 469). This also signals that complying with the partnership principle – as a special mode of governance – required a longer learning period even in the old member states. This chapter will examine whether the same is the case in the new member states.

EMERGING ELEMENTS OF NEW MODES OF GOVERNANCE IN THE NEW MEMBER STATES

The application of the new modes of governance has been introduced gradually in the new EU member states. These countries only adopted the EU *acquis* as part of a process that involved complex legal and institutional changes. Understandably, the challenge was concerned more with regulatory and other requirements that reflect the traditional side of governance in the EU structures than with introducing new modes of governance. With the possibility of accession at stake for several years, these countries obviously sought first and foremost to meet the formal requirements for implementing the regulatory system. The elements of the old modes of governance received priority over those of the new. Indeed, in many cases, initiatives for new modes of governance have come from private actors and civil society, not just from central or regional government (Dezséri, 2007: 29).

As financial assistance after accession was conditional on well-functioning structural or regional and cohesion policies, it was important to plan and implement the programmes that would be eligible for financial support. The new member states took over all regulations related to the Structural Funds and the Cohesion Fund (Council Regulations 1260/1999 and 1164/1994, respectively). As these provide significant financial support, it was greatly in their interest to abide by the EU regulations on establishing the regional administrative structure and an adequate institutional set-up, and to elaborate development plans and documents of various types, that is, the governance of the structural and cohesion policies.

Before accession all the candidate countries endorsed basic government regulations on the establishment and functioning of national institutions of the Structural Funds and Cohesion Fund. The common feature of these is that rules about all funds are treated together. At the same time, the establishment of institutions and the methods of financial implementation are regulated in different legal acts for the Structural Funds and the Cohesion Fund, although there is some institutional overlap in the smaller new member states (Dezséri, 2007: 21).

The new member states have long traditions of strongly centralized nation-state administration and governance. Their regions[2] were created only recently, so that regional authority, infrastructure and expertise are still relatively weak (Ágh, 2005: 22–4). Similarly, four decades of socialism left no room for a bottom-up approach to targeting regional policy and fostering economic convergence and cohesion among regions. These traditions and conditions may still limit the effective involvement of regional institutions in planning and deciding programmes and implementation.

All the new member states except Poland are small or medium-sized countries. They all have different historical traditions and different institutional and administrative structures. Not surprisingly, they faced various problems when establishing their regional administrative structures to conform to EU regulations and requirements. Some introduced legislation to support regional development and defined areas of responsibility for delegation to regions. These determined regional policy in a broader sense and constituted a further step towards harmonization with EU regulations. Responsibilities allocated to the regions included the coordination, development and implementation of regional development programmes, and cooperation with central government and coordination of the interests of municipalities in cases where development went beyond the sphere of one municipality. Decisions were made as to how far the regions could take part in decision-making on the allocation of public funding to support regional development, including the funding of some regional development agencies.

The placing of the Cohesion and Structural Funds Managing Authority (MA) in relation to the state administrative structure can be a crucial issue from many points of view. As the experience of old member states shows, the MA can be placed within or outside the state administration. In most cases, the MAs were placed within the public administrative structure and only rarely (for example in Portugal) outside it. In the latter case, there were not many intermediate bodies involved in implementation, while in the former a significant proportion of the tasks were delegated to intermediate bodies.

In every new member state, the administrative structure for implementing development plans is based on rational, mainly centralized, organization and experience gained before accession. The key institution for executing EU cohesion policy is the MA, whose position in the public administration structure sheds light on the importance of the decision-makers during the implementation of structural policy. The practice in old member states which incorporated their MA into the public administration varied. Some set it up within their Finance Ministry, others within their Ministry of Economy, and yet others set it up under another portfolio (for example planning or European relations). This suggests that priority was given to the financial aspects in the former cases, and to development aspects in the others.

Most new member states put more emphasis on the development aspects of policy and established the MA within the public administration, under the Prime Minister's office, a line ministry (for economy, regional development, and so on) or a separate development office, with several intermediate bodies involved in the execution (Dezséri, 2007: 33–4). Some selected the Ministry of Finance for the MA (for example Estonia, Latvia and Lithuania). Generally the new member states established a single MA, although some have a single paying authority within the Ministry of Finance and others have paying authorities in different ministries, according to types of activities (for example Lithuania). There are special cases as well, such as that of Estonia, where the Ministry of Finance is concurrently the MA, the paying authority and the auditing authority (Artner, 2007: 130).

Experience shows that it is harder to ensure institutional effectiveness for the Structural Funds than it is for the Cohesion Fund, as the Structural Funds operate with greater amounts of money and cover wider fields of the economy. Thus diverse development priorities have to be treated within a single system, where numerous, fragmented projects have to be evaluated, processed, checked and monitored. Cohesion Fund financing, on the other hand, covers large, concentrated investments in two main fields of the economy (environmental protection and infrastructure), so that an effective institutional system can be set up more easily. To achieve stronger coherence and coordination between the management of the two types of funds' operations, their MAs may be placed in the same institutions. Thus implementation of tasks takes place inside the same ministries that deal with environmental protection and transport. This relatively concentrated system is applied by the new member states. With Cohesion Fund operations, this solution can be considered the most effective under prevailing conditions (Dezséri, 2007: 35).

The MA in a new member state represents a relatively new centre of power inside the government structure and has important competences in the decision-making process on development policy. In some new member states, the superior body of the MA is the Prime Minister's office, which increases the political importance of the economic development and structural policy, and the decision-making process takes place at cabinet level or close to it, as well as close to the head of government, to whom a minister without portfolio may be directly responsible. In other new member states, the superior body is a ministry. This separates the management of development policy from the direct control of the prime minister or his office and may make it an administrative unit in its own right within the government (Dezséri, 2007: 35).

One main feature of the management systems in the new member states is that national-level management of structural and cohesion policies is relatively concentrated within central government, and the regional level does not have a significant role. This means that management is centralized, as programming, implementation and financing take place inside central government, but several ministries gain relatively significant individual control over the utilization of EU resources, giving them more power than they had before accession.

Implementation of EU structural assistance to member states under the structural policy is based on seven-year programming periods that follow the EU budget system of financial planning. The aims and mechanisms are laid down during the programming process. One of the main characteristics of the Structural Funds is that they aim at financing multi-year development programmes, not individual projects. Another important feature of programming (the process of programme preparation) is that it should ensure coordination among the activities and priorities of the Structural Funds and between them and other EU financial instruments (for example the Cohesion Fund and the European Investment Bank, EIB). A further aim of programming is to ensure that the activities of the Structural Funds and the co-financed development programmes are compatible with other EU policies and comply with EU legislation (Dezséri, 2007: 35).

It is clear that in the first phase of implementation the EU has allowed member states broad freedom to shape their priorities and set the basic guidelines of their co-financed plans. On the one hand, there are the strict Community rules about the general principles to be respected, while on the other hand strong consideration is given to the specific circumstances in member states.

In practice, there is a profound difference between the implementation process of the Structural Funds and that of the Cohesion Fund. Programmes financed out of the former are managed in a decentralized way and are based on the subsidiarity and partnership principles, while the latter employs a more centralized system. This difference between the two funds is clearest in their project selection processes. With the Structural Funds, member states or their government-appointed authorities make the final decision on project funding. With the Cohesion Fund, the selection of projects for financing is done by the Commission. Before this final decision, member states have the right and the responsibility to identify and sift projects that will apply for financing from the fund.

The selection procedures for financial assistance from the Structural Funds and from the Cohesion Fund require different authorities, tasks and responsibilities of member states. There are therefore different patterns or systems of governance in the structural and cohesion policies, which may provide room for different solutions and practices in their management. In practical terms this means that with the Cohesion Fund beneficiary, countries carry out the identification of projects to be financed, either during the preparation of reference frameworks, which may include a project portfolio, or in other ways, such as evaluation using scoring systems, or decisions by pre-selection committees. This situation certainly implies that not all projects will receive financing (Dezséri, 2007: 42–3).

In all new member states, monitoring committees (MCs) have been established especially to perform monitoring tasks during the whole process of implementing development programmes. These committees are explicitly required by the EU regulations establishing these specific funds. No other advisory bodies for the EU funds (for example working groups, steering committees) are required by the regulations. These Council regulations define the general responsibilities and compositions of the MCs, which may monitor the implementation of programming documents or of particular projects (Council of the European Union, 1994, 1999).

In both cases, the composition of the MCs is of particular importance to the mode of governance. Member states are in charge of appointing the members of these committees. The EU regulations require that representatives of the authorities responsible for managing EU financial assistance (MAs, ministries as intermediate bodies) be MC members and provide places for representatives of the European Commission and the EIB. The regulation implies that for assistance from the Structural Funds the partnership principle should apply both to the preparation and implementation phases of the process of financial assistance and to monitoring and appraisal. It can therefore be deduced from the regulation that representatives of social and economic partners, as well as Non-governmental Organizations (NGOs), must be included in the work of MCs (Council of the European Union, 1999). The provisions for financial assistance for the Cohesion Fund do not require the authorities of beneficiary member states to invite representatives of the social and economic partners into the MCs, although some countries have decided to apply the partnership principle to monitoring financial assistance from the Cohesion Fund and invited representatives of NGOs into these committees as well (Dezséri, 2007: 45).

Centralization is a dominant feature of the institutional structure and working systems of cohesion policy in the new member states, for several reasons, the main ones being the short programming period, limited experience with decentralization and regional institutions in most countries, the absence of fully-fledged regional administrative systems in some, and the small size of four of the countries. This centralization leaves their regional administrations in a weak political, financial and institutional position and limits their capacity to make policy. The role of sub-national actors in managing and implementing programmes is limited in most cases to a few areas, usually the process of programming and certain activities relating to the beneficiaries of assistance financed by the funds. The sub-national actors in the larger new member states (Poland, Hungary and the Czech Republic) may be more active and influential. These countries have some forms of joint or integrated regional operational programmes (OPs). Slovakia has a regional element in the OP for basic infrastructure. In these cases, the regional authorities are more involved in policy-making (Dezséri, 2007: 45).

One of the main requirements for the new modes of governance is the existence of social actors who are able to assert their interests and those of wider communities. Such social partners include local and regional authorities, employers' associations, civic groups and NGOs, and trade unions. Civil societies must also be subject to the principles of good governance,[3] so that internal organization, openness and representation are concerns when aiming to involve civil society in these norms of governance.

Civil society in the new member states is much less developed than it is in the old. Moreover, different social groups in different countries have different capacities to represent their interests, which makes the situation more complex. For various reasons, some new member states (such as the Czech Republic and Poland) assign a more important role to citizens because their traditions of civil society have different roots and features. Czech society in the nineteenth century and the first half of the twentieth century had a more substantial middle class than other Central and Eastern European societies did, and these civil traditions survived the ensuing decades to re-emerge gradually (Bassa, 2007: 81). In Polish society, bottom-up action by private actors in politics emerged in the 1980s as trade unionism mushroomed (Wisniewski, 2007: 186). This kind of experience of private/civil action can influence the present state of affairs as well.

Historical experience shows that the genesis and activity of civil society in Central and Eastern Europe is fundamental to the new mode of governance. It can bring about socioeconomic transformation and offset the failures of the state. Where central actors have been unable to fulfil certain tasks and carry out certain actions, the private/civil sector has come to the fore with alternative ways and means (Rhodes, 2005). The introduction of the new mode of governance is most successful when it is supported by national and/or international institutions. Both national and international factors were present in the new member states as they implemented the governance of cohesion policy, with EU requirements acting as the driving force.

According to the general provisions on the Structural Funds, the process of programme preparation must respect the partnership principle. Article 8 of Council Regulation 1260/1999 stated explicitly that national governments must include regional and self-government, businesses and other social and economic partners in the process of programming. The provisions of the Council regulation 1083/2006 continue to include the partnership principle: 'Partnership shall cover the preparation, financing, monitoring and evaluation of assistance'. However, the national rules and regulations of several new Central European member states do not include binding and enforceable mechanisms to implement this. NGOs are often unable to influence the preparation, implementation and monitoring of development projects (Dezséri, 2007: 47–9).

The implementation process for projects receiving financial assistance from EU funds usually involves several bodies which are responsible for project evaluation and appraisal. These were either specially created for the purpose (for example special working groups or steering committees) or existing committees already engaged in similar activities (for example departments of ministries, other bodies, agencies and authorities appointed to participate in project implementation). Most bodies in the new member states were set up for the purpose.[4] NGO representatives on MCs may contribute to enforcing compliance in every element of these development projects with EU policy recommendations, agreements and directives on sustainable development, environmental sustainability, public participation and transparency (Dezséri, 2007: 51).

MCs have important roles in monitoring implementation and in the programming of projects supported by EU financial assistance. This means that they may approve or adjust programme components, consider and approve the criteria for selecting operations for financing, and approve or adjust indicative lists of eligible activities. NGO representatives on the MCs may shift the use of public resources in a more sustainable direction. This influence on decision-making can be particularly important for environmental and sustainability aspects and issues, as experience shows that MCs often focus on the financial aspects and progress of the projects and ignore or pay insufficient attention to environmental aspects and issues. NGO participation on MCs can ensure that monitoring activity leads to compliance with EU and national environmental legislation and standards.

As mentioned above, except in Poland and the Czech Republic, civil society was still underdeveloped in the new member states in the first years of the new millennium, as discussions between the state authorities and representatives of social partners were due to start. Yet neither Poland nor the Czech Republic did substantially better than the other six new member states.

Partnership should, however, remain a core element of future cohesion policy even if it creates new challenges. The responses to those challenges are likely to continue to differ between member states, even between new member states. Some of the latter will make observable efforts to follow the main trend of developing mechanisms for increasing participation, including more wide-ranging and intensive processes of consultation, in which partners from sectoral and regional interest groups are involved. Such an approach would reflect increased awareness of the value of incorporating stakeholders' perspectives in programme implementation.

EVALUATING COHESION POLICY GOVERNANCE: A THEORETICAL APPROACH

From the governance point of view, cohesion policy has gone through a very interesting course of development in recent decades. At the European level it can be stated that new (or alternative) modes of governance emerged and evolved for three reasons (Dezséri and Vida, 2008). First, there was a *tension* between the member states wanting to act at Community level but showing reluctance to cede sovereignty. Thus, new (that is other than the classical) modes could serve as a 'learning path' before more decisive steps were taken towards deepening: this was the case in the pre-1987 period. Second, after cohesion policy became a common, treaty-based policy, greater *efficiency* was needed in its implementation. Efficiency is crucial given that the European taxpayers' money is at stake. Implementation of cohesion policy can be more efficient if the potential beneficiaries have a say in the process: this is why the partnership principle was introduced and has been reinforced in all the successive key regulations. Third, after cohesion policy became a fully-fledged Community policy, more *democracy and legitimacy* were needed in its implementation. Again, partnership complies with these requirements: this is why there is ever-increasing pressure from the partners involved for this principle to be respected and reinforced at the EU level as well as at the national level. Thus cohesion policy provided the ground for applying new modes of governance in a great variety across the member states throughout the last two decades – which also served as a learning period for the beneficiary countries.

The initial experience of cohesion policy governance in the eight new member states can well be theorized along the three dimensions of emergence, evolution and evaluation (Dezséri and Vida, 2008).

Starting with the framework conditions for the *emergence* of new governance modes, two aspects must be highlighted. First, the new member states have all inherited a centralized and unitary type public administration and governance system from the past. This phenomenon of *haunting centralization* could be regarded as a handicap when implementing a region-centred Community policy. Second, those countries which became a new sovereign state or regained statehood after 1989 had the advantage of building up national institutions from scratch. Those countries with a legal continuity faced more problems given the old vested interests of the actors in the public administration, accompanied by inter-ministerial rivalries. All this of course affected cohesion policy governance too, reflecting the fact that *the age of statehood matters* when comparing the performance of the new member states.

As regards the framework conditions for the *evolution* of new modes of governance, five aspects can be identified: the state remaining the gate-keeper; the continuous pressure for EU conformity; the phenomenon of defensive over-bureaucratization; instability coupled with complexity of the institutional set up; as well as an ongoing process of regionalization. First, there is the states' role as a *gatekeeper*, as the central/key position of the state remained practically unchallenged in the framework of cohesion policy in the new member states. Furthermore, due to *pressure for EU conformity*, all the new member states have been making continuous efforts to reach high-level legal, procedural and institutional conformity with the relevant EU rules of cohesion policy; in fact, to avoid any procedural mistakes when receiving EU money, some new member states initially introduced highly complex mechanisms into the tendering/application and funds management system, leading to unnecessary over-bureaucratization. In many countries this phenomenon of *defensive over-bureaucratization* was coupled with the *instability* (due to trial and error practice or due to political changes) and *complexity* (low transparency) of the institutional framework. Achieving 'literal' EU conformity seemed at this stage to enjoy higher priority than introducing new governance modes in the spirit of partnership, even if this is encouraged by the EU. Increasingly, however, EU conformity seems to pave the way for using new governance modes. Besides legal harmonization and institutional capacity-building, most new member states have also engaged in the process of regionalization and eventual devolution. The first step was the delimitation of the NUTS-2 regions, but even this has not come to a definitive end yet. The second step in some new member states is the potential devolution of power to the newly created regions – requiring even longer time, accompanied by political debates (*ongoing regionalization*). All this points to the fact that the new member states are going through a learning process where finding the proper modes for successful cohesion policy implementation can be perceived as a moving target.

Finally, the framework conditions for *evaluation* can be described with two main phenomena: *initial weaknesses in partnership* and *slow gradualism*. In the midst of institutional capacity-building coupled with unfolding public administration reform, and under the time pressure for the first national development plans to be delivered to the European Commission, most new member states did not really comply with the partnership principle. In such a context, recourse to any kind of new modes of governance has so far been rather sporadic (Grosse and Kolarska-Bobinska, 2008). The other side of the coin is that the potential partners seem in many cases to lack the necessary information, as well as the capacity, to play the role of a competent partner in the whole process of national/regional development. Despite the initial weaknesses, however, there are clear signs that in most new member states the introduction of the partnership principle – as an obvious element of new governance modes in our interpretation – could gradually be reinforced as a result of both supranational and sub-national pressures. This process is accompanied by an increasing willingness on the part of the public administrations to open up, and by an increasing awareness on the part of the partners concerned.

CONCLUSIONS

The European Union has recognized that the catching-up process of less-developed member states leads to appreciable convergence in their per capita gross domestic product (GDP) on a national level, but not to a reduction in regional inequalities within the countries concerned. As the main aim of EU regional policy is to narrow regional differences, its effectiveness has been questioned. Many research studies in the past have stated that regional inequalities can be reduced only if the regions themselves gain more competence to shape their own priorities and have at their disposal the necessary financial resources to realize their own development aims (Lakatos, 2007: 178).

This experience calls for a general decentralization process and the involvement of as many partners as possible, to enhance the efficiency of structural policy. This was not only recognized but also advocated by the Union, although the EU has no competence to instruct member states to restructure their public administration systems or organize their social dialogue in the way it deems optimal. Instead, in the past two decades the EU has managed to create legal, procedural and financial framework conditions that actually initiate a kind of decentralization and involvement of civil society and regional and local government in order to enable member countries to absorb EU assistance effectively under cohesion policy. There are no EU institutions or rules binding member states to decentralize and maximize participation, yet effective utilization of the funds calls for compliance with these principles (Lakatos, 2007: 178).

Thus, in the field of EU cohesion policy in general, new modes of governance appear as the 'indirect effect' of EU legislation on implementation of the Structural Funds (Lakatos, 2007: 157). This indirect effect means that the EU provides only the framework and general principles of implementation, leaving member states relative freedom of action to establish their own institutions and methods of management. It has been seen that programming documents submitted to the European Commission can be approved even if some of the basic principles are not complied with in full, for three basic reasons (Lakatos, 2007: 177–8): (1) because the principle of regionalism and partnership can be interpreted broadly and the absence of a strict legal definition makes it hard to enforce in practice; (2) because national decision-makers may refer to the principles mentioned in their programming documents, yet ignore them during implementation, without incurring EU sanctions; and (3) because these principles cannot be implemented in a uniform way, as each member state has its own state structure and traditions. This means in theory that it is enough to meet the minimum criteria required by EU legislation. Strict fulfilment of some of the principles is not obligatory.

This raises the question why most member states do not follow this practice. Why do they not derogate from the basic EU principles, even where this would technically be the easiest solution? One of the main indicators of successful membership is the absorption ratio of EU assistance. Member countries sooner or later realize that it is not enough to meet only the minimum criteria if structural and cohesion policy is to be implemented efficiently. It is vital for them to demonstrate such efficiency, because citizens tend to measure successful membership by the amount of money they receive from the Union, and the EU can cut back its financial commitments to certain member states if they prove inefficient in absorbing EU support. So the answer is very simple. The EU has given member states an interest in complying with the basic principles of its cohesion policy (Lakatos, 2007: 178).

This is where new modes of governance can be detected. Shaping the state structure and the method of social dialogue is an exclusive competence of member states, but the Union has persuaded most of them to launch some measure of decentralization. As the experience of the Central European new member states has shown, here the emergence of new modes of governance in cohesion policy can occur in three phases (Lakatos, 2007: 178–9):

1. Member states set up a system that meets EU minimum requirements.
2. Member states recognize that effective absorption of EU support can be achieved by complying with EU principles and start giving more competence to regional units, introducing a decentralization process that delegates more tasks and resources to regions, for shaping and implementing development policy.
3. Member states start to reorganize their state structure according to EU principles and engage in a decentralization process. Naturally, states that have stronger traditions of regionalism and civil society start with the second phase. And it should be remembered that decentralization and the emergence of civil society are not stimulated exclusively by the EU.

As the analysis of the experience of the new member states shows, these countries are slowly and gradually passing from phase 1, mainly characterized by pressure for EU conformity against the background of a heritage of centralization and the states as gatekeepers, to phase 2. The new member states entering phase 2 seem to be engaging in a more thoroughgoing regionalization and in a deepening and widening of dialogue with the stakeholder partners – especially during the elaboration and implementation of their second national development plans.

On the basis of empirical evidence and theory, the entry into phase 3 presupposes the existence of well organized regions, and social, civil and economic partners, which are able to join the process of planning, monitoring and evaluation of national development activities under EU assistance. The emergence of such a multi-level and multi-actor type governance in the new member states would to a great extent be the result of pressure for EU conformity promoting and favouring new governance modes.

NOTES

1. This chapter is based on team research carried out in the framework of NEWGOV Cluster One. The research focused on the evolution of cohesion policy at the European level as well as on its implementation in eight new member states, namely, Poland, Czech Republic, Slovakia, Hungary, Slovenia, and the Baltic states of Estonia, Latvia and Lithuania. The complete results have been published in a volume to which reference is recurrently made here (Dezséri, 2007).
2. See the initial NUTS-classification of the new member states: Regulation (EC) No 1888/2005 of the European Parliament and of the Council of 26 October 2005 (OJ L309/1) http://eur-lex.europa.eu/LexUriServ/LexUriServ.do?uri=OJ:L:2005:309:0001:0 008:EN:PDF.
3. In conformity with the European Commission's White Paper on European Governance, published in July 2001.
4. For example, in Poland the environmental infrastructure projects to be co-financed by the Cohesion Fund have first to be evaluated by the National Fund for Environmental Protection and Water Management, which is the largest and a long-standing body responsible for financing environmental protection and water management infrastructure.

REFERENCES

Ágh, Attila (2005), 'Europeanization: from accession deficit to partnership principle', in Attila Ágh (ed.), *Institutional Design and Regional Capacity-Building in the Post-Accession Period*, Budapest: Hungarian Centre for Democracy Studies, pp. 17–26.

Artner, Annamária (2007), 'EU cohesion policy and new governance: the example of the Baltic states', in Kálmán Dezséri (ed.), *New Modes of Governance and the EU Structural and Cohesion Policy in the New Member States*, Budapest: Akadémiai Kiadó, pp. 113–53.

Bache, Ian (1998), *The Politics of European Union Regional Policy: Multi-level Governance or Flexible Gatekeeping?*, Sheffield: Sheffield Academic Press.

Bassa, Zoltán (2007), 'New modes of governance and the EU structural and cohesion policy in the Czech Republic and Slovakia', in Kálmán Dezséri (ed.), *New Modes of Governance and the EU Structural and Cohesion Policy in the New Member States*, Budapest: Akadémiai Kiadó, pp. 61–85.

Council of the European Union (1994), 'Council Regulation 1164/1994 establishing a Cohesion Fund', Official Journal, L 130, 16 May.

Council of the European Union (1999), 'Council Regulation 1260/1999 laying down general provisions on the Structural Funds', Official Journal, L 161/1, 21 June.

Council of the European Union (2006), 'Council Regulation 1083/2006 laying down general provisions on the European Regional Development Fund, the European Social Fund and the Cohesion Fund and repealing Regulation (EC) No 1260/1999', Official Journal, L210/25, 11 July.

Dezséri, Kálmán (2007), 'The new member states and the structural and cohesion policy', in Kálmán Dezséri (ed.), *New Modes of Governance and the EU Structural and Cohesion Policy in the New Member States*, Budapest: Akadémiai Kiadó, pp. 21–59.

Dezséri, Kálmán and Krisztina Vida (2008), 'New modes of governance within cohesion policy at the European and new member states' level', available at: http://www.eu-newgov.org/database/PUBLIC/Policy_Briefs/NEWGOV_Policy_Brief_no16.pdf.

European Commission (2001), 'European Governance: A White Paper', COM(2001) 428 final, 25 July, Brussels.

Grosse, Tomasz Grzegorz and Lena Kolarska-Bobinska (2008), 'New modes of governance in new member states', available at: http://www.isp.org.pl/files/1741 8526190869443001207919391.pdf.

Hooghe, Liesbet (1998), 'EU cohesion policy and competing models of European capitalism', *Journal of Common Market Studies*, **36**(4), December.

Lakatos, Gábor (2007), 'New modes of governance and the EU structural and cohesion policy in Hungary', in Kálmán Dezséri (ed.), *New Modes of Governance and the EU Structural and Cohesion Policy in the New Member States*, Budapest: Akadémiai Kiadó, pp. 155–81.

Rhodes, Martin (2005), 'The scientific objectives of the NEWGOV project: a revised framework', paper presented at NEWGOV Consortium Conference, Florence, 30 May 2005.

Treib, Oliver, Holger Bähr and Gerda Falkner (2005), 'Modes of governance: a note towards conceptual clarification', available at: http://www.connex-network.org/eurogov/pdf/egp-newgov-N-05-02.pdf.

Vida, Krisztina (2007), 'New modes of governance in EU cohesion policy: emergence, evolution, evaluation', in Kálmán Dezséri (ed.), *New Modes of Governance and the EU Structural and Cohesion Policy in the New Member States*, Budapest: Akadémiai Kiadó, pp. 87–112.

Wisniewski, Anna (2007), 'New modes of governance and the EU structural and cohesion funds in Poland', in Kálmán Dezséri (ed.), *New Modes of Governance and the EU Structural and Cohesion Policy in the New Member States*, Budapest: Akadémiai Kiadó, pp. 183–212.

7. Modes of governance in the EU's Common Foreign and Security Policy

Udo Diedrichs

THE EMERGENCE AND EVOLUTION OF THE LEGAL BASE FOR EU FOREIGN POLICY GOVERNANCE

EPC as the Run-up to the CFSP: Shaping Modes of Governance

Studies on European Political Cooperation (EPC) and on the Common Foreign and Security Policy (CFSP) have been characterized by a growing interest in theoretical questions over recent years (Bretherton and Vogler, 1999; Smith, 2001; Tonra, 2001; Schmalz, 2004; Wagner and Hellmann, 2003). When academic analysis of EPC started in the 1970s and 1980s, the level of interest in theoretical and conceptual issues was fairly low (Allen and Wallace, 1978; de Schoutheete, 1980, 1986; Nuttall, 1992), but ever since, and particularly since the 1990s, the literature on European foreign policy has become a booming industry (White, 2001; Zielonka, 1998; Nuttall, 1992, 1997; Hill and Smith, 2000; Regelsberger et al., 1997). A growing number of scholarly contributions are describing, analysing and assessing the EU's foreign policy system, its interplay with the external environment and the conceptual framing of the Union's international role, focusing to a great extent – albeit not exclusively – on the CFSP. In this growing corpus of literature, it is still rather difficult to find a consensus about how a European foreign policy can be defined and what the shaping factors are.

The rationalist–constructivist debate has added new impetus to the theoretical analysis of European foreign policy. A growing number of scholars have rejected the traditional juxtaposition of intergovernmentalism and supranationalism, and introduced a conceptualization of the CFSP as a European form of governance in foreign policy: 'EFP [European Foreign Policy] as a system of foreign policymaking is a collective enterprise through which national actors conduct partly common, partly separate international actions' (Ginsberg, 2001: 32). Many authors regard the CFSP as a system that has gone well beyond classical intergovernmental patterns of decision-making and is heading towards a 'transgovernmental' mode of governance. It may be described as a way of decision-making marked by regular and familiar contacts among the governmental actors of the CFSP, based upon a coordination reflex and a high degree of trust which has been built up over the years (Schmalz, 2004). The CFSP is increasingly seen as being shaped by processes of 'Europeanization' (White, 2001: 20ff.; Ginsberg, 2001: 37ff.), 'Brusselization' (White, 2001: 21; Regelsberger and Wessels, 2003; Allen, 1997) or 'institutionalization' (Smith, 2004: 17ff.) of actors that have traditionally not belonged to the framework of the EU. Still, these developments have not produced a European supranational authority in security and defence matters, but were rather built on the institutional logics of cooperation which started with EPC (de Schoutheete, 1986; Pijpers et al., 1988; Nuttall, 1992).

In the CFSP there has so far been no broad academic debate about 'new' modes of governance or about 'innovative' elements in decision-making – except for the introduction of *flexibility*, which has been discussed as a way out of the impasse created by the potentially paralysing effect of unanimity (Diedrichs and Jopp, 2003b). In this context, modes of governance in EPC and the CFSP have been reviewed in order to find institutional and procedural patterns that would go beyond the classical notion of intergovernmentalism (Smith, 2004, 2001; Tonra, 2001). At the same time, a higher degree of differentiation has been reached in the study of EU foreign policy, emphasizing formal and informal rules, soft law, or socialization processes, which all convey the impression that the governance of EPC/the CFSP is far from being driven merely by national interests and dominated by consensus in decision-making.

Long before the CFSP came into being, the member states had developed modes of interaction within the framework of EPC (de Schoutheete, 1980), and even EPC did not start from scratch, but was able to make use of the reliable and well-defined rules and practices of diplomatic intercourse which were familiar to the member states' foreign policy services. The European Communities had already seen earlier attempts to create a federalized political organization, including a military dimension in the shape of the European Defence Community (EDC) which failed in 1954 (Duke, 2000); in contrast to those efforts, the Gaullist Fouchet plans of the early 1960s sketched an intergovernmental framework for interstate contacts covering foreign and security policy as well. Both models failed due to the lack of consensus among the member governments (de Schoutheete, 1980: 18ff.). These historical examples reveal the high degree of contention that marked the creation of a 'European foreign policy', torn between federalist and intergovernmentalist aspirations.

In a pragmatic sense, the objective of European Political Cooperation was defined by the creation of a community of 'information', of 'views' and of 'action', the latter being the most difficult and cumbersome exercise (de Schoutheete, 1986: 49). This formula, which is often repeated in the literature, serves as a rather rough description of the functional features of EPC, while leaving open a number of crucial questions.

The establishment of European Political Cooperation in the early 1970s was possible because any definition of the '*finalité*' of foreign policy cooperation was avoided; instead, the focus lay on pragmatic cooperation among the diplomats and ministers of the member states. A particular set of rules and procedures, formally and informally, but not treaty-based, were created for that purpose (Smith, 2001; Tonra, 2001). In terms of policy content, East–West relations, the Conference on Security and Co-operation (CSCE) process and the Middle East conflict were high on the agenda during the first years of EPC (de Schoutheete, 1980: 29). These topics called for a degree of expertise that was not available in the original Communities.

As regards the motivations for creating EPC, a series of factors and forces may be mentioned (Nuttall, 1992; de Schoutheete, 1986; Regelsberger, 2004):

- the functional need to expand the scope of EC policy-making, driven by the completion of the customs union and the establishment of a common external tariff;
- the growing sense of a common identity among the member states as a result of dense and intensive interaction within the European Communities;
- the increasing number of international contacts and formalized forms of dialogue that had been developed by the EC and the need to provide a political framework for and orientation to numerous external relationships;
- the demand for a European profile within the East–West conflict, which had moved to a period of détente and mutual arrangements between the superpowers;
- the interest of key member states in using the EC to develop a more global role between the superpowers and in this way to enhance national influence via Brussels.

Thus, the impetus for the emergence of EPC came from internal as well as external factors. It responded to a demand for more consistency among the member states without involving the framework of institutions created by the EC.

Laying the Ground for EPC: The EPC Reports and Beyond

EPC was able to grow and to develop its own institutional and procedural profile in the shadow of the European Communities and their well-structured institutional set-up (Pijpers et al., 1988). The need for more formally defined rules of the game became apparent and led to the adoption of the Luxembourg/Davignon Report in 1970, the Copenhagen Report in 1973 and the London Report in 1980. These three documents, far from including any legally binding commitment, provided the basis for what would later be inscribed into the Single European Act (SEA) in 1986, and later into the Treaty of Maastricht (1992).

The Luxembourg Report was a response to the task formulated by the 1969 Hague Summit and stressed the common ground in values and principles to which all EU member states were able to subscribe. Foreign policy coordination was regarded as a step towards the fulfilment of the political dimension of the integration process, which should complement and complete the economic aspects of unification (Luxembourg Report 1970). In contrast, the Copenhagen and London reports put the emphasis on the procedural and institutional expansion and differentiation of EPC, which had outgrown its original form and function during the 1970s (Copenhagen Report 1973; London Report 1980). Still, it remains to be stressed that not only was EPC conceived and built up as an exercise in efficient coordination; it also to the same extent appeared as a process of adoption and internalization of common norms and principles, and as an answer to the need for a European voice in the international system.

As Ben Tonra points out, the creation of EPC was designed as a starting point for creating a 'stronger political identity' (Tonra, 2001: 2), paving the way for the deepening of the integration process. In this regard, EPC had a double relevance for the Communities. It represented the emergence of cooperation in a specific policy area – diplomatic, foreign and security policies – and was also seen as an acronym capturing the political dimension of the integration process. These two spheres of relevance were not always neatly separated; they are still today a particular feature of the EU's CFSP and Common Security and Defence Policy (CSDP).

The belief in the *political dimension* of the integration process, which was expected to follow from steps taken in the economic field, was a recurrent topic in the EPC reports. Furthermore, an explicit aspiration on the part of the member states to organize a *new kind of international relations* became visible in the Copenhagen Report of 1973: 'What is involved in fact is a new procedure in international relations and an original European contribution to the technique of arriving at concerted action' (Copenhagen Report 1973). The peculiar European vision of both the substance and the procedure of foreign policy coordination constituted a long-term objective, representing the ambition to deliver more than the usual and familiar patterns of diplomatic contacts, without crossing the line towards a communitarized system of policy-making. The early success and the swift progress in establishing the first formal mechanism for foreign policy concertation encouraged the member governments to look for further ways of enhancing and enriching EPC. The London Report in 1980 ratified a number of institutional habits and innovations which had already been introduced into EPC on the basis of pragmatic agreements, such as the working groups which had been set up to prepare and implement decisions in EPC at civil servant level. The Copenhagen Report introduced the practice of taking stock of EPC: ever since, the achievements and failures have been reported and evaluated at regular intervals.

From EPC to the CFSP: Institutionalization of EU Foreign Policy

According to Simon Nuttall (1997: 20ff.), the development of EPC can be divided into four phases.

The first was from 1970 to the mid-1970s and was characterized by successful cooperation among the governments and a stabilization of the new procedures and institutions.[1] Not only had the ministers found their role, but the political committee, the working groups, and the European correspondents had also given proof of their efficiency and effectiveness.

From the mid-1970s until the early 1980s (the second period), EPC was in a period of stagnation caused by international crises (for example the Soviet occupation of Afghanistan) and by institutional stalemate because there was not sufficient political interest on the part of the key member states in boosting political integration in the EC (Nuttall, 1997: 21). The London Report, intended to inject fresh dynamics into EPC, rather confirmed the established practices, while the Genscher–Colombo initiative of 1981 was watered down into the Solemn Declaration of Stuttgart (1983).

From 1982, EPC entered a period of renewed activity, driven by a fresh impulse from the international system. The introduction of martial law in Poland, the occupation of the Falklands by Argentina, and the violent conflict in Central America provided opportunities for the member states to sharpen their international profile (Nuttall, 1997: 21ff.). At the same time, the combined use of EPC and Community instruments became an attractive operational option. In the case of Argentina, political solidarity of the member states with the United Kingdom was backed by a trade embargo against the South American country, bringing EC instruments into play. In the case of Central America, where in 1984 the San José Dialogue was inaugurated, political dialogue with international partners was supported by a scheme of substantial development cooperation measures. The conclusion of the Single European Act, which for the first time endowed EPC with official legal status (although outside the Community framework), represented the institutional highlight of EPC's development in that period. In substance, the SEA confirmed most of the institutional and procedural practice developed in the past 15 years; it literally took over numerous elements from the reports, and stuck to the basic political and institutional principles of EPC, which remained fundamentally intergovernmental (Nuttall, 1997: 21–2).

The fourth and final phase of EPC came between 1989 and the Treaty of Maastricht, when the historic upheavals caused serious problems to which EPC was unable to respond effectively. German unification was dealt with outside this framework, and major international crises such as the first Gulf War, the breaking up of the former Yugoslavia (Edwards, 1997) or the disintegration of the Soviet Union were widely regarded as a failure for European foreign policy.

Although the phase model as described here looks rather conventional, it contains an important insight into the factors shaping EPC: the dynamics triggered by the interrelation between EPC and the Community system, the role of the external environment and the impact of crises on EU foreign policy.

Michael E. Smith identifies a trend towards 'legalization', which he defines as a process in which rules or standards of behaviour in a social setting are clarified, codified and invested with the status of law (Smith, 2001: 81), representing a type of institutionalization, which means the development of expectations of social behaviour (Smith, 2001: 82). While EPC was endowed with a treaty base only with the conclusion of the Single European Act (Ifestos, 1987), the first years of operation reflected the emergence of a kind of customary law: 'EPC increasingly functioned as a body of soft law before acquiring full legal status with the SEA. Its officials conducted their relations according to improvised habits which became an increasingly binding set of rules; thus over time, soft law matured into hard law' (Smith, 2001: 83). Smith assumes that the actors in EPC behaved according to certain rules and norms which they perceived as legally valid, proving 'that European legal integration can also proceed through intergovernmental (or, more appropriately, transgovernmental) interactions, and not just those taking place at the summit level during intergovernmental conferences or treaty negotiations' (Smith, 2001: 84).

The idea of legalization in the sense of progress towards the legally binding nature of the rules of social and political behaviour provides an important supplement to the conceptualization of EPC/the CFSP as an intergovernmental process that is neatly separated from the supranational structures of the Communities. Although Smith's use of the term could be criticized for suggesting a too rigid approach which in this ideal-type form never existed, it sheds light on the peculiar features of foreign policy coordination which has always been more than diplomatic ad-hocery among national governments, deciding voluntarily whether or not they wish to respect the rules enshrined in their common effort to define a European voice in international politics.

Two levels of interaction can be distinguished: (a) the summit-level legalization which according to Smith stalled from the mid-1970s until the 1980s; and (b) the process by which informal customs emerged, which later matured into written rules (Smith, 2001: 87): 'As EC governments could not agree at this time to establish and codify their own procedural rules for EPC, these eventually developed as working habits in behind-the-scenes discussions among regular EPC participants' (Smith, 2001: 87). The most important of these habits have been confidentiality, consensus and consultation. In addition to these norms, the value of reputation was widely appreciated among the partners, leading to solutions beyond the lowest common denominator level: 'These fundamental norms or customs (among others), practised and reinforced in a dense transgovernmental network of experts, gradually gave substance to the EPC process' (Smith, 2001: 87).

The dynamics of EPC thus resulted less from the formal text adopted than from the need to implement and operationalize decisions, leading to the densification of 'transgovernmental' networks.

In parallel, a growing rapprochement between EPC and the Community way of doing things became evident in a number of institutional areas. The Copenhagen Report provided for the Commission to be contacted on EPC matters that affected the European Communities (Tonra, 2001: 2). The London Report went a step further by stating that the Commission would in general be fully integrated in the conduct of EPC, making it officially a player in the process, which it had de facto already become.

The Creation of the CFSP: A New Stage in the Development of EU Governance

When the CFSP came into existence with the entry into force of the Treaty of Maastricht, the modes of decision-making and interaction in this policy domain were already well defined and working efficiently (Regelsberger,

2003). Still, a 'new threshold' (Tonra, 2001: 3) in EU foreign policy cooperation was reached. Although there was no radical change with regard to the modes of governance used, the legal base had been fundamentally altered. The establishment of a strengthened institutional and procedural framework for what had been foreign policy cooperation among the member states of the European Communities meant above all that new potentials and perspectives could be activated (although it had a rather modest impact on the daily routines and the deep-rooted practices in Europe's diplomatic community).

In the negotiations leading up to the Treaty of Maastricht, the experience of 'Black Monday', when the Dutch presidency dramatically failed to replace the three-pillar approach with a Community-based model, highlighted the lack of federal aspirations among the member governments, and also indicated that the three-pillar structure which had initially been so heavily criticized would represent a feasible formula (Laursen and Vanhoonacker, 1992; Diedrichs, 1996).

The following features of the CFSP in comparison to EPC are of crucial importance:

- the integration of foreign policy cooperation into the framework of the treaties as the second pillar of the EU, including the single institutional framework, with the European Council and the Council as the key bodies;
- a certain 'scope enlargement' of the CFSP, in particular by covering security policy and by introducing closer relations with the Western European Union (WEU) as an integral part of the process of European integration;
- the expansion and differentiation of legal instruments, which should include joint actions and common positions. These were de facto already in existence under EPC, but were given a more systematic appreciation;
- a differentiation of procedures in the sense of defining a possibility for majority voting, while consensus remained the rule.

The CFSP from Maastricht to Lisbon: Confirming the Long-term Trends

Since the entry into force of the Maastricht Treaty, the provisions on the CFSP have been adapted and revised by various treaty reforms (Regelsberger and Jopp, 1998; Schmalz, 1998; Regelsberger, 2001; Wessels, 2004). Additional impetus also came from outside the treaties, when the European Security and Defence Policy was introduced in the late 1990s (Andréani et al., 2001). The trends which had become visible in the decades before were reinforced and strengthened by these developments.

The legalization and institutionalization reached a new stage with the creation of the office of High Representative for the CFSP in the Amsterdam Treaty of 1997 (Regelsberger and Jopp, 1998). The High Representative may be seen as one of the most successful institutional innovations of the EU as a whole along its entire history. In the Lisbon Treaty of 2010 the post of the High Representative has been reshaped in order to cover two basic functions hitherto separated: the role of a Commission member and of a Council representative (Art. 27 TEU Lisbon version). This 'double hat' coupled with enhanced competencies might lead into an institutional merger and thus render EU external action more coherent and efficient, but it could also cause an over-stretch. Interinstitutional friction with the new President of the European Council might further weaken the High Representative for Foreign Affairs and Security Policy.

The establishment of a European External Action Service (Art. 27 (3) TEU Lisbon version) represents an ambitious project which would overcome the institutional separation of Council and Commission services in order to tackle foreign policy issues from a comprehensive viewpoint.

Also the scope enlargement was a crucial trend when in 1998 the door was opened to include security and defence issues on the agenda. The ESDP represents perhaps the most important policy expansion of the EU after 1989 (Howorth, 2007). The Petersberg tasks had already been introduced into the treaty at Amsterdam. With the European Council meetings of Cologne and Helsinki in 1999, the process of institutionalizing ESDP was inaugurated, which found a final step in the Lisbon Treaty in 2010 with a number of explicit and detailed provisions on what is now called the Common Security and Defence Policy (CSDP). The EU's capability to undertake civilian and military missions in crisis management has been tested in 24 operations undertaken since 2003, of which 14 were still in place in February 2010. Along with the increasing legal formalization and policy expansion went a changing nature of instruments. CFSP and ESDP/CSDP have become much more operational than had been the case with EPC.

But also the differentiation of procedures was a major trend. With the introduction of constructive abstention in the Amsterdam Treaty, the classical consensus machinery was not turned upside down, but became more flexible (Diedrichs and Jopp, 2003b). Member states were allowed to disagree without necessarily halting the decision-making process. In a more pronounced manner, different forms of flexibility or enhanced cooperation also found their way into CFSP since Amsterdam, with the exeption of military and defence matters (Schmalz, 1998). The Treaty of

Lisbon has again enriched the menu by introducing permanent structured cooperation (Art. 46 TEU Lisbon version), allowing enhanced cooperation in security and defence and by encouraging group-building when it comes to implementing crisis management operations (Art. 42 (5) TEU Lisbon version).

The major factors that accounted for the emergence and evolution of the CFSP having been described, it is now necessary to assess the importance of decision-making procedures and the patterns of interaction. The CFSP provides an excellent example of the distinction between decision-making procedures and mode of governance, the latter being more comprehensive than the former. The legal provisions of the treaty were rather sparse. Consensus was the rule; that is, every member government was expected to agree to a decision before it could be taken. On the other hand, the style of interaction was greatly influenced by the rules of diplomatic intercourse and marked by a considerable degree of collegiality, informal practice and confidentiality.

THE EXECUTION OF THE CFSP: MODES OF GOVERNANCE IN ACTION

The Legal Output in the CFSP

After the coming into force of the Treaty of Maastricht, the institutional reform debate on the CFSP did not come to an end. There was continuing pressure for further reform, mainly under the label of efficiency, effectiveness and legitimacy (Regelsberger, 2004: 13ff.). The prospect of enlargement was increasingly regarded as a catalyst for major procedural and institutional modifications. In the end, the result of the treaty reforms was a modification of the set-up of the CFSP without changing its basic features. The creation of a High Representative for the CFSP and the introduction of constructive abstention for decision-making, and of common strategies as a new instrument in the Treaty of Amsterdam (1997), in the end led to a perfection of a 'rationalized intergovernmentalism' (Wessels, 1997a), which sought to improve the working of the mechanism of the CFSP.

In parallel, the implementation of the Treaty on European Union revealed an intensive use of CFSP provisions by the EU. In particular, joint actions and common positions belong to the usual repertoire of the CFSP, while, since 2001, agreements with third countries have also become increasingly important (see Figure 7.1). These reflect the growing activities of the EU in the field of crisis management, where the Union invites third countries to participate in military and civilian operations.

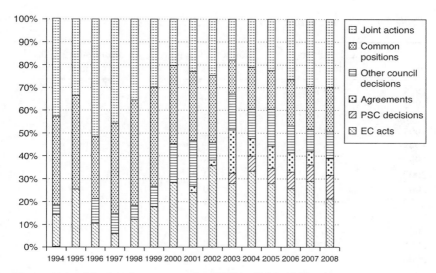

Figure 7.1   The legal output in the CFSP, 1994–2008

Most of the agreements concluded so far have been devoted to fixing the terms of participation of third countries in crisis management operations, while others have been concluded with the governments of those states where an operation took place.

The Political and Security Committee (PSC) has become a decision-making body with growing activism over the last years (see Figure 7.1). PSC decisions concern in particular the setting up of a committee of contributors of EU member states and third countries for carrying out a crisis management operation, and the appointment of force commanders or heads of missions for such operations.

Legal acts in the CFSP are also increasingly linked to legislation in the sphere of the European Community. Since the end of the 1990s a real surge in the amount of CFSP-related EC legislation has been seen. In this respect, it is not only the Council that has played an active role; the Commission has also been involved to an increasing degree.

The first remarkable push in CFSP-related EC legislation came after 1998 with the crisis in Kosovo, which triggered a number of CFSP acts that subsequently required EC action in the shape of restrictive measures directed against the regime in Belgrade. In later years such measures were adopted against transnational organizations and natural persons as well, most prominently in the case of Usama bin Laden, the Al-Qaida network and the Taliban (Council of the European Union, 2002). Table 7.1 highlights these developments.

Table 7.1   EC legislation related to the CFSP, 1994–2008

	EC legal acts total	Council EC legal acts	Commission EC legal acts
1994	3	3	
1995	3	3	
1996	3	3	
1997	2	2	
1998	6	6	
1999	14	8	6
2000	21	14	7
2001	19	10	9
2002	29	12	17
2003	51	18	33
2004	52	16	36
2005	52	10	42
2006	37	10	27
2007	45	15	30
2008	38	12	26
Total	375	142	233

Source: EURLEX data 1994–2008.

The legal basis for most of the regulations on restrictive measures has so far been provided by Articles 60 TEC, 301 TEC and 308 TEC (Nice version). Article 60 TEC stipulated that '[i]f, in the cases envisaged in Article 301 TEC, action by the Community is deemed necessary, the Council may, in accordance with the procedure provided for in Article 301, take the necessary urgent measures on the movement of capital and on payments as regards the third countries concerned'.

Article 301 TEC provided the link to the CFSP by stating that

> (w)here it is provided, in a common position or in a joint action adopted according to the provisions of the Treaty on European Union relating to the common foreign and security policy, for an action by the Community to interrupt or to reduce, in part or completely, economic relations with one or more third countries, the Council shall take the necessary urgent measures. The Council shall act by a qualified majority on a proposal from the Commission.

Finally, the general clause of Article 308 TEC was also used, enabling the Council to take decisions even without an explicit authorization in the EC Treaty:

If action by the Community should prove necessary to attain, in the course of the operation of the common market, one of the objectives of the Community and this Treaty has not provided the necessary powers, the Council shall, acting unanimously on a proposal from the Commission and after consulting the European Parliament, take the appropriate measures.

The most prominent case of an EC regulation providing for restrictive measures directed against legal or natural persons has been the regulation against Usama bin Laden, Al-Qaida and the Taliban; amendments concerned the list annexed to the regulation naming the persons and entities to be subjected to restrictive measures. Regulation EC 881/2002 (Art. 7) empowers the Commission to adjust the list on the basis of decisions by the UN Security Council or the UN Sanctions Committee. In a similar manner, restrictive measures against third countries have been updated and adjusted in recent years, producing a dynamic set of regulations.

There is thus a link between the quantitative development of common positions, and their amendments or repeal, on the one hand, and subsequent Community legislation on the other. The adoption of common positions explains the activities in EC legislation related to these positions.

Financing the CFSP: Mixed Sources of Financing

Until the entry into force of the Lisbon Treaty, the 'hardest' competences of the EC in the CFSP were to be found in the budgetary field. The EC budget under subsection B 8 contained the operational expenditure for the CFSP, while the associated administrative expenditure was covered within the Council's budget line and not subject to interference by the European Parliament (EP), according to a gentleman's agreement between the institutions.

In addition to the treaty, the Interinstitutional Agreement of 17 May 2006 between the EP, the Council and the Commission contains particular provisions on financing the CFSP (European Parliament et al., 2006). It states that the three institutions will engage in a conciliation procedure through a 'trilogue' in which they will try to arrive at a common understanding on CFSP spending.

Agreement must be reached on the overall amount as well as on the distribution between the different articles of the CFSP budgetary chapter. The Interinstitutional Agreement also confirms that the Commission is authorized to transfer appropriations on its own initiative between different articles within one chapter, so that the necessary flexibility in implementing the budget shall be assured (Ibid.: para. 42). Two further important points deserve attention. Should the amount of the CFSP budget prove to be insufficient during the financial year, the EP and the Council are called upon to search for a solution on the grounds of a Commission proposal. This means that without the EP's approval no further financial appropriations will be allowed. Second, the Council has to send the EP a financial statement for any decision it takes involving expenditure, including a specific cost estimate. Once a year the Council presents its report on the main aspects and basic choices of the CFSP, including the financial implications for the EC budget. The Commission is committed to informing the Council and the EP in a quarterly report about the implementation of CFSP actions and about the financial forecast for the remainder of the year (Ibid.: para. 43).

In the past, disputes between the Council and the Parliament were caused by different interpretations and preferences where financing the international actions of the Union was concerned. In 2002, a conflict emerged over the amount of the operational CFSP budget, which the Council wished to increase, while the EP threatened to reduce the budget line unless the Council adopted a commitment to inform the Parliament in timely fashion before taking action. The sources of financing for civilian crisis management were also extensively discussed; while the EP intended to finance measures for the European Union Police Mission (EUPM) in Bosnia by resorting to the Community Assistance for Reconstruction, Development and Stabilization (CARDS) programme, the Council insisted on using the CFSP chapter.[2]

As a result, the provisions of the 1999 Interinstitutional Agreement were specified by a joint declaration of the Parliament, the Council and the Commission from 25 November 2002, which strengthened the EP in particular by introducing concrete deadlines and procedures for the budgetary coordination process. The Council report on the main aspects and basic choices of the CFSP should arrive at the Parliament by 15 June of the year in question. As to CFSP decisions entailing financial expenditure, the Council committed itself to inform the EP no later than five working days after taking a decision. Furthermore, an 'early warning' by the Council to the EP was provided for in the context of a regular 'political dialogue' whenever a joint action might have important financial implications.

The 2006 Interinstitutional Agreement further tightened the coordination mechanism between the Council, the Commission and the Parliament. The Council was called upon to consult the EP each year, by 15 June, on the basis of a forward-looking document including the main aspects and basic choices of the CFSP and the implications for the budget of the EU (European Parliament et al., 2006). At least five times a year the Council commits itself to consultations with the EP, in the context of the regular political dialogue, and on a level specified in the Interinstitutional Agreement, including the bureaux of the EP committees concerned, the Council at ambassador level (chairman of the Political and Security Committee) and members of the Commission (European Parliament et al., 2006).

In practice, these arrangements have not worked in a satisfactory manner from the EP's point of view. The EP complained in the past that the Council report did not contain an adequate focus on the financial implications of the CFSP, and insisted that these should be laid down in a separate document. Also, the information provided by the Council was regarded as incomplete and far from timely. The EP tried to use its financial competences to create a political dialogue, while the Council has traditionally tried to keep CFSP business at a technical level, avoiding any substantial political consultation. The new Interinstitutional Agreement will thus have to prove its viability for all the institutional players.

The issue of financing is not only a playground for interinstitutional quarrels, but also reveals in reality the highly complex nature of the CFSP in practice. De facto, the CFSP and the ESDP/CSDP have been financed by different sources in the past: by Community programmes in support of CFSP actions, or by the CFSP chapter of the EC budget for operational expenditure, or by the member states, either through the ATHENA mechanism (Council of the European Union 2004) for common costs (mostly incremental costs for operations-, force- and component headquarters, essential infrastructure and equipment) or by national spending on the basis of the principle that costs lie where they fall (see Table 7.2). ATHENA is managed by a Special Committee, enjoys certain legal privileges, and includes an early financing mechanism.

These different modes of financing entail divergent forms of institutional participation and influence. Going from left to right of Table 7.2, the powers of the EP decrease, while member states' autonomy increases. In particular, crisis management operations reveal a multiple and complex institutional and financial environment that makes it rather difficult to separate the single items of the overall expenditure on the ground.

As an example, the EU military operation EUFOR RD Congo (in the DRC) was embedded into the broader objectives and principles of the EU-ACP (Africa, the Caribbean and the Pacific) cooperation, which had been redefined by the Cotonou Agreement in 2000 and had been prominently focused on democracy-building and institutional stability. The Commission strategy paper on the DRC from 2003 stressed the promotion of democracy and the building up of reliable security forces as a key objective of EC support to the country. In particular, the organization of elections was regarded as a key step towards achieving these goals (Commission Européenne, 2003, 2005). The Commission also sent an electoral observer mission to the DRC.

Table 7.2   Financial sources of EU external action

	Financial sources of EU action (before entry into force of Lisbon Treaty)			
	EC budget Community programmes	EC budget CFSP chapter	ATHENA (based upon member states' contributions)	Member states' contributions
Legal base	Budgetary procedure and inter-institutional agreement EC and EU Treaty	Budgetary procedure; EU Treaty with special provisions on CFSP in inter-institutional agreement	Council decision 2004/197/ CFSP	EU Treaty
Cases of application	External aid and support programmes (e.g. CARDS, ENPI)	Joint actions without military or defence implications	Common costs for crisis management missions having military or defence implications	Costs lie where they fall (member states pay the bill)

EUFOR RD Congo was financed both from the EC budget, to the amount of 9.9 million euros, while the member states contributed 6 million euros. This mixed financing does not open up immediate sources of influence for the EC but reveals the de facto hybrid nature of crisis management when it comes to the implementation of an operation. On the spot, EC financial support is administered by EuropeAid and controlled by the Commission delegation in Kinshasa.

The different forms and mixtures of financing the CFSP, and in particular ESDP operations, could lead to a hidden and incremental increase in the number and size of jointly financed actions, which could help the member states to save money, improve their planning security and share the risk with other participants. The creation of ATHENA is a clear sign that even in the strictly intergovernmental sphere of the CFSP/ESDP/ CSDP there is a growing demand for pooling of resources.

Ultra-soft Coordination in the ESDP/CSDP: Shaming without Naming?

Since the summits of Cologne and Helsinki in 1999, the EU has defined a set of military and later also civilian goals that should be achieved in order to become fully operational in conducting crisis management operations (Lindley-French, 2002). The Helsinki Force Catalogue contained a list of resources deemed necessary in terms of staff, equipment and weapon systems which would be used to implement the Petersberg tasks. As the guiding principle of the ESDP/CSDP was voluntary national contributions to crisis management, in particular regarding the deployment of troops, it was clear that neither a supranational authority nor procedural patterns borrowed from the EC would be applied. The result was a tension between intergovernmentalism in institutional terms and the need for more effectiveness in capability terms. The capabilities commitment conferences which started in November 2000 in Helsinki aimed to list the range of resources and staff which would be available for operations, while leaving the final decision on delivery to the member states. At the same time it became clear that the pledges made by national governments would fall far short of matching the needs identified.

The Helsinki Force Catalogue revealed a number of strategic gaps and shortcomings which would have to be overcome if the ESDP/CSDP were not to suffer an early and sudden loss of credibility. As the door towards more binding supranational mechanisms in decision-making was not open, a particular process of capability improvement was developed that was intended to avoid naming certain countries and their failings, but was designed to increase the pressure on governments so as to make them act. The first element of this process has been the existence of regular reports on the ESDP by the presidency since 1999, describing the state of the art, the gaps and the prospects. After December 2001, the European Council inaugurated the European Capabilities Action Plan (ECAP), which led to the creation of panels composed of national experts who were to discuss the existing shortcomings and gaps and try to find solutions for sensitive capability deficits. ECAP made it possible to mobilize technocratic expertise from the ministries of defence and also promoted a discourse on the capabilities of the ESDP which led to a kind of semi-public pressure upon the member states to enhance their national contributions.

The coordination of these panels was entrusted to a Headline Goal Task Force, which was supported by the EU Military Staff (Schmitt, 2005: 1ff.). As a next step, in 2003 a new stage in the definition of the headline goals was taken, leading to the adoption in June 2004 of the Headline Goal 2010; these goals focused more on qualitative improvements for addressing the more demanding Petersberg tasks, and on multinational projects between the member states in order to mobilize synergies.[3]

In March 2003 the Capability Development Mechanism (CDM) started to operate, including mid-year progress reports as well as the publication of the Capabilities Improvement Chart. Thus, due to the functional need to improve the military capabilities of the member states, a process of reporting emerged, reflected in national media and expert publications, and hinting at the capabilities–expectations gap in European security and defence policy. There is no explicit naming of specific national shortcomings, so that no 'naming and shaming' is taking place, which would be unacceptable for member states governments. On the other hand, the information and data on defence spending that are regularly published allow for comparisons and make it possible to identify compliers and non-compliers. This is less a question of objective criteria which can be applied, but much more one of political will. So far the mechanism has proved not to be very effective, mostly because of its cautious approach and the political resistance against binding obligations. On the other hand, there seems to be a mechanism of good practice and efforts to lead the flock which found its expression in the initially French–British initiative of February 2004 on battle groups and which was hastily taken up by Germany before including almost all the EU countries.

Regime-building in the ESDP/CSDP: Creating a Market without a Supranational Authority

The creation of the European Defence Agency (EDA) has so far had a double effect: it has introduced a new institutional player in the CFSP/ESDP/CSDP arena, and it has led to the creation of a specific regime under the authority of the agency: an emerging European procurement and defence equipment market. It is basically an experiment in creating market structures by opening national procurement systems while rejecting the classical Monnet method; instead, a strictly intergovernmental set of rules and principles was established. The EDA has been put in charge of four main tasks:

- defence capabilities development;
- armaments cooperation;
- the defence technological and industrial base;
- the defence equipment market, research and technology.

It is a crucial actor in the process of capability improvement, and responsible for the coordination of ECAP, and it is also the supervising authority for the defence equipment market (Keohane, 2004).

Initially a child of the Convention, the EDA was put on the agenda of the European Council in July 2003; its establishment was approved before the draft Constitutional Treaty entered the negotiations at the Intergovernmental Conference (IGC) in 2003/2004. The European Council of Thessaloniki defined the objective of creating an intergovernmental agency, and it was set up on 12 July 2004 after a preparatory phase had been concluded. The High Representative was installed as the head of the EDA, while a chief executive was to manage its daily work, and the Council would preserve a guiding and supervising function. The steering board of the EDA is composed of the defence ministers or their representatives who thus for the first time gained a formal arena in the EU institutional set-up (which could lead to tensions with the foreign ministers in the Council).

The EDA, initially conceived as a network, has increasingly become a focus for defence cooperation among the member states. The Western Europe Armaments Group soon disappeared, while the EDA became a crucial player in the creation of an EU defence market. On 1 July 2006 the regime for a European defence equipment market came into force, which tried to open up national procurement systems and currently includes 22 out of the 25 member states. The basis of the market is the *Code of Conduct on Defence Procurement*,[4] which constitutes a voluntary commitment by the participating states on the opening up of their defence markets. It is explicitly non-binding, intergovernmental and aimed at encouraging competition based upon reciprocity between the participating states. Member states will offer – with some exceptions – fair and equal opportunities to suppliers in other participating countries, thus accepting tenders to be published by the EDA on the Electronic Board Bulletin (EBB). This would constitute a first cautious step in the direction of overcoming the impediments of Article 296 TEC which has prevented the application of the single market rules in the defence sector. The crucial question will be whether market structures can develop under such a regime without binding rules and a strong supranational authority supervising the application of the rules established, and whether the EDA could grow into a regulatory agency that would be able to compensate for the lack of such an authority. The gains in efficiency could in the end represent an incentive for governments to open up their national procurement systems further or to choose multinational projects where their home companies are represented so that a 'juste retour' is guaranteed.

THE EVOLUTION OF MODES OF GOVERNANCE IN THE CFSP

The assessment of the evolution of governing modes in EPC/the CFSP depends to a great extent upon the theoretical standpoint. A number of assumptions may be made in this regard.

From an intergovernmentalist point of view, the basic trend since the creation of the EPC has never been reversed or fundamentally changed. Both EPC and the CFSP are intergovernmental spheres of action, and will probably remain so in the foreseeable future (Pijpers, 1990). From this perspective, the processes of legalization, institutionalization or Brusselization described above would not even be denied or called into question; they would simply not be taken as an indicator for a fundamental change. In this sense, nothing really new under the sun would be observed. Even the notion of transgovernmentalism may not be rejected, as it refers primarily to the administrative and not to the political level of interaction.

Major international crises regularly prove that the processes of institutionalization are comparatively weak and too fragile to shape EU foreign policy modes (Hill, 2003, 2004).

From a constructivist point of view, which puts the emphasis on the socialization dynamics within a network of contacts in EPC/the CFSP, it is also hard to find clear-cut landmarks. With the creation of EPC, a process of increasing socialization was triggered off which has fundamentally influenced national foreign policy (Schmalz, 2004) and contributed to the emergence of a foreign policy mode of governance that is marked by intensive contacts and interrelations among diplomats (Tonra, 2001; Schmalz, 2004). This trend may have intensified, although there is still a tension between different systems of identification, but in the end there is little leeway for dramatic reversals. Thus what a constructivist approach would probably sustain is that the CFSP represents the emergence of a new mode of interstate relations, different from classical diplomacy, and that this trend has been going on since the early 1970s.

It is in the field of institutionalist approaches that changes and turning points can be identified with greater precision. Wessels (2004) describes a process of 'ratchet fusion' that started in EPC, with intergovernmental cooperation outside the treaty framework, but then reached a new plateau with the formal inclusion of EPC/the CFSP in the single institutional framework of the Treaty on European Union (see Figure 7.2). Ever since, more binding forms of cooperation have been developed: 'In each IGC . . . the "Masters of the Treaty" have regularly revised the legal constitution upwards on a ladder with ever more refined modes of intergovernmental governance from soft to harder variations' (Wessels, 2004: 47).

The remarkable changes in the development of EU foreign policy governance represent a process of reaching new 'plateaux' in the sense of 'ratchet fusion', marked by a new quality of decision-making.

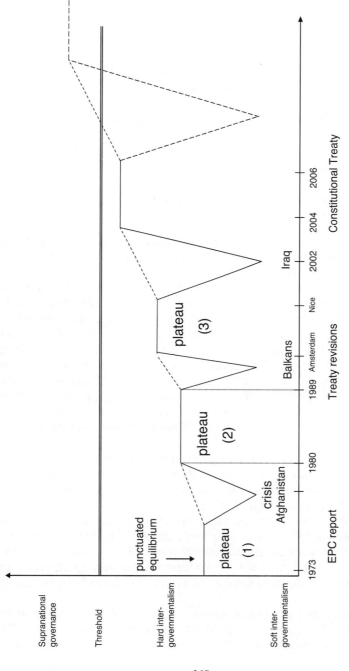

Source: Wessels (2004: 47).

Figure 7.2 Ratchet fusion and the CFSP

Stage						
V						Governance
IV				Organizations		
III				Norms		
II			Information-sharing			
I	Intergovernmental Forum					
	1970		1973	1981	1986–1991	1993–present

Source: Smith (2004: 39).

Figure 7.3   Stages in EU foreign policy institutionalization

From a different institutionalist perspective, Michael E. Smith has developed a model which divides the evolution of EPC/the CFSP into five stages (see Figure 7.3).

These scholarly contributions identify a number of criteria which could lead in the direction of changing modes of governance in EPC/ the CFSP. The emergence of governing modes in the CFSP represents a case of novelty and a difference between the EU and other international organizations. Then, the evolution from a loose intergovernmental form of cooperation to more consistent and more strictly binding forms of decision-making within the legal framework of the EU represents a next important step. In this direction, the creation of a supranational foreign policy – including majority decisions, sanctions for non-compliance, or the structures of a European army – could represent a substantial next step forward.

In sum, the emergence of new governing modes in the CFSP implied the creation of a new framework for diplomatic interaction and foreign policy formulation, of which the innovative feature was the result not so much of the decision-making procedures at ministerial level but rather of the dense contacts, relations and interactions on different levels of foreign policy activity. Second, although the basic structure of EPC/the CFSP was and remains intergovernmental, it reveals a number of points of contact with the EC framework. While formally they are neatly separated, the two spheres of interaction have been politically interrelated.

The debates on the EU Constitution have revealed the potential for further institutional and procedural reform existent in the CFSP/CSDP, which is taken up by the Lisbon Treaty. Thus important changes (Wessels,

2004; Diedrichs and Jopp, 2005; Jopp and Regelsberger, 2003) will take effect if and when the Lisbon Treaty comes into force:

- further legal densification of the CFSP, and closer relations between the EP, the Commission and the Council;
- greater consistency between EC and the CFSP by opening the possibility of resort to the EC in the case of economic sanctions as a result of foreign policy decisions;
- increased institutional coherence and effectiveness through the creation of a High Representative for Foreign Affairs and Security Policy of the EU, and a common external service;
- more potential for flexibility in the CFSP and the CSDP, for example, by structured cooperation;
- a differentiation of procedures and mechanisms for decision-making.

Still, the key question is whether there is sufficient reason to talk about new modes of governance in these areas. Basically, intergovernmentalism/transgovernmentalism remains intact, but most of the dynamics for the future may well come from a field which few observers might have expected some time ago: the ESDP. The ESDP could result in a dynamic engine for the CFSP, generating more innovative solutions in terms of connections between the EC and the CFSP, or with regard to flexible modes of decision-making and participation. It remains to be seen whether the ESDP even without the Constitutional Treaty will continue to be a most attractive field of research in EU foreign policy.

CONCEPTUALIZING CHANGE: HYBRIDIZATION, MIXTURE AND INNOVATION?

The trends and developments observed within the CFSP and ESDP since the early 1990s lead to a number of conclusions that might enable us to answer the question of new versus old modes of governance in this particular policy area.

- First of all, it seems plausible to define modes of governance in a policy-specific and a time-dynamic perspective. The CFSP has its own rules and traditions in decision-making, and has developed forms and modes of governance which are typical for its path of institutional and procedural evolution; this path is clearly distinct from the developments observed in the classical Community areas of legislation.

- The traditional conceptualization of the CFSP as an intergovernmental policy area is not out of date or out of touch; however, except for times when there is an exceptional and dramatic crisis, the daily political and institutional reality of the CFSP is open to innovation 'beyond intergovernmentalism'.
- A major source of innovation and dynamics lies in the creation of the ESDP, which has not, as many observers expected, strengthened the intergovernmental nature of the CFSP, but has led to new 'windows of opportunity' by opening up new fields of activity. Crisis management operations rely on mixed sources of financing, even when they are primarily military in nature; the creation of a defence equipment market is an unprecedented experiment in the EU; extremely soft forms of coordination might even be identified in the ESDP/CSDP when it comes to the capability improvement mechanism.
- The legal spheres of action and application have so far not been combined, but they have moved closer together; the creation of the first double-hatted special representative might be regarded as a sign of growing coherence even before the stage is reached of creating a European external service *avant la lettre*.
- The differentiation of instruments applied in the sphere of the CFSP has increased dramatically since the early 1990s. Today, more diversity is visible in the legal acts adopted under the CFSP. The increase in the numbers of agreements with third countries on crisis management operations, and the growing correlation of common positions and EC regulations providing for economic sanctions, seem to be particularly interesting.
- The result is a CFSP which has not developed in a supranational direction as such, but uses the range of possibilities included in the treaties and operates in a pragmatic, flexible and sometimes mixed way, not by confusing legal spheres of application, but by combining instruments from these spheres and by creating opportunities for joint or common resources.

NOTES

1. See also Barbé (2000: 109ff.) with a slightly different time frame.
2. Agence Europe, 23 November 2002.
3. Council of the European Union, Headline Goal 2010, approved by General Affairs and External relations Council on 17 May 2004 endorsed by the European Council of 17 and 18 June 2004.
4. Code of Conduct on Defence Procurement: The Code of Conduct on Defence Procurement of the EU Member States participating in the European Defence Agency, approved on 21 November 2005.

REFERENCES

Algieri, Franco (2001), 'Die europäische Sicherheits- und Verteidigungspolitik – erweiterter Handlungsspielraum für die GASP', in Werner Weidenfeld (ed.), *Nizza in der Analyse*, Gütersloh: Bertelsmann Foundation, pp. 161–201.

Allen, David (1997), 'EPC/CFSP, the Soviet Union, and the former Soviet republics: do the twelve have a coherent policy?', in Elfriede Regelsberger, Philippe de Schoutheete de Tervarent and Wolfgang Wessels (eds), *Foreign Policy of the European Union: From EPC to CFSP and Beyond*, Boulder, CO and London: Rienner, pp. 219–37.

Allen, David and William Wallace (1978), 'Der geschichtliche Hintergrund der EPZ – Vom Problemkind zum Musterknaben europäischer Politik', in Reinhardt Rummel and Wolfgang Wessels (eds), *Die Europäische Politische Zusammenarbeit*, Bonn: Europa Union, pp. 52–73.

Andréani, Gilles, Christoph Bertram and Charles Grant (2001), *Europe's Military Revolution*, London: Centre for European Reform.

Barbé, Esther (2000), 'La PESC: Desafíos Políticos y Límites Institucionales', in Esther Barbé (ed.), *Política Exterior Europea*, Barcelona: Ariel, pp. 107–28.

Blair, Tony (2000), 'Europe's political future', Speech to the Polish Stock Exchange, 6 October 2000, available at http://www.fco.gov.uk/en/newsroom/latest-news/?view=Speech&id=2037261.

Bretherton, Charlotte and John Vogler (1999), *The European Union as a Global Actor*, London: Routledge.

Bull, Hedley (1995), *The Anarchical Society: A Study of Order in World Politics*, 2nd edn, London: Macmillan.

Cameron, Fraser (1997), 'Where the European Commission comes in: from Single European Act to Maastricht', in Elfriede Regelsberger, Philippe de Schoutheete de Tervarent and Wolfgang Wessels (eds), *Foreign Policy of the European Union: From EPC to CFSP and Beyond*, Boulder, CO and London: Rienner, pp. 99–108.

Commission Européenne (2003), 'Stratégie de cooperation et programme indicative, 2003–2007, République Démocratique du Congo – Communauté Europénne', 2 September, Brussels.

Commission Européenne (2005), 'Addendum au document de Stratégie de cooperation et programme indicatif national, Communauté Européenne et République Démocratique du Congo', 21 June, Brussels.

Council of the European Union (2002), 'Council Regulation (EC) No 881/2002 of 27 May 2002 imposing certain specific restrictive measures directed against certain persons and entities associated with Usama bin Laden, the Al-Qaida network and the Taliban, and repealing Council Regulation (EC) No 467/2001 prohibiting the export of certain goods and services to Afghanistan, strengthening the flight ban and extending the freeze of funds and other financial resources in respect of the Taliban of Afghanistan', Official Journal, L 139, 29 May.

Council of the European Union (2004), 'Council decision 2004/197/CFSP establishing a mechanism to administer the financing of the common costs of European Union operations having military or defence implications', Official Journal, L 63, 23 February, p. 68.

Davignon Report (1970), Luxembourg, 27 October, *Bulletin of the European Communities*, November 1970, No 11, pp. 9–14.

de Schoutheete, Philippe (1980), *La Coopération Politique Européenne*, Brussels: Labor.

de Schoutheete, Philippe (1986), *La Coopération Politique Européenne*, 2nd edn, Brussels: Labor.

de Schoutheete, Philippe (2002), 'The European Council', in John Peterson and Michael Shackleton (eds), *The Institutions of the European Union*, Oxford: Oxford University Press, pp. 21–46.

Diedrichs, Udo (1996), 'National views and European cleavages: from the Single European Act to the Treaty on European Union', in Franco Algieri and Elfriede Regelsberger (eds), *Synergy at Work: Spain and Portugal in European Foreign Policy*, Bonn: Europa Union, pp. 233–58.

Diedrichs, Udo (2003a), 'The provisions on ESDP in the Constitutional Treaty: no revolution in military affairs', *CFSP Forum*, **1**(1).

Diedrichs, Udo (2003b), 'Die Entwicklung der ESVP – wissenschaftliche und politische Diskussionen', *Integration*, 2/03, 166–70.

Diedrichs, Udo (2004), 'The European Parliament in CFSP: more than a marginal player?', *International Spectator*, **2**, 31–46.

Diedrichs, Udo and Mathias Jopp (2003a), 'Flexibility in ESDP: from the Convention to the IGC and beyond', *CFSP Forum*, **2**(2).

Diedrichs, Udo and Mathias Jopp (2003b), 'Flexible modes of governance: making CFSP and ESDP work', *International Spectator*, **3**, 15–30.

Diedrichs, Udo and Mathias Jopp (2005), 'Die Sicherheits- und Verteidigungspolitik der EU nach dem Verfassungsvertrag: Innovationen, Experimente, Impulse', *Europäische Schriften des Instituts für Europäische Politik*, **83**, 343–66.

Diedrichs, Udo, Mathias Jopp and Sammi Sandawi (2004), 'Möglichkeiten und Grenzen der Integration von Streitkräften in der EU, Studie für das Bundesministerium der Verteidigung', *Integration*, 3/04, 223–33.

Dûchene, François (1973), 'Die Rolle Europas im Weltsystem: Von der regionalen zur planetarischen Interdependenz', in Max Kohnstamm and Wolfgang Hager (eds), *Zivilmacht Europa – Supermacht oder Partner?*, Frankfurt am Main: Suhrkamp, pp. 19–26.

Duke, Simon (2000), *The Elusive Quest for European Security: From EDC to CFSP*, London: Macmillan.

Edwards, Geoffrey (1997), 'The potential and limits of CFSP: the Yugoslav example', in Elfriede Regelsberger, Philippe de Schoutheete de Tervarent and Wolfgang Wessels (eds), *Foreign Policy of the European Union: From EPC to CFSP and Beyond*, Boulder, CO and London: Rienner, pp. 173–97.

European Parliament, European Commission and Council of the European Union (2006), 'Interinstitutional Agreement between the Parliament, the Council and the Commission on budgetary discipline and sound financial management', *Official Journal*, C 139, 14 June.

Fligstein, Neil, Wayne Sandholtz and Alec Stone Sweet (2001), 'The institutionalization of European space', in Alec Stone Sweet, Wayne Sandholtz and Neil Fligstein (eds), *The Institutionalization of Europe*, Oxford: Oxford University Press, pp. 1–29.

Forster, Anthony and William Wallace (2000), 'Common foreign and security policy', in Helen Wallace and William Wallace (eds), *Policy-making in the European Union*, 4th edn, Oxford: Oxford University Press, pp. 461–92.

Frisch, Thomas (2000), *Der Hohe Vertreter für die GASP – Aufgaben und erste Schritte*, Ebenhausen: Stiftung Wissenschaft und Politik.

Gablentz, Otto von der (1977), 'Wege zu einer europäischen Außenpolitik', in Heinrich Schneider and Wolfgang Wessels (eds), *Auf dem Weg zur Europäischen Union*, Bonn: Europa Union, pp. 85–117.

Galtung, Johan (1973), *Kapitalistische Großmacht Europa oder die Gemeinschaft der Konzerne?*, Reinbek: Rowohlt.

Garden, Timothy (2003), 'The future of ESDP: defence capabilities for Europe', *International Spectator*, **XXXVIII** (3), July/September, 7–15.

Gasteyger, Curt (1996), *An Ambiguous Power: The European Union in a Changing World*, Gütersloh: Bertelsmann Foundation.

Ginsberg, Roy H. (1999), 'Conceptualizing the European Union as an international actor: narrowing the theoretical capability–expectation gap', *Journal of Common Market Studies*, **37**(3), September, 429–54.

Ginsberg, Roy H. (2001), *The European Union in International Politics: Baptism of Fire*, Lanham, MD et al.: Rowman & Littlefield.

Hill, Christopher (1993), 'The capability expectation gap, or conceptualizing Europe's international role', *Journal of Common Market Studies*, September, pp. 305–28.

Hill, Christopher (1998), 'Closing the capabilities–expectation gap?', in John Peterson and Helen Sjursen (eds), *A Common Foreign Policy for Europe?*, London: Routledge, pp. 18–38.

Hill, Christopher (2001), 'The EU's capacity for conflict prevention', *European Foreign Affairs Review*, Autumn 2001.

Hill, Christopher (2003), *The Changing Politics of Foreign Policy*, Basingstoke and New York: Palgrave.

Hill, Christopher (2004), 'Renationalizing or regrouping? EU foreign policy since 11 September 2001', *Journal of Common Market Studies*, **42**(1), 143–63.

Hill, Christopher and K.E. Smith (eds) (2000), *European Foreign Policy: Key Documents*, London: Routledge.

Holland, Martin (1997), *Common Foreign and Security Policy: The Record and Reforms*, London and Washington: Pinter.

Howorth, Jolyon (2001), 'European defence and the changing politics of the EU: hanging together or hanging separately?', *Journal of Common Market Studies*, **39**(4), 765–89.

Howorth, Jolyon (2002), 'CESDP after 11 September: from short-term confusion to long-term cohesion?', *EUSA Review*, Winter 2002, pp. 3–4.

Howorth, Jolyon (2007), *Security and Defence Policy in the European Union*, Basingstoke: Palgrave Macmillan.

Hudemann, Rainer, Hartmut Kaelble and Klaus Schwabe (eds) (1985), *Europa im Blick der Historiker, Europäische Integration im 20. Jahrhundert: Bewußtsein und Institutionen*, Historischen Zeitschrift supplement, Munich: Oldenburg Wissenschaftsverlag.

Ifestos, Panayiotis (1987), *European Political Cooperation: Towards a Framework of Supranational Diplomacy?*, Aldershot et al.: Avebury.

Jopp, Mathias (1997), 'The defence dimension of the European Union: the role and performance of the WEU', in Elfriede Regelsberger, Philippe de Schoutheete de Tervarent and Wolfgang Wessels (eds), *Foreign Policy of the European Union: From EPC to CFSP and Beyond*, Boulder, CO and London: Rienner, pp. 153–69.

Jopp, Matthias (2000), 'Gemeinsame Europäische Sicherheits- und Verteidigungspolitik', in Werner Weidenfeld and Wolfgang Wessels (eds), *Jahrbuch der Europäischen Integration 1999/2000*, Bonn: Europa Union, pp. 243–50.

Jopp, Mathias and Elfriede Regelsberger (2003), 'GASP und ESVP im Verfassungsvertrag – eine neue Angebotsvielfalt mit Chancen und Mängeln', *Integration*, 4/03, October, 550–63.

Jopp, Mathias, Barbara Lippert and Elfriede Regelsberger (2003), 'Europäische Außen- und Sicherheitspolitik der erweiterten Union – interne und externe Herausforderungen an Politik und Institutionen in GASP und ESVP', in Matthias Chardon, Ursula Göth, Martin Große Hüttmann and Christine Probst-Dobler (eds), *Regieren unter Neuen Herausforderungen: Deutschland und Europa im 21. Jahrhundert*, Baden-Baden: Nomos.

Keating, Patrick (1997), 'The twelve, the United Nations, and Somalia: the mirage of global intervention', in Elfriede Regelsberger, Philippe de Schoutheete de Tervarent and Wolfgang Wessels (eds), *Foreign Policy of the European Union: From EPC to CFSP and Beyond*, Boulder, CO and London: Rienner, pp. 275–97.

Keohane, Daniel (2004), 'Europe's new defence agency', London: Centre for European Reform, Policy Brief.

Krenzler, Horst G. and Henning C. Schneider (1997), 'The question of consistency', in Elfriede Regelsberger, Philippe de Schoutheete de Tervarent and Wolfgang Wessels (eds), *Foreign Policy of the European Union: From EPC to CFSP and Beyond*, Boulder, CO and London: Rienner, pp. 133–51.

Laursen, Finn and Sophie Vanhoonacker (eds) (1992), *The Intergovernmental Conference on Political Union: Institutional Reforms, New Policies and International Identity of the European Community*, Dordrecht: Nijhoff.

Lindley-French, Julian (2002), 'Combined and joint? The development of a security and operational doctrine for the European Union', in Erich Reiter, Reinhardt Rummel and Peter Schmidt (eds), *Europas ferne Streitmacht, Chancen und Schwierigkeiten der Europäischen Union beim Aufbau der ESVP*, Hamburg: Mittler, pp. 86–118.

Maull, Hanns W. (1997), 'Europa als Weltmacht? Perspektiven für die gemeinsame Außen- und Sicherheitspolitik', in Thomas Jäger and Melanie Piepenschneider (eds), *Europa 2020: Szenarien Politischer Entwicklung*, Opladen: Leske + Budrich, pp. 81–95.

Maull, Hanns (2000), 'Germany and the use of force: still a civilian power?', *Survival*, **2**, 56–80.

Maull, Hanns (2002), 'Die "Zivilmacht Europa" bleibt Projekt: Zur Debatte um Kagan, Asmus/Pollack und das Strategiedokument NSS 2002', *Blätter für Deutsche und Internationale Politik*, **12**, 1467–78.

Monar, Jörg (1997a), 'The European Union's foreign affairs system after the Treaty of Amsterdam: a strengthened capacity for external action?', *European Foreign Affairs Review*, **2**, 413–36.

Nuttall, Simon (1992), *European Political Cooperation*, Oxford: Clarendon Press.

Nuttall, Simon (1997), 'Two decades of EPC performance', in Elfriede Regelsberger, Philippe de Schoutheete de Tervarent and Wolfgang Wessels (eds), *Foreign Policy of the European Union: From EPC to CFSP and Beyond*, Boulder, CO and London: Rienner, pp. 19–39.

Nuttall, Simon (2000), *European Foreign Policy*, Oxford: Oxford University Press.

Partnership agreement between the members of the African, Caribbean and Pacific Group of States of the one part, and the European Community and its Member States, of the other part, signed in Cotonou on 23 June 2000: Protocols/Final Act/Declarations (2000), Official Journal, L 317, 15 December, pp. 3–353.

Pijpers, Alfred (1990), *The Vicissitudes of European Political Cooperation: Towards a Realist Interpretation of the EC's Collective Diplomacy*, Leiden: Leiden University.

Pijpers, Alfred, Elfriede Regelsberger and Wolfgang Wessels (eds) (1988), *A Common Foreign Policy for Western Europe? European Political Cooperation in the 1980s*, Dordrecht: Nijhoff.

Regelsberger, Elfriede (1986–91), 'Die Europäische Politische Zusammenarbeit', in Werner Weidenfeld and Wolfgang Wessels (eds), *Jahrbuch der Europäischen Integration, 1986–1991*, Bonn: Europa Union.

Regelsberger, Elfriede (2000), 'Gemeinsame Außen- und Sicherheitspolitik', in Werner Weidenfeld and Wolfgang Wessels (eds), *Jahrbuch der Europäischen Integration 1999/2000*, Bonn: Europa Union, pp. 233–42.

Regelsberger, Elfriede (2001), 'Die Gemeinsame Außen- und Sicherheitspolitik nach "Nizza" – begrenzter Reformeifer und außervertragliche Dynamik in der ESVP', *Integration*, 2/01, 156–66.

Regelsberger, Elfriede (2002), 'Gemeinsame Außen- und Sicherheitspolitik', in Werner Weidenfeld and Wolfgang Wessels (eds), *Jahrbuch der Europäischen Integration 2001/2002*, Bonn: Europa Union, pp. 233–42.

Regelsberger, Elfriede (2003), 'Gemeinsame Außen- und Sicherheitspolitik', in Werner Weidenfeld and Wolfgang Wessels (eds), *Jahrbuch der Europäischen Integration 2002/2003*, Bonn: Europa Union.

Regelsberger, Elfriede (2004), *Die Gemeinsame Außen- und Sicherheitspolitik der EU (GASP), Konstitutionelle Angebote im Praxistest 1993–2003*, Baden-Baden: Nomos.

Regelsberger, Elfriede and Mathias Jopp (1998), 'Die Stärkung der Handlungsfähigkeit in der Gemeinsamen Aussen- und Sicherheitspolitik,' in Mathias Jopp, Andreas Maurer and Otto Schmuck (eds), *Die Europäische Union nach Amsterdam*, Bonn: Europa Union, pp. 155–77.

Regelsberger, Elfriede and Uwe Schmalz (2001), 'The Common Foreign and Security Policy of the Amsterdam Treaty: towards an improved EU identity on the international scene', in Jörg Monar and Wolfgang Wessels (eds), *The European Union after the Treaty of Amsterdam*, London and New York: Continuum, pp. 249–66.

Regelsberger, Elfriede and Wolfgang Wessels (2003), 'The evolution of the Common Foreign and Security Policy: a case of an imperfect ratchet fusion', in Amy Verdun and M. Croci (eds), *Institutional and Policy-Making Challenges to the European Union in the Wake of Enlargement*, Manchester: Manchester University Press.

Regelsberger, Elfriede, Philippe de Schoutheete de Tervarent and Wolfgang Wessels (eds) (1997), *Foreign Policy of the European Union: From EPC to CFSP and Beyond*, Boulder, CO and London: Rienner.

Rummel, Reinhardt and Wolfgang Wessels (eds) (1978), *Die Europäische Politische Zusammenarbeit*, Bonn: Europa Union.

Sabá, K. (1996), 'Spain: evolving foreign policy structures: from ECP challenge to CFSP management', in F. Algieri and E. Regelsberger (eds), *Synergy at*

Work: Spain and Portugal in European Foreign Policy, Bonn: Europa Union, pp. 181–206.

Schmalz, Uwe (1998), 'The Amsterdam provisions on external coherence: bridging the Union's foreign policy dualism?', *European Foreign Affairs Review*, **3**, 421–42.

Schmalz, Uwe (2004), *Deutschlands Europäisierte Außenpolitik, Kontinuität und Wandel Deutscher Konzepte zur EPZ und GASP*, Wiesbaden: VS.

Schmitt, Burkard (2005), 'European capabilities action plan', Briefing Paper, Paris: EU Institute for Security Studies.

Schubert, Klaus and Gisela Müller-Brandeck-Boucquet (eds) (2000), *Die Europäische Union als Akteur der Weltpolitik*, Opladen: Leske + Budrich.

Second report on European political cooperation on Foreign Policy (1973), Copenhagen, 23 July, *Bulletin of the European Communities*, September 1973, No. 9, pp. 14–21.

Smith, Michael E. (2001), 'Diplomacy by decree: the legalisation of EU foreign policy', *Journal of Common Market Studies*, **1**, 79–104.

Smith, Michael E. (2004), *Europe's Foreign and Security Policy: The Institutionalisation of Cooperation*, Cambridge: Cambridge University Press.

Solemn Declaration on European Union (1983), Stuttgart, 19 June, in *Bulletin of the European Communities*, June 1983, No. 6, pp. 24–9.

Stone Sweet, Alec, Wayne Sandholtz and Neil Fligstein (eds) (2001), *The Institutionalization of Europe*, Oxford: Oxford University Press.

Tonra, Ben (2001), *The Europeanisation of National Foreign Policy: Dutch, Danish and Irish Foreign Policy in the European Union*, Aldershot: Ashgate.

Volkmann, Hans-Erich und Walter Schwengler (eds) (1995), *Die Europäische Verteidigungsgemeinschaft, Stand und Probleme der Forschung*, Boppard: Boldt.

Wagner, Wolfgang and Gunther Hellmann (2003), 'Zivile Weltmacht? Die Außen- und Sicherheits- und Verteidigungspolitik der Europäischen Union', in Markus Jachtenfuchs and Beate Kohler-Koch (eds), *Europäische Integration*, Opladen: Leske + Budrich, pp. 569–96.

Wallace, Helen (2000a), 'The policy process', in Helen Wallace and William Wallace (eds), *Policy-Making in the European Union*, Oxford: Oxford University Press, pp. 39–64.

Wallace, Helen (2000b), 'The institutional setting', in Helen Wallace and William Wallace (eds), *Policy-Making in the European Union*, Oxford: Oxford University Press, pp. 3–37.

Weiler, Joseph and Wolfgang Wessels (1988), 'EPC and the challenge of theory', in Alfred Pijpers, Elfriede Regelsberger and Wolfgang Wessels (eds), *A Common Foreign Policy for Western Europe? European Political Cooperation in the 1980s*, Dordrecht: Nijhoff, pp. 229–58.

Wessel, Ramses A. (1999), *The European Union's Foreign and Security Policy: A Legal Institutional Perspective*, The Hague: Kluwer Law International.

Wessels, Wolfgang (1978), 'Die EPZ – Ein neuer Ansatz europäischer Aussenpolitik', in Reinhardt Rummel and Wolfgang Wessels (eds), *Die Europäische Politische Zusammenarbeit*, Bonn: Europa Union.

Wessels, Wolfgang (1997a), 'An ever closer fusion? A dynamic macropolitical view on integration processes', *Journal of Common Market Studies*, **35**(2), 267–99.

Wessels, Wolfgang (1997b), 'Der Amsterdamer Vertrag – Durch Stückwerksreformen zu einer effizienteren, erweiterten und föderalen Union?', *Integration*, 3/97, 117–35.

Wessels, Wolfgang (2001), 'Nice results: the millenium IGC in the EU's evolution', *Journal of Common Market Studies*, **39**(2), 197–219.

Wessels, Wolfgang (2002), 'Security and defence of the European Union: the institutional evolution: trends and perspectives', Contribution to the 6th ECSA World Conference, December 2002.

Wessels, Wolfgang (2003), 'Eine institutionelle Architektur für eine globale (Zivil-) Macht? Die Artikel zur Gemeinsamen Außen- und Sicherheitspolitik des Vertrags über eine Verfassung für Europa', *Zeitschrift für Staats- und Europawissenschaften*, **3**, 400–29.

Wessels, Wolfgang (2004), 'A "*saut constitutionnel*" out of an intergovernmental trap? The provisions of the Constitutional Treaty for the Common Foreign, Security and Defence Policy', paper presented at the Jean Monnet Conference: Altneuland: The EU Constitution in a Contextual Perspective, NYU, Working Paper 5/04, available at http://www.jeanmonnetprogram.org/papers/04/040501-17.rtf.

White, Brian (2001), *Understanding European Foreign Policy*, Basingstoke and New York: Palgrave.

Whitman, Richard (2002), 'The fall and the rise of civilian power Europe', National Europe Centre Paper No. 16, paper presented to conference on 'The European Union in International Affairs', National Europe Centre, Australian National University, 3–4 July 2002, available at http://dspace.anu.edu.au/bit-stream/1885/41589/2/whitman.pdf.

Zielonka, Jan (1998), *Paradoxes of European Foreign Policy*, The Hague: Kluwer Law International.

INTERNET SOURCES

Agence Europe: www.agenceeurope.com.

8. Modes of EU governance in the justice and home affairs domain: specific factors, types, evolution trends and evaluation*

Jörg Monar

INTRODUCTION

Since the entry into force of the Treaty of Amsterdam in 1999, EU justice and home affairs (JHA) in the context of the 'area of freedom, security and justice' (AFSJ) has developed into one of the major policy-making areas of the EU: developing the EU as an AFSJ has become one of the fundamental treaty objectives (Article 2 TEU). Since 1999 the Council has adopted on average ten new texts each month on JHA issues and there is no JHA field left which is not now covered by multi-annual programmes or action plans. JHA objectives have also 'penetrated' other policy areas of the EU, such as EU external relations and the internal market. As a result the JHA domain appears as the most rapidly developing and expansionist EU policy area in the post-Amsterdam era.

The rapid expansion of the JHA domain as an EU policy area can in itself be regarded as an interesting phenomenon of EU governance, but in this chapter – in line with the questions presented in the introduction to this volume – we will focus on the questions regarding which specific factors determine EU modes of governance in the JHA domain, which types can be identified and distinguished, what main evolution trends can be observed and how those modes appear from an evaluation point of view.[1]

Because of the wide range of different definitions of the concepts of 'governance' and 'modes of governance', it will be useful to clarify at the outset the meaning of these terms as used in this chapter.

a. Following broadly the general definition provided by Arthur Benz (2003) we understand by 'governance' *the steering and coordination of*

interdependent actors through institution-based systems of internal rules.
As there is as yet no significant involvement of non-governmental/
private actors in EU JHA policy-making,[2] we understand by 'interdependent actors' public authorities both at the national level (governments, ministries, police forces, courts and so on) and at the European
level (EU institutions, coordinating structures and special agencies)
which as a result of the EU framework and EU objectives have to
cooperate in one way or another. It should be noted that this definition covers only 'internal' rule systems and not 'external governance'
issues in relation with third countries.

b. Building on this working definition of 'governance', we understand
by 'modes of governance' *the different types of instruments (legislative or non-legislative) used for the steering and coordination of
interdependent actors through institution-based internal rules systems.*
This working definition comes very close to Adrienne Héritier's
analysis of governance as consisting of the use of different
types of 'steering instruments', whether legally binding or operating through various forms of common target-setting (Héritier,
1987).

SPECIFIC FACTORS OF THE EMERGENCE OF MODES OF GOVERNANCE IN THE JHA DOMAIN

The Particular Sensitivity of JHA Policy Fields from a Sovereignty, Territoriality and Political Point of View

EU action in the JHA domain touches upon core functions of the state:
providing security and justice for citizens and sovereign control over the
national territory are not only central prerogatives of the modern nation-
state but also essential elements of its *raison d'être* and legitimacy. The
principle that the exercise of law enforcement is strictly limited to national
authorities within the national territory – a traditional expression of state
sovereignty – continues to be a major problem for JHA cooperation.[3] In
addition, some of the key issues of the JHA domain, especially internal
security and the control of migration, are highly sensitive issues at the
domestic level with a great potential to cause national governments to
win or lose elections. Most EU governments have therefore been reluctant
to relinquish control over national governance instruments in the JHA
domain. Rather than seeking any form of 'integration'[4] of their systems
and policies, they have opted for gradually increasing interaction and
synergy between their national systems while limiting as far as possible

legislation and common structures which can interfere with national control over JHA instruments. This has major implications for current EU governance in the JHA domain, as follows.

The EU has so far only been vested with rather limited powers in the JHA domain; the powers it has come nowhere near the competences in 'classic' EC 'common policies'. There is, in fact, so far not a single common policy within this domain, and even in the case of the 'common asylum system' – which may be regarded as coming closest to a common policy – the treaty does not provide for a comprehensive transfer of competences. This in itself is an indication of the member states' reluctance to proceed with real 'integration' in this domain. A further indicator is the fact that the member states have shown a strong preference for mutual recognition and minimal(ist) harmonization as far as legislative action is concerned rather than pursuing any major harmonization project such as the gradual introduction of a European criminal or civil law code. It is also noteworthy that the member states have so far not transferred operational powers to any of the special agencies they have set up in this domain (Europol, Eurojust, Frontex), so that in a domain where operational action is central to many objectives the EU as such does not as yet have any capabilities at its disposal. The political preference for cooperation rather than integration has thus entailed (a) a certain preference for governance instruments which are 'lighter' in the sense of being less invasive upon the national systems; and (b) the development of specific mechanisms and structures which make it possible to enhance cooperation and coordination while leaving the national systems largely unchanged.

The Diversity of the JHA Policy Fields

One particular feature of the JHA domain is that it comprises a set of rather diverse policy fields: asylum, immigration, border controls, judicial cooperation in civil matters, judicial cooperation in criminal matters and police cooperation. Both the objectives pursued and the instruments used to achieve them are necessarily rather different if one compares, for instance, the fields of asylum policy, judicial cooperation in civil matters and police cooperation. In the first the main focus is on the common definition of minimum guarantees and procedures regarding asylum seekers; in the second it is essentially on the facilitation of the cross-border administration of civil justice; and in the third it is on enhanced interaction between national law enforcement authorities. In each case different governance approaches are clearly needed, which makes it practically impossible to apply a 'one-size-fits-all' mode of governance. This diversity has increased with the expansion of the policy-making objectives in the individual areas since the 1990s.[5] As a result of all this, EU governance in the JHA domain is necessarily in itself more diverse than more homogeneous policy domains such as agricultural or environmental policy.

The Strong Operational Dimension of the JHA Domain

The progress of EU integration has traditionally been strongly linked with an extensive use of legislation for setting common rules. While there are some areas, such as asylum and migration, where legislative instruments are also very important for progress in the JHA domain, there are others, especially police cooperation and external border controls, where operational information exchange and coordination as well as the carrying out of joint operations are more important. Legislative measures on the one hand and operational measures on the other obviously have substantially different rationales and requirements – as regards flexibility and speed, for instance. As a result rather different instruments of governance are needed, often enough in one and the same field. Judicial cooperation in the fight against cross-border crime needs, for instance, both legislative action for minimum harmonization of certain procedural and substantive provisions of criminal law and operational coordination of prosecution services. This obviously adds to the very special nature of the governance requirements of the JHA domain.

Differentiation as a Characteristic of the JHA Domain

Although the AFSJ is formally designed as a single 'area' it is the most differentiated of all the constructions which the EU integration process has produced so far: currently only 12 of the member states[6] participate fully in all the instruments and structures of governance which have been developed within the AFSJ. The UK, Ireland and Denmark all have 'opt-out' arrangements to various degrees, and the ten new member states will only be fully integrated into the Schengen arrangements in December 2007. Further differentiation is generated by the 'association' of three non-EU member states – Iceland, Norway and Switzerland – with the Schengen system. This major differentiation in the JHA domain has substantial implications for EU governance in the sense that some instruments of governance are designed to serve only part of the member states (that is the Schengen countries) and that the form and the use (in a more or less binding way) of instruments can vary depending on whether or not all member states participate.

The Divide between the First- and the Third-Pillar Fields

This is the last, but certainly not the least, of the factors determining EU governance in the JHA domain: although linked together by the common objective of the AFSJ and the common institutional framework (in particular the JHA Council), the First-Pillar fields (asylum, immigration, border controls, and judicial cooperation in civil matters) are separated from the Third-Pillar fields (police and judicial cooperation in criminal matters) not only by virtue of their having a different legal basis (cf. Title IV TEC and Title VI TEU) but also because they have different decision-making procedures,[7] separate decision-making structures in the Council below the level of COREPER, and different legal instruments (to which we will come back below). This divide, which cuts through the entire domain, means that the current treaty framework – as a result of a political compromise between the member states as 'masters of the Treaties' – imposes a distinct cleavage on EU governance in the JHA domain such as cannot be found in this form in any other EU policy field. The artificiality of this divide becomes particularly clear in cases in which different procedures and instruments have to be used separately in parallel for the same objective, which is the case, for instance with First- and Third-Pillar legislative measures against illegal immigration. Yet, artificial or not, this legal divide currently clearly belongs to the inherent nature of EU governance in the JHA domain.

The Impact of the Treaty of Amsterdam Reforms

The JHA domain as it exists today is very much determined by one fundamental revision of the 'constitutional' context: the 1997 Treaty of Amsterdam transformed what, since the Maastricht reforms of 1993, had been a domain of loose intergovernmental cooperation – marked by an inhibiting lack of clear objectives, adequate competences and appropriate instruments – into one with a range of ambitious goals under the heading of the AFSJ, much extended possibilities of taking action both internally and externally, and better instruments, with the communitarization of the current First-Pillar areas and the incorporation of the Schengen system also adding to new strength and importance of this domain (de Lobkowicz, 2002). Here we can speak of a 'revolution of the legal constitution' which accounts for much of the expansion since 1999, already mentioned, and a significantly more fertile 'living constitution'. At the same time this also accounts for some of the more problematic aspects of EU governance in this domain, especially the 'pillar divide' and the formal acceptance and codification of differentiation within the AFSJ.

THE MAIN TYPES OF EU GOVERNANCE IN THE JHA DOMAIN

A Suitable Typology of Modes of Governance in the JHA Domain

Since the end of the 1990s the General Secretariat of the Council – as part of a laudable effort to increase public transparency regarding EU action in the JHA domain – has been providing annual lists of texts adopted by the JHA Council on the Council's website. These lists are very useful for identifying the main modes of governance in the JHA domain as only less than half of these texts – most of which are not formally binding – are published in the *Official Journal* and/or appear on EUR-Lex. Adopted by the JHA Council as the supreme decision-making body in the JHA domain, they comprise, for instance, the rather large number of action plans, evaluation reports, situation assessments and studies which play an important role in the JHA domain for targeting common action and ensuring better implementation. The following analysis of EU governance modes in the JHA domain is based on these annual JHA Council lists of texts, starting with the Treaty of Amsterdam in 1999 because of the massive changes this treaty introduced to the JHA domain.

In the context of the NEWGOV integrated project, Oliver Treib, Holger Bähr and Gerda Falkner have suggested a 'new typology of four modes of governance' (Treib et al., 2005) which is partly based on the typology used by Christoph Knill and Andrea Lenschow (2000). It distinguishes between four basic types of modes of governance: 'coercion' (legally binding and rigid in terms of implementation); 'framework regulation' (legally binding but with flexible implementation); 'targeting' (soft law and rigid implementation); and 'voluntarism' (soft law and flexible implementation). With some modifications, this model can be usefully applied to the JHA domain.

The 'Tight Regulation' Mode

The JHA domain clearly has its own set of 'coercive' instruments of government, that is fully binding legal instruments which, if used, allow for little or no flexibility when it comes to implementation by the EU or its member states. These are the EC regulations, applied in the First-Pillar fields, formal Council decisions or common positions based on Article 34 TEU,[8] and any other formal Council decisions, which often regulate rather detailed individual issues such as amendments to the Schengen Border Manual. Also in this category belong conventions concluded by the member states – such as the 1995 Europol Convention (Council of the European Union, 1995) or the 2000 Convention on Mutual Assistance in Criminal Matters (Council of the European Union, 2000) – and Council Acts amending those conventions. Unlike the other instruments in this category, conventions require national parliamentary ratification, which is one of the reasons why they have rarely been used since the entry into force of the Treaty of Amsterdam. In order to distinguish this category of fully binding instruments from the following, which also has its 'coercive' side, we call this *tight regulation* rather than using the term 'coercion'.

Neither the instruments used under this mode nor their content differ substantially from those of hard or coercive governance applied in other domains of EU policy-making. The statistical analysis of the Council texts adopted from 1 May 1999 to 31 December 2006 shows that, with 219 out of 868 texts or 25.2 per cent of the total, tight regulation texts form – by a very narrow margin – the largest group (see Figure 8.1 and Table 8.1). This may at first sight seem surprising if one thinks of the political preference for instruments of cooperation rather than integration (see above). Yet a relatively large number of the texts in this category are related to technical aspects of border control and visa policy matters as well as the functioning of the Schengen system[9] (SIS) and the regulatory framework of special agencies, such as Europol, which because of their legal implications are in need of tight regulation in order to ensure adequate legal certainty. 'Major' legal instruments such as EC regulations and EU conventions only account for a fraction of this body of 'tight regulation' texts. The large number of measures of technical implementation therefore make the 'tight regulation' effort appear much broader than it actually is.

The 'Framework Regulation' Mode

The second mode of the typology of Treib, Bähr and Falkner can be applied without difficulty. The JHA domain has two instruments of *framework regulation* – directives in the First-Pillar areas and 'framework decisions' in the Third-Pillar areas – which are binding (coercive) on the member states as to their objectives, but leave it to them to adopt implementing legislation within the normally more or less broad framework of rules set by the EU, thereby offering a considerable degree of flexibility. Framework decisions are in essence the Third-Pillar parallel to First-Pillar directives, the only major difference being that by virtue of Article 34(c) TEU the probably most supranational feature of EC legislative acts – the principle of direct effect – does not apply to *decisions* and *framework decisions* under Title VI TEU, as this is provided for by Article 34(b) and (c)

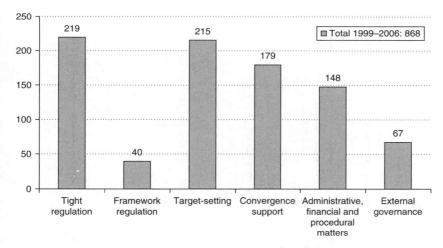

Figure 8.1   Texts adopted in the JHA area, 1 May 1999–31 December 2006 (post-Amsterdam period): total numbers in all categories

TEU.[10] As in other domains of EU policy-making, the framework regulation mode is used to reduce the costs of adapting the national systems to EU regulatory objectives by allowing for wider margins of implementation. Directives have so far served as the primary instrument for putting the EU's common asylum system in place[11] and framework decisions for providing a minimum level of harmonization of the constituent elements of criminal acts and of penalty levels in the fight against serious forms of cross-border crime.[12]

Instruments of the framework regulation type are used comparatively rarely. With 40 out of a total of 868 texts adopted by the Council from 1999 to 2006 (see Figure 8.1 and Table 8.1) they account for only 4.6 per cent of the total. This can be explained by a tendency of member states in the Council to give preference – if tight regulation can be avoided at all – to the 'softer' and most heavily used mode of target-setting (see below) which allows them in many cases to proceed without comprehensive national implementing legislation by simply using executive regulatory powers or issuing different instructions and guidelines to ministries, law enforcement agencies and other implementing authorities. The *framework regulation* mode has, it should be recalled, a clear 'hard' side in the fields of the First Pillar as national implementation there is subject to both the control of the Commission and potential judicial review by the ECJ.

Table 8.1   *Texts adopted in the JHA area, 1 May 1999–31 December 2006 (post-Amsterdam period): total numbers per mode and field*

	Asylum	Immigration	Frontiers	Visa	Civil law	Criminal law	Police co-operation	Customs co-operation (Third Pillar)	Horizontal issues. Title IV[1]	Horizontal issues. Title VI[2]	Horizontal issues. Titles VI and VI[3]
Tight regulation[4]	10	4	26	32	25	15	27	1	21	18	40	**219**
Framework regulation[5]	4	8	1	0	2	15	1	0	2	4	3	**40**
Target-setting[6]	5	13	17	15	6	10	45	4	14	41	45	**215**
Coordination support[7]	0	3	9	0	3	12	54	5	10	27	56	**179**
Administrative, financial and procedural matters[8]	2	2	43	2	15	9	46	0	4	10	15	**148**
External governance[9]	1	5	2	1	3	5	34	0	7	4	5	**67**
	22	**35**	**98**	**50**	**54**	**66**	**207**	**10**	**58**	**104**	**164**	**868**

Notes:

1. Asylum, immigration (including integration), border controls, judicial cooperation in civil matters.
2. Police and judicial cooperation in criminal matters.
3. Schengen, enlargement, data protection and other texts with 'cross-pillar' reach such as action plans on drugs.
4. These include regulations, decisions, common positions under Article 34 TEU, Acts of the Council according to the Schengen Convention, the Europol Convention, the mutual legal assistance conventions, the Convention on the use of information technology for customs purposes and other conventions and other formal decisions.
5. Directives and framework decisions under Article 34 of TEU.
6. These include Council resolutions, recommendations and conclusions, action plans, strategies, programmes, guidelines (including programmes of institutions), best practice manual and so on.
7. These include crime situation reports, evaluation reports, information studies, assessments adopted or taken note of, implementation papers and so on.
8. These include administrative documents, appointments, budgetary matters, documents on institutional working methods, authorizations to forward documents, audit reports and so on.
9. These include international agreements including drafts under both Title IV TEC and Title VI TEU, letters to third countries, joint declarations with third countries and so on.

The 'Target-setting' Mode

The third mode, *target-setting*, also makes sense in the JHA domain, as there is a wide range of adopted Council texts which set common targets or guidelines. We can broadly distinguish between two sub-categories of texts.

The first may be described as *functional target-setting* texts. This group includes Council resolutions, recommendations and conclusions as well as guidelines and best practice manuals. It focuses on the setting of targets for improving the functioning of often fairly specific aspects of cross-border cooperation between the member states. An example is the Council Recommendation of 30 March 2004 (Council of the European Union, 2004a) regarding guidelines for taking samples of seized drugs. Targets or guidelines in this sub-category are often quite detailed and can sometimes resemble legislative texts in the density of their provisions.

The second sub-category of target-setting texts can be described as *programme target-setting*, and comprises action plans, programmes and strategies which define in a multi-annual perspective common measures – whether legislative or operational – which the member states are planning to adopt, often in combination with specific deadlines. The extensive use of such programming documents is one of the most characteristic features of EU governance in the JHA domain. The development of the AFSJ as a whole is governed by such a programming document: after the Tampere Programme,[13] which ran from 1999 to 2004, this is currently the 2005 to 2010 Hague Programme on the 'strengthening of freedom, security and justice in the European Union' (Council of the European Union, 2005a). However, the Council has also adopted a whole range of similar documents for major fields of the AFSJ – often with a cross-pillar dimension – containing broad descriptions of objectives to be achieved and individual measures to be adopted in the light of those objectives. The most detailed of these is the repeatedly amended EU Action Plan on Combating Terrorism (Council of the European Union, 2007) which comprises over 200 measures extending to all three pillars of the EU. Other examples are the 2002 Council Plan for the management of external borders (Council of the European Union, 2002c), the 2005–2008 EU Action Plan on Drugs (Council of the European Union, 2005c) and the 2005 EU Plan on best practices, standards and procedures for combating and preventing trafficking in human beings (Council of the European Union, 2005g).

What all types of target-setting in the JHA domain – both functional and programming – have in common is that target-setting does not take the form of legislative Acts. Whereas some of the instruments in this category – especially the recommendations, resolutions and conclusions

– may entail an indirect legal effect, for instance, as a preliminary to a subsequent binding instrument or as a source of interpretation for the provisions of binding instruments, such effects are highly dependent on the individual case and can certainly not be generalized. The programming documents have in any event no binding effects. It is therefore not possible to classify this whole mode as 'soft law' – a rather problematic category anyway – as is suggested in the Treib et al. typology. However, there is a relatively high degree of rigidity in most of the targeting texts in the sense that they prescribe a line of action that the member states and the institutions are expected – though not in the legal sense obliged – to follow.

In the target-setting mode, EU governance in the JHA domain clearly shows some particular characteristics. The statistical analysis of the Council texts adopted between 1 May 1999 and 31 December 2006 reveals that, with 215 out of 868 texts, or 24.8 per cent of the total, target-setting texts come in second position after 'tight regulation' texts by a very narrow margin (see Figure 8.1 and Table 8.1). The political preference for 'lighter' forms of governance and for coordinating and cooperative instruments can be regarded as the main reasons for this. However, the strong operational dimension of the JHA domain is also a contributory factor as tight or even framework regulation on operational matters regarding national law enforcement authorities would be regarded as highly invasive upon national practices and likely to encounter much opposition. National governments therefore prefer to agree targets or guidelines for areas such as police cooperation or horizontal operational coordination.

The extensive use of multi-annual programming instruments merits special consideration. It can be explained by the need for the member states to agree on a longer-term path of common action in fields which are affected by the diversity of the JHA policy areas, much differentiation and the artificial divide between the pillars. These specific problems or at least challenges of the JHA domain account for a particular need for cross-cutting common objectives, scheduling and prioritization of action to be taken.

The 'Convergence Support' Mode

It is with regard to the fourth mode of governance that the JHA domain deviates most from the Treib et al. typology. Because of the focus of EU governance on coordination of and cooperation between the national systems, a significant number of measures have been adopted to support such coordination through evaluation mechanisms and reports. The texts adopted under this mode do not set any rules or even just guidelines to be complied with, but rather identify performance or implementation weaknesses at the European and/or the national level and/or needs for further action, or simply provide situation assessments on the basis of which action can be taken. They comprise, for instance, the regular (classified) evaluation reports on the implementation of the Schengen rules by current Schengen member states (so-called Schengen evaluations), the collective evaluation reports on the state of preparedness of candidate countries for implementing the JHA *acquis*,[14] and evaluation reports on specific issues, for instance, on the exchange of information and intelligence between Europol and the member states and between the member states.[15] Also into this category fall situation or monitoring reports and threat assessments regarding specific forms of crime[16] or illegal immigration and facilitation, reports on data protection issues and information studies. Although none of these texts entail any legal effect – a negative evaluation report cannot legally 'force' a member state to take action to remedy its own weaknesses – they contribute in a varying degree to convergence in the coordinated space of national systems which the AFSJ constitutes. They do so by 'encouraging' member states to address identified weaknesses because of peer pressure resulting from a negative report and by contributing to a common perception of problems and needs for action through common situation assessments. Reports can also serve as an instrument of 'collective discipline', reminding member states collectively that they need to make additional efforts to meet agreed objectives.[17]

This mode of governance is certainly a weaker one than that of target-setting, but it is not entirely 'voluntary' either, as all member states submit to these rules-based procedures and as reports and situation assessments can at the very least support convergence in both the implementation of agreed measures and decision-making on further measures/rules in the Council. As a result we call this mode *convergence support* rather than 'voluntarism', the term used in the typology of Treib et al.

With 179 out of 868 texts (20.6 per cent) over the period 1999–2006 (see Figure 8.1 and Table 8.1), the *convergence support* mode accounts for the third-largest group of texts adopted by the Council. It can also be regarded as a rather specific feature of EU governance in the AFSJ domain. Again, the political preference for 'lighter' forms of governance and coordinating and cooperative instruments can be regarded as the main reason for the extensive use of instruments in this category. A cynical view could lead to the conclusion that national governments prefer to be reminded by evaluation reports that they are failing to respect certain obligations rather than to face possible judicial sanctions in a tight or even framework regulation context. It has to be acknowledged, however, that the strong operational dimension is also of some importance in this context as it is often only through detailed reports or situation assessments 'on the ground' that certain deficits of operational cooperation and coordination and/or needs for new forms of operational coordination and cooperation can be identified.

Administrative, Financial and Procedural Matters and External Governance Measures as Separate Categories

There are two further broad groups of measures in the JHA domain which – although they do not fall within our definition of governance, with its focus on the steering of actors through internal rules systems – nevertheless should be mentioned as they account for a substantial part of the texts adopted by the Council.

A very significant number of the texts adopted by the Council between 1999 and 2006 – 148 out of 868, or 17.1 per cent of the total – do not set rules for the member states or regulate matters concerning their inter-action, but deal with the EU administrative, financial and procedural framework in the JHA domain. The texts adopted for this purpose often have a legal status, but either only regulate specific administrative matters (such as appointing the Director of a special agency) or financial issues (such as approving the annual budget of a special agency), or emanate from intermediary steps of a legislative process (such as Commission or member state legislative initiatives or Council common positions under the co-decision procedure). They therefore do not establish any 'rules' for steering or coordinating national or EU authorities, and we have therefore listed them under a separate heading (see Figure 8.1 and Table 8.1).

During the last few years the Council has adopted an increasing number of texts – 7.7 per cent of the total – which relate to EU external relations in the JHA domain, such as agreements concluded with third countries (for example return agreements or agreements on judicial assistance) and the decisions of the Council regarding negotiating mandates or authoriza-tions. As these are aimed at establishing rules or cooperation objectives between the EU, its member states or agencies on the one hand and third countries on the other, rather than being rules internal to the EU system, they do not fall within our definition of governance. In our statistical analysis they are therefore listed separately under the heading of 'external governance' (see Figure 8.1 and Table 8.1).

The Specific Institutional Dimension of EU Governance in the JHA Domain

The annual lists of texts adopted by the Council cannot fully account for one rather important dimension of the EU governance in the JHA domain: the extensive institutionalization of cooperation and coordination which has emerged since the beginning of the 1990s. Not only has the JHA domain seen the establishment of more than 30 specialized Council committees and working parties within the decision-making hierarchy of the JHA Council and the establishment of two fully-fledged directorates-general in the Council and Commission, but it has also been populated with an increasing number of institutional structures quite specific to this area of EU policy-making.[18] These include the special agencies Europol, Eurojust and Frontex,[19] which all have information exchange and analysis as well as coordination functions, the office of the EU Anti-Terrorism Coordinator in the General Secretariat of the Council, the monitoring centres for drugs[20] and racism and xenophobia[21] – the latter having been transformed since March 2007 into the EU Agency for Fundamental Rights (FRA) – and the European Police College (CEPOL). All these structures contribute to a varying degree to the 'steering and coordination' of the national authorities operating within the AFSJ 'through institution-based internal rules' in the sense of our definition of governance. Although this contribution is of a non-regulatory nature it is nevertheless significant for cooperation and coordination. A few examples will illustrate this.

Through its assessments of serious forms of cross-border crime in the EU as a whole, *Europol* contributes not only to a common assessment of major internal security risks but also to the identification of cross-border crime networks and related targets in several member states. Europol also provides analytical and technical support for coordinated operational activities in response to these targets and contributes to the initiation of joint investigation teams (Europol, 2007b). *Eurojust* not only facilitates the cross-border interaction between national prosecution authorities, but can also request national prosecution authorities to initiate prosecution, coordinate prosecution activities across borders, help avoid conflicts of jurisdiction, push for the setting up of joint investigation teams, identify, facilitate and monitor the application of the European Arrest Warrant, and promote best practices in cooperation between prosecutors.[22] In the case of *Frontex*, the youngest of the EU's special agencies, the coordination role is even more pronounced: on the basis of integrated external border risk assessments and demands formulated by national authorities, Frontex sets up and coordinates joint operations of member states on external border control and security matters and initiates pilot projects on testing new techniques and elements of border management. It also plays an important role in defining common training standards and spreading best practices in external border management (Frontex, 2007). The definition of common training standards and best practices can well be regarded as a kind of target-setting at an operational level. Although the EU *Anti-Terrorism Coordinator*[23] has not been vested with any 'hard' coordination powers, he has played a significant role in the monitoring of the implementation of the EU Action Plan on Combating Terrorism and the identification of weaknesses in both the implementation of the plan and interaction between national authorities.[24] Through training courses aimed at the transfer of advanced policing techniques and best practices, the *European Police College* also contributes to a certain approximation of standards and practices in a cross-border policing context.[25]

All these institutional structures and their respective roles have primarily grown out of the need to create steering and coordination instruments for the strong operational dimension of the JHA domain. Extensive regulatory activity of cross-border cooperation between national law enforcement authorities would not only encounter strong resistance because of the sensitivity of this area from the national sovereignty, territoriality and political points of view, but it would also in many cases not be efficient as in operational cooperation shared best practices, pragmatic cooperation through trusted channels and the common identification of weaknesses and resulting changes to working procedures can often be more effective than inflexible rules imposed by EU legislation. Institutionalized cooperation and coordination can therefore be regarded as an essential instrument of EU governance in the JHA domain.

MAJOR EVOLUTION TRENDS OF EU GOVERNANCE IN THE JHA DOMAIN

Trends in Total Volume of Activity in the JHA Domain

Council activity in terms of numbers of texts adopted has gone through one major cycle in the post-Amsterdam period. As Figure 8.2 shows, overall activity rose steeply from 1999 to 2002 when it reached a peak, which was maintained as regards activity in the tight regulation and target-setting modes in 2003, but dropped in 2004 and even more sharply in 2005, to start rising again in 2006. This curve can mainly be explained by the impact of the end of the five-year transitional period provided for by the Treaty of Amsterdam, which ended on 30 April 2004 and had provided for a whole range of deadlines for adopting certain measures. This deadline was reinforced by the Conclusions of the Tampere European Council of 15 October 1999, which set additional targets to be achieved by the end of the transitional period. There was therefore considerable pressure on the Council and the Commission to adopt a large number of decisions before 30 April 2004, which contributed much to the high output in 2002 and especially 2003, and also contributed a great deal to the high

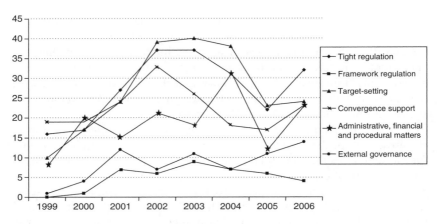

*Figure 8.2   Texts adopted in the JHA area, 1 May 1999–31 December 2006
(post-Amsterdam period): evolution per year, all texts included*

number of administrative, financial and procedural measures which had
to be taken in 2004 in order to fully implement the many decisions taken
during 2002 and 2003. The Tampere European Council Conclusions actually amounted to the first multi-annual programme for the development
of the AFSJ, covering the period of 1999–2004 and being the predecessor
of today's 2005–2010 Hague Programme. Looking at the statistics of the
period 1999–2006, one can draw the conclusion that one of the effects
of multi-annual programming as part of the *target-setting* governance
mode is that output increases with the progress of the programme cycle,
as member states tend to postpone many decisions until deadlines draw
closer. The slightly rising curve of activity in 2006 suggests that the Hague
Programme period will follow the same pattern.

Exogenous factors can also have an impact on governance output in
the JHA domain: the terrorist attacks in New York of 11 September
2001 led during 2001/2002 to the adoption of a whole range of measures
– such as the European Arrest Warrant and the Framework Decision
on Combating Terrorism – which otherwise would probably have been
adopted much later (or even not at all). This contributed to the peak of
regulatory activity reached in 2002.

**Trends in the Overall Use of the Different Modes of Governance in the
JHA Domain**

If we look at the four modes of governance identified above – leaving
aside the administrative and external governance texts – it is clear that

overall the 'softer' legally non-binding governance modes, that is *target-setting* and *convergence support*, exceed by a significant margin of 3.12 to 2.0 (394 to 252 texts) the 'harder' legally binding modes of *tight regulation* and *framework regulation* (see Figure 8.1). As indicated, the absorption of much of the tight regulation activity by technical implementation measures relating to a relatively small number of 'major' measures makes this mode appear slightly more important in the JHA domain than it actually is. Overall the statistical analysis demonstrates the member states' overall preference for 'lighter' forms of governance in this domain, which can be explained primarily by the sensitivity of the JHA policy fields, although the strong operational dimension must also be regarded as a contributory factor.

The continuously high usage of *tight regulation* and *target-setting* instruments contrasts sharply with the constantly rather flat curve of the *framework regulation* mode (see Figure 8.2). It seems that the member states – if they want to give themselves a wider margin of flexibility – greatly prefer a target-setting instrument rather than a framework regulation instrument. This can partly be explained by the fact that many target-setting actions cannot sensibly be transformed into framework regulation instruments. It would make no sense, for instance, to cast multi-annual political programming instruments, such as the action plans, into framework legislation. However, certain Council resolutions, recommendations and conclusions could be developed into framework legislation if the member states were willing to do so. Although this is obviously not spelled out in any official texts, one can safely assume that the reason for them preferring target-setting texts in these cases is that this makes it possible to avoid the more cumbersome legislative process (which would also involve the European Parliament), potential jurisdiction by the Court of Justice and precise commitments regarding potential national implementing legislation which might cause difficulties at the national level.

Another notable trend is the steep increase of the number of texts of the *convergence support* mode up to 2002 and its gradual but clear decrease afterwards (see Figure 8.3). The main explanation for this is the considerable effort made at the beginning of the decade to monitor the progress made by the ten candidate countries in the JHA domain: every accession candidate went through several evaluation phases, and reporting on their progress peaked in 2002 as the final decision whether or not to admit the candidates had to be taken in 2003. This contributed to an exceptionally large number of reports – which we have identified as one of the convergence support instruments – adopted by the Council in 2002, with a corresponding decline afterwards as the pressure generated by the final accession decision decreased.

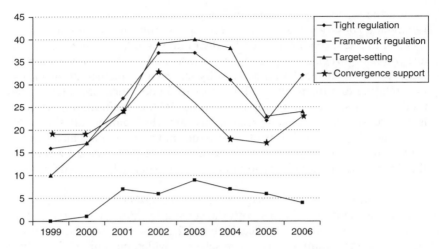

*Figure 8.3   Texts adopted in the JHA area, 1 May 1999–31 December
2006 (post-Amsterdam period): evolution per year under the
four governance modes*

**Trends in the Use of the Different Governance Modes in the Different
Fields of the JHA Domain**

Because of the diversity of the JHA policy fields it is hardly surprising
that trends in the usage of governance instruments vary considerably from
one field to the other. In order to arrive at a clearer picture, we show in
Figure 8.4 on the one hand the texts falling under the *tight regulation* and
framework regulation modes as legally *binding* texts, and on the other those
falling under the *target-setting* and *convergence support* modes as legally
non-binding texts, again leaving aside the administrative and external governance texts. The result shows that within the AFSJ domain the balance
between binding and non-binding measures does indeed vary considerably
from one field to the other. Fields such as visa policy, civil law cooperation, police cooperation, and horizontal issues show differences which are
both significant and revealing.

Visa policy
Here the number of binding texts exceeds the number of non-binding texts
by a ratio of just over 2 to 1 (32 to 15). In visa matters the 'legal constitution' very much determines the 'living constitution' as Article 62(2)(b)
TEC provides for a high degree of harmonization of visa policy as regards
country lists, procedures for issuing visas and the uniform format for

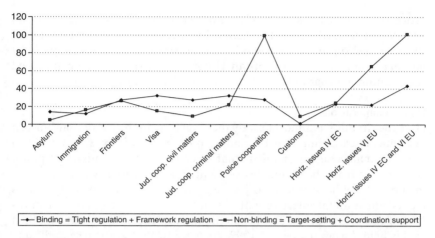

Figure 8.4   Texts adopted in the JHA area, 1 May 1999–31 December 2006 (post-Amsterdam period): numbers of binding and non-binding texts per policy field

visas. Treaty-defined objectives in this field cannot be attained without the use of legislative instruments, so that non-binding instruments are relegated to secondary usage. It should be noted that visa policy is a field of high differentiation as the countries with Schengen opt-outs are not participating in legislative measures in this field, which has made it slightly easier for the Council to use binding instruments in this field.

Civil law cooperation
In this field the number of binding texts exceeds that of non-binding texts by a ratio of 3 to 1 (27 to 9). The main reason for this is that civil law cooperation has always had a close link with the construction and completion of the internal market, where the use of binding instruments is widely accepted as necessary for creating sufficient legal certainty for cross-border economic activities. Long before the introduction of JHA as a formal policy-making domain, important binding texts had already been adopted in the field of civil law, such as the – now transformed – 1968 Brussels Convention on Jurisdiction and the Enforcement of Judgments in Civil and Commercial Matters. One can therefore say that in this field there has been a 'path dependency' of using binding instruments, and that a shift towards non-binding instruments would have run against an established method, an already quite substantial binding *acquis* and the need for legal certainty of economic actors within the internal market, as well as parents and children involved in cross-border divorce and parental responsibility

proceedings. Measures in the civil law field also received a quite distinct orientation towards legislative action by virtue of the 2000 multi-annual 'Programme' on mutual recognition of decisions in civil and commercial matters (Council of the European Union, 2001), so that one can indeed speak about a 'programmed' strong use of binding instruments.

Police cooperation

Here the situation is almost exactly the reverse, with the use of non-binding instruments exceeding that of binding ones by a ratio of 3.5 to 1 (99 to 28). The main reason for this is that, because of the sensitivity of police cooperation from the national sovereignty and territoriality point of view, member states have tended to be highly reluctant to use binding instruments which might interfere with the autonomous control and organization of the police forces. The broad majority of the binding texts adopted in this field during the period 1999–2006 are related to the role and functioning of Europol and the European Police College, institutions which have not substantially changed or interfered with the role of national police forces. Whenever the Council considers it necessary to establish guidelines for cross-border police cooperation, target-setting instruments are preferred.[26] The considerable number of reports drawn up by Europol for the Council – which are classified here under the convergence support mode – also add to the high overall number of non-binding instruments.

Horizontal issues

A significantly higher use of non-binding rather than binding instruments can also be observed in horizontal issues under Title VI TEU – with a ratio of 3 to 1 (68 to 22) – and cross-pillar horizontal objectives which extend to both Title IV TEC and Title VI TEU – with a ratio of 2.3 to 1 (101 to 43). Horizontal issues under Title VI TEU – police and judicial cooperation in criminal matters – concern in most cases general aspects of the fight against certain serious forms of cross-border crime, which often involve questions of strategy and broad coordination for which the use of legislative regulatory instruments would make little sense.[27] Frequent reports on certain forms of crime also contribute to the higher figure of non-binding texts in this horizontal area.

As regards horizontal issues stretching across the Title IV TEC/Title VI TEU divide, the comparatively low number of binding texts can be explained by the fact that the legal divide between the First and the Third Pillar normally requires the use of separate legal instruments for different aspects of the same issue. In the fight against illegal immigration, for instance, First-Pillar legal instruments are required for measures at external borders, whereas Third-Pillar instruments are required for penal law measures against traffickers and facilitators, with the result that the respective measures 'count' under the respective individual policy fields. The comparatively high number of non-binding instruments can be explained by the facts that (a) many of the reports adopted or taken note of by the Council apply to both the Title IV TEC and the Title VI TEU fields – for instance, all evaluation reports on candidate countries – and (b) that many of the target-setting texts, including some of the multi-annual programming documents,[28] have a cross-pillar dimension.

The 'Blurring' of the Pillar Divide

The analysis of the texts adopted in the JHA domain contradicts to some extent the traditional assumption that 'communitarization' tends to lead to a greater use of binding instruments than is normally the case in 'intergovernmental' areas of cooperation. Figure 8.4, however, shows that in one of the 'communitarized' JHA fields of Title IV TEC – immigration – more non-binding than binding instruments have been used, whereas in one of the 'intergovernmental fields' of Title VI TEU – judicial cooperation in criminal matters – more binding than non-binding instruments have come to be applied. Furthermore the communitarized field of external border controls has seen a nearly equal use of both binding and non-binding measures. This points towards a rather pragmatic attitude on the part of the member states: instead of a systematic preference, for instance, in the 'intergovernmental' context of Title VI TEU for non-binding measures, member states are prepared to use binding instruments extensively if they are dealing with a field which, because of the nature of the procedural and substantive issues at stake, requires a high degree of legal regulation – which is certainly the case for judicial cooperation in criminal matters. On the other hand they may use non-binding instruments heavily even in the 'communitarized' context of Title IV TEC if binding instruments appear less appropriate. The higher number of non-binding measures in the field of immigration is a case in point as it results from the reluctance of several member states to accept binding measures on the sensitive issue of legal immigration. In terms of the usage of the different governance modes we can therefore speak of a certain blurring of the much-discussed pillar divide.

The 'Hybridization' of Governance Instruments and the Question of 'New' versus 'Old' Instruments

Contributing to the blurring of the pillar divide is what may be termed the 'hybridization' in the JHA domain of governance instruments traditionally assigned to either the 'Community' or the 'intergovernmental' method. As already indicated, the instruments under Title VI TEU (decisions, framework decisions) introduced by the Amsterdam Treaty are largely similar to the equivalent First-Pillar instruments (regulations, directives) – a notable difference from the instruments of the pre-1999 'old Third Pillar', which were much more in line with classic intergovernmental cooperation.[29] Some of the post-1999 Third-Pillar measures – such as the 2002 framework decisions on the European Arrest Warrant and on Combating Terrorism – have had significant mutual recognition and harmonization effects, governance outcomes which have traditionally been more associated with the Community than with the intergovernmental method. While governance modes in the intergovernmental fields of Title VI TEU have thus become more similar to those used in the First Pillar, there are also some instruments that had initially been used in the Third Pillar, which have now made their appearance in the First-Pillar JHA fields. A key example in this respect is the establishment in 2005 of Frontex as a First-Pillar border management agency with analysis and operation support functions which are in many respects similar to those of Europol as the oldest Third-Pillar agency. In this case a type of governance instrument originally developed in the intergovernmental context of Title VI TEU has been 'copied' (and improved in terms of possibilities for action) in the First Pillar.

As a result of the above, since the entry into force of the Treaty of Amsterdam, governance instruments in the JHA domain have become 'hybrids' as far as the First/Third pillar divide is concerned. While they take different legal forms and have been arrived at under different legal procedures under Title IV TEC and Title VI TEU, they are aimed at generating rather similar governance outcomes in terms of tight or framework regulation, target-setting or convergence support, the use of the different modes depending primarily on field-specific functional and political considerations. This reduces the explanatory value of the pillar and Community/intergovernmental-method divide for the understanding of EU governance in this domain.

The 'hybridization' also makes the distinction between 'old' and 'new' modes of governance difficult to apply. The new legally binding instruments under Title VI TEU, introduced by the Treaty of Amsterdam, were 'new' for the Third-Pillar JHA fields but because of their similarity to traditional First-Pillar instruments they can also be regarded as 'old' instruments from a First-Pillar perspective. The spillover – in the case of Frontex – of the agency type providing operational support from the Third to the First Pillar was in a sense 'new' to the First Pillar but already a comparatively 'old' feature of the Third Pillar. Generally it seems more appropriate to classify the evolution of governance in the JHA domain as one of modification and adaptation of governance instruments, both ways across the pillar divide rather than of the emergence of real 'new' modes.

THE EVALUATION OF EU GOVERNANCE IN THE JHA DOMAIN – AND ITS LIMITS

The evaluation of EU governance in the JHA domain by the EU institutions and governments is primarily – and pragmatically – focused on the question of how well 'it works'. This means asking the question of both its *effectiveness*, that is whether it is successful in producing the intended results, and its *efficiency*, that is whether it is producing these results on the basis of an acceptable cost–benefit ratio.

As regards the question of *effectiveness*, the various scoreboard and evaluation mechanisms put into place suggest a mixed balance sheet. On the one hand – in line with the ambitious Amsterdam and Tampere objectives – there has since 1999 been a massive expansion of EU activity in the JHA domain to nearly all fields and issues of relevance previously not touched upon. Also in some areas – such as mutual recognition in judicial cooperation in criminal matters, and support and coordination of cooperation between law enforcement agencies – innovative and substantial progress has been achieved. On the other hand, some objectives have either not been met – in the field of legal immigration, in particular – or only on the basis of a minimalist approach – in the fields of asylum policy and harmonization of criminal law, for instance. Probably the most problematic aspect on the effectiveness side is the huge deficits on the implementation side, in the form of both delayed and blocked decisions implementing agreed objectives at EU level and failures of the member states to transpose measures at the national level effectively and in time, which is a particular problem in the Third-Pillar fields because of the absence of effective infringement procedures.[30] The extensive use of 'softer' non-legally binding instruments, which has certainly facilitated the huge increase of governance output because of the lower level of constraints it imposes on member states, is obviously not helping with implementation discipline. It must be said, however, that EU implementation monitoring has so far focused on formal transposition of legal measures – which does not take into account the effects of 'soft governance' measures such as guidelines, recommendations and best practice transfers. In June 2006 the Commission proposed a new system of in-depth impact assessment of JHA policies based on an evaluation of the effects of all measures at the national level (European Commission, 2006). It is currently being implemented and could allow for a better assessment of the overall effectiveness of EU governance in this domain.

As regards the issue of *efficiency* it is much more difficult to arrive at a sensible assessment because of the absence of clear objective criteria and means of comparison. Those, for instance, who criticize the proliferation of groups and committees in the JHA domain as excessive[31] may have a point in regarding this as an efficiency problem. Yet this immediately raises the question of how one assesses efficiency in a complex policy-making domain such as EU JHA where it is methodologically extremely difficult to make meaningful direct efficiency comparisons with other EU policy-making areas – which all have their fair share of proliferation of structures – and even more so with national policy-making contexts.

Legitimacy must be regarded as an additional evaluation criterion of particular importance in the JHA governance domain because of the particular sensitivity of JHA measures from a fundamental rights and civil liberties perspective. As at the national level, adequate *democratic accountability* through parliamentary control as well as adequate *judicial control* can be regarded as crucial elements of such legitimacy.

As regards the latter, the judicial review procedures introduced by the Treaty of Amsterdam have removed most, if not all, of the judicial review deficits of the 'old Third Pillar'. With the ECJ having repeatedly asserted its competence to review JHA legal acts across the pillar divide in spite of persisting restrictions on its role under Title VI TEU on grounds of rule of law and legal coherence considerations,[32] the legitimacy of EU governance in the JHA domain can no longer be questioned on grounds of judicial review deficits.

Yet the picture is different on the parliamentary control side as the absence of co-decision rights of the European Parliament in the Third-Pillar fields – which are particularly sensitive from the point of view of the rights of individuals – constitutes a real deficit of the democratic control of collective decision-making in the Council. This deficit cannot be compensated for by the national parliaments which, at best, can exercise such control over their ministers. This deficit in democratic accountability is exacerbated by the extensive use of target-setting and convergence support instruments which fall outside parliamentary control rights under legislative procedures. The multi-annual programming texts, for instance, which have a decisive impact on overall strategy, the timetabling of measures and the form they will take do not need the European Parliament's approval. National parliaments fare no better as they tend to be informed only after negotiations in the Council have already been completed – even in the case of a major strategic programme like the Hague Programme.[33] The new Lisbon Treaty[34] retains the extension of the co-decision procedure provided for by the original Constitutional Treaty, so that the deficit in legislative control by the EP is likely to be removed. Yet this does not have an immediate impact on the non-binding governance modes, so that in this respect – for the sake of the legitimacy of EU governance in the JHA domain – the 'legal constitution' will have to be complemented by an improved democratic culture in the 'living constitution'.

NOTES

*   This chapter was completed in 2007.
1. The author thanks Anya Dahmani, NEWGOV Research Associate at the Université Robert Schuman in Strasbourg, for her excellent work on the statistics and tables of this chapter.
2. The consultation of interest groups carried out by the Commission in certain fields, especially asylum and immigration, and the frequent criticisms raised by civil liberties organizations, such as Statewatch, may have an occasional impact on the content of Commission proposals, but there is as yet no evidence that they have any decisive influence on overall governance and the modes of governance in this area.
3. On the national sovereignty issue in the context of the AFSJ see Barbe (2002: 23).
4. The term 'integration' is used here along the lines of the definition of economic integration developed in Belassa (1961) with the very basic meaning of a process leading to the creation of single new system through the merging of several separately existing ones, as opposed to 'cooperation' as a process where these systems interact but remain essentially separate.
5. On this growth of diversity and differentiation see Müller (2003).
6. These are the 'old' 13 Schengen member states without Denmark which, because of its Amsterdam 'opt-out' protocol, enjoys a special status.
7. Mainly qualified majority under Title IV TEC and unanimity under Title VI TEU.
8. Article 34 TEU decisions can also be used to establish or change institutional structures of the AFSJ. A major example is the Council Decision of 28 February 2002 setting up Eurojust, OJ L63, 6 March 2002 (Council of the European Union, 2002a).
9. Examples are the Council decisions 2005/451/JHA of 13 June 2005 and 2005/719/JHA, 2005/727/JHA and 2005/728/JHA of 12 October 2005 concerning the introduction of some new functions for the Schengen Information System: OJ L158, 21 June 2005, L271, 15 October 2005 and L273, 19 October 2005 (Council of the European Union, 2005b, 2005d, 2005e, 2005f).
10. Although this has been slightly nuanced by the 2005 judgment of the ECJ in the *Pupino* case (Case C-105/03 *Pupino* ECR-I-5285) (European Court of Justice, 2003).
11. A recent example is the Council Directive on minimum standards on procedures in member states for granting and withdrawing refugee status: OJ L326, 13 December 2005 (Council of the European Union, 2005h).
12. A major example is the June 2002 Framework Decision on combating terrorism: OJ L164, 22 June 2002 (Council of the European Union, 2002b).
13. We come back to this in the section titled 'Trends in total volume of activity in the JHA domain' below.
14. A good summary of the collective evaluation process and its reporting mechanisms is given in Council of the European Union (2006b).
15. For a rare (and not completely declassified) example, see Council of the European Union, 'Evaluation of the third round of mutual evaluations – report on Spain', Council document 1410/05, 19 April 2006 (Council of the European Union, 2006a).
16. For example the annual Europol threat assessment report on organized crime (OCTA) which exists in a full version, which is classified, and an abridged version, which is public (see Europol, 2007a).

17. Examples of these are the regular reports of the EU Anti-Terrorism Coordinator on the implementation of the EU Action Plan to Combat Terrorism, which each time identifies major deficits in the implementation of legislative acts, in information supply and in coordination. See, for instance, Council document 15266/1/06, 24 November 2006 (Council of the European Union, 2006c).
18. For the main elements of this institutionalization process see Monar (2002).
19. The EU Agency for the Management of Operational Cooperation at the External Borders which was established in Warsaw in June 2005.
20. European Monitoring Centre for Drugs and Drug Addiction (EMCDDA), Lisbon.
21. European Monitoring Centre on Racism and Xenophobia (EUMC), Vienna.
22. Examples are given in Eurojust (2007).
23. The office is currently vacant and has been since March 2007 after the departure of Mr Gijs de Vries.
24. See, for example, the Coordinator's report of November 2006, Council document 15266/1/06, 24 November 2006 (Council of the European Union, 2006c).
25. For examples, see the 2007 list of courses and seminars organized by CEPOL, available at http://www.cepol.net/KIM/plaatjes/pictemp185162.pdf.
26. Good examples are the Council Conclusions on police professional standards concerning international police cooperation (Council document 14633/04) and the Council recommendation concerning the reinforcing of police cooperation especially in the areas surrounding the internal borders of the EU (Council document 15105/04), both adopted on 2 December 2004 (Council of the European Union, 2004c, 2004d).
27. Examples are the Council Conclusions on the fight against organized crime originating from the Western Balkans (Council document 14703/04 adopted on 19 November 2004) and the Council Conclusions on the development of a strategic concept with regard to tackling cross-border organized crime in the EU (Council document 15050/04, adopted on 2 December 2004) (Council of the European Union, 2004b, 2004e).
28. A recent example is the 2005–2008 EU Action Plan on Drugs, OJ C168, 8 July 2005 (Council of the European Union, 2005c).
29. On the 'old' Third-Pillar instruments see Peers (2006: 13–17).
30. For an official analysis and relevant detail see the latest Commission report on the implementation of the Hague Programme during 2006, COM(2007) 373, 3 July 2007 (European Commission, 2007).
31. See, for instance, the remarks of Lord Wright of Richmond, Chairman of the House of Lords Subcommittee dealing with EU JHA, on the proliferation of EU structures in the anti-terrorism field in the House of Lords debate of 20 June 2005 (Lord Wright of Richmond, 2005).
32. Most recently in cases C-354/04 P, *Gestoras pro Amnestia* [2007], and C-355/04 P, *Segi* [2007], judgments of 27 February 2007, both not yet reported (European Court of Justice, 2007a, 2007b). For a general analysis of the Court's self-assertion in this respect see Hatzopoulos (2007).
33. The British Houses of Parliament, for instance, only received a note from their government on the content of the Hague Programme in November 2004 on the very day that the European Council was to approve it. House of Lords, Select Committee on the European Union (2005, paragraphs 2–4).
34. Amending the Treaty on European Union and the Treaty establishing the European Community, signed at Lisbon, 13 December 2007, OJ C 306 (Official Journal of the European Union, 2007).

REFERENCES

Barbe, Emmanuel (2002), *Justice et Affaires Intérieures dans l'Union Européenne*, Paris: La Documentation Française.
Belassa, Bela (1961), 'Towards a theory of economic integration', *Kyklos*, **14**(1), 1–17.
Benz, Arthur (2003), 'Governance: Modebegriff oder nützliches sozialwissenschaftliches Konzept?', in Arthur Benz (ed.), *Governance: Regieren in komplexen Regelsystemen. Eine Einführung*, Wiesbaden: VS Verlag, pp. 13–32.
Council of the European Union (1995), 'Convention based on Article K.3 of the Treaty on European Union, on the establishment of a European Police Office (Europol Convention)', Official Journal, C 316, 27 November.
Council of the European Union (2000), 'Communication by the Secretary-General of the European Union under Article 30(2) of the Convention, established by the Council in accordance with Article 34 of the Treaty on European Union, on Mutual Assistance in Criminal Matters between the Member States of the European Union', Official Journal, C 197, 12 July.
Council of the European Union (2001), Draft programme of measures for implementation of the principle of mutual recognition of decisions in civil and commercial matters, Official Journal, C 12, 15 January.
Council of the European Union (2002a), 'Council Decision of 28 February 2002 setting up Eurojust with a view to reinforcing the fight against serious crime', Official Journal, L 63, 6 March.
Council of the European Union (2002b), 'Council Framework Decision of 13 June 2002 on combating terrorism', Official Journal, L 164, 13 June.
Council of the European Union (2002c), 'Plan for the management of the external borders of the Member States of the European Union', Official Journal, 10019/02, 14 June.
Council of the European Union (2004a), 'Council Recommendation of 30 March 2004 regarding guidelines for taking samples of seized drugs', Official Journal, C 86, 6 April.
Council of the European Union (2004b), 'Council Conclusions on the fight against organized crime originating from the Western Balkans', Official Journal, 14703/04, 19 November.
Council of the European Union (2004c), 'Council Conclusions on police professional standards concerning international police cooperation', Official Journal, 14633/04, 2 December.
Council of the European Union (2004d), 'Council recommendation concerning the reinforcing of police cooperation especially in the areas surrounding the internal borders of the EU', Official Journal, 15105/04, 2 December.
Council of the European Union (2004e), 'Council Conclusions on the development of a strategic concept with regard to tackling cross-border organized crime in the EU', Official Journal, 15050/04, 2 December.
Council of the European Union (2005a), 'The Hague Programme: strengthening freedom, security and justice in the European Union', Official Journal, C 53, 3 March.
Council of the European Union (2005b), 'Council Decision 2005/451/JHA of 13 June 2005 fixing the date of application of certain provisions of Regulation (EC) No 871/2004 concerning the introduction of some new functions for the

Schengen Information System, including in the fight against terrorism', Official Journal, L 158, 13 June.

Council of the European Union (2005c), 'EU Drugs Action Plan (2005–2008)', Official Journal, C 168, 8 July.

Council of the European Union (2005d), 'Council Decision 2005/719/JHA of 12 October 2005 fixing the date of application of certain provisions of Decision 2005/211/JHA concerning the introduction of some new functions for the Schengen Information System, including in the fight against terrorism', Official Journal, L 271, 12 October.

Council of the European Union (2005e), 'Council Decision 2005/727/JHA of 12 October 2005 fixing the date of application of certain provisions of Decision 2005/211/JHA concerning the introduction of some new functions for the Schengen Information System, including in the fight against terrorism', Official Journal, L 273, 12 October.

Council of the European Union (2005f), 'Council Decision 2005/728/JHA of 12 October 2005 fixing the date of application of certain provisions of Decision 2005/211/JHA concerning the introduction of some new functions for the Schengen Information System, including in the fight against terrorism', Official Journal, L 273, 12 October.

Council of the European Union (2005g), 'EU plan on best practices, standards and procedures for combating and preventing trafficking in human beings', Official Journal, C 311, 9 December.

Council of the European Union (2005h), 'Council Directive 2005/85/EC of 1 December 2005 on minimum standards on procedures in Member States for granting and withdrawing refugee status', Official Journal, L 326, 13 December.

Council of the European Union (2006a), 'Evaluation of the third round of mutual evaluations: report on Spain', Official Journal, 1410/05, 19 April.

Council of the European Union (2006b), 'Enlargement: statement by the Collective Evaluation Group', Official Journal, 14264/2/03, 11 May.

Council of the European Union (2006c), 'Implementation of the Strategy and Action Plan to Combat Terrorism', Official Journal, 15266/1/06, 24 November.

Council of the European Union (2007), 'EU Action Plan on combating terrorism (update)', Official Journal, 7233/07, 9 March.

de Lobkowicz, Wenceslas (2002), *L'Europe de la Sécurité Intérieure': Une Élaboration par Étapes*, Paris: La Documentation Française.

Eurojust (2007), *Annual Report 2006*, The Hague.

European Commission (2006), 'Communication from the Commission to the Council and the European Parliament: Evaluation of EU Policies on Freedom, Security and Justice', COM (2006) 332, 28 June, Brussels.

European Commission (2007), 'Communication from the Commission to the Council and the European Parliament: Report on the implementation of The Hague Programme for 2006', COM (2007) 373, 3 July, Brussels.

European Court of Justice (2003), 'Criminal proceedings against Maria Pupino', Case C-105/03, Luxembourg.

European Court of Justice (2007a), 'Judgment of the Court (Grand Chamber) of 27 February 2007: Gestoras Pro Amnistía, Juan Mari Olano Olano, Julen Zelarain Errasti v Council of the European Union, Kingdom of Spain, United Kingdom of Great Britain and Northern Ireland', Case C-354/04, Luxembourg.

European Court of Justice (2007b), 'Judgment of the Court (Grand Chamber) of 27 February 2007: Segi, Araitz Zubimendi Izaga, Aritza Galagara v Council of the European Union, Kingdom of Spain, Kingdom of Great Britain and Northern Ireland', Case C-355/04, Luxembourg.

Europol (2007a), 'EU organised crime threat assessment 2007 (OCTA)', June, The Hague.

Europol (2007b), *Annual Report 2006*, The Hague.

Frontex (2007), *Annual Report 2006*, Warsaw.

Hatzopoulos, Vassilis (2007), 'With or without you . . . judging politically in the field of area of freedom, security and justice?', *College of Europe Research Papers in Law*, 3 (2007), Bruges: College of Europe.

Héritier, Adrienne Windhoff- (1987), *Policy Analyse. Eine Einführung*, Frankfurt and New York: Campus.

Héritier, Adrienne (2002), 'New modes of governance in Europe: policy-making without legislating?', Working Paper no. 81 of the Political Science Series, Vienna: Institut für Höhere Studien, available at http://www.ihs.ac.at/publications/pol/pw_81.pdf.

House of Lords, Select Committee on the European Union (2005), 'The Hague Programme: A Five Year Agenda for EU Justice and Home Affairs', Session 2004/2005, Tenth Report, London: The Stationery Office.

Knill, Christoph and Andrea Lenschow (eds) (2000), *Implementing EU Environmental Policy: New Directions and Old Problems*, Manchester: Manchester University Press.

Lord Wright of Richmond, Chairman of the House of Lords Subcommittee dealing with EU JHA (2005), 'Remarks on the proliferation of EU structures in the anti-terrorism field in the House of Lords debate of 20 June', in *Hansard*, (672) 18, column 1435.

Monar, Jörg (2002), 'Institutionalising freedom, security and justice', in John Peterson and Michael Shackleton (eds), *The Institutions of the European Union*, Oxford: Oxford University Press, pp. 186–209.

Müller, Thorsten (2003), *Die Innen- und Justizpolitik der Europäischen Union*, Opladen: Leske & Budrich.

Official Journal of the European Union (2007), 'Treaty of Lisbon amending the Treaty on European Union and the Treaty establishing the European Community, signed at Lisbon, 13 December 2007', C 306.

Peers, Steve (2006), *EU Justice and Home Affairs Law*, 2nd edn, Oxford: Oxford University Press.

Treib, Oliver, Holger Bähr and Gerda Falkner (2005), 'Modes of governance: a note towards conceptual clarification', European Governance Papers, no. N-O5-02, Mannheim (EUROGOV), available at http://www.connex-network.org/eurogov/pdf/egp-newgov-N-05-02.pdf.

9. New modes of governance: perspectives from the legal and the living architecture of the European Union

Udo Diedrichs

A FRAMEWORK FOR ANALYSIS

Modes of Governance in the EU: Dynamics and Change

The analysis and discussion of modes of governance in the European Union (EU) is one of the most exciting and fascinating issues of relevance for the academic as well as the political world (Tömmel, 2007; Kohler-Koch and Rittberger, 2006; Schuppert, 2005; Jachtenfuchs, 2001). Although there are some variations of detail in the consensus on how to define modes of governance, it still appears useful to start from the 'classical' triple set of hierarchy, negotiation and competition as ideal-type basic models which help us to structure our research (Börzel et al., 2008: 63).

With regard to the EU, these basic models have to be refined and differentiated in order to account for the specific features of the integration process and its systemic configurations. While Tanja Börzel regards hierarchy, negotiation systems and competition as useful models for categorizing EU governance modes more specifically (Börzel, 2007: 69), Bähr et al. (2007) prefer the triad of market, network and hierarchy as fundamental categorizations, with different implications for EU governance. Ingeborg Tömmel (2007) deviates from this triple set and introduces the model of cooperation into the definition of EU governance modes, referring to the voluntary adaptation by actors towards common goals and norms, which are specifically, though not exclusively, relevant to the debate on new modes of governance (Tömmel, 2007: 28).

These categories may serve as a useful starting point, but they need to be further specified and adjusted; modes of EU governance are emerging and evolving in a particular context which is marked by the legal and the living architecture of the EU and which provides opportunities and constraints for the use of specific forms of decision-making. Therefore, after defining a categorization of EU modes of governance, I will investigate the context of the new EU Treaty law and how far these provisions can be used for assessing the framework and context in which governing modes are embedded and in which they develop.

EU Modes of Governance: Proposal for a Categorization

I apply a categorization which divides modes of governance in the EU into four main categories, described as hierarchy, negotiation, coordination and competition (see Table 9.1). At the same time, I consider the space between the poles of hierarchy and competition as a field of dynamic interaction (Börzel, 2007), in the sense that the transition from hierarchy to less hierarchical forms takes place in steps and stages which make it rather difficult to delineate an exact frontier, but which is characterized as sometimes fuzzy and mixed.

To distinguish these categories, three key indicators are used:

- the level of competence (ranging from exclusive EU competence to 'purely' national competence);
- the decision-making procedures regarded from an intra-institutional (majority voting versus unanimity) and interinstitutional (involving different models of interaction between the Council, the European Parliament and the Commission) perspective;
- the nature of the legal output (between binding and non-binding (soft) legal acts).

Two extreme poles thus become visible which may not find rich empirical evidence, but will serve as points of orientation: on the one side of the spectrum is the highly hierarchical, supranationally centralized mode which is characterized by an exclusive EU competence, leaving little choice or voice to the member states, where decisions on legally binding instruments are taken unilaterally by a supranational institution using majority voting (Börzel, 2007). On the other side of the spectrum, we see areas where the EU has no formal or informal competence, where nation states would not even coordinate their positions, while any kind of formal or informal decision-making on the adoption of joint instruments is excluded.

New modes of governance emerge in this context if and when there are changes in the constellation of the different categories over time, for example in the sense of an increasing 'hierarchization', or trends towards more mixed forms of governance where one mode is combined with

Table 9.1   Modes of governance in the European Union: forms and features

Basic models	Hierarchy	Negotiations		Coordination	Competition
EU modes of governance	Supranational centralization	Supranational decision-making	Joint decision-making	Trans-/inter-governmental governance	(Open) Method of Coordination	System competition
Level of EU competence	Exclusive EU competence	Exclusive or shared EU competence	Exclusive, shared EU competence, coordination or supporting EU activities	Shared EU competence, coordinating and supporting activities	No or weak EU competence	National competence
Decision-making provisions	Unilateral decisions by supranational institutions	Co-decision/ OLP majority Council	Mixed combinations of voting in Council and EP participation	Consensus/ unanimity in Council/ European Council	Voluntary adaptation member states	No common decision-making
Legal instrument	Binding acts	Binding legislation (directives, regulations, laws)	Binding and non-binding legal acts	Non-binding legal acts and acts with limited bindingness; no judicial review	Non-binding commitments	Voluntarism no instruments
		Community Method				

Decrease in hierarchy

Note: OLP = ordinary legislative procedure.

Source: Own findings by author.

212

others. These changes may take place on the level of EU Treaty provisions (legal architecture) or in the use of such provisions by EU institutions and member states (living architecture). The analysis presented here therefore does not try to apply an exhaustive definition of governing modes, but will look at key developments and trends of the EU system and assess their importance. The results may serve as a basis and a background for more refined investigations of and within particular policy areas of the European Union.

Hierarchy exists when we observe an asymmetrical constellation of actors, in the sense that decisions may be taken by an institutional player that does not formally come under another, as is the case when the Commission takes autonomous decisions in trade or competition policy (for example state aid, mergers), or when the Court of Justice decides finally and without any further resort for the parties involved. Exclusive competence in this context does not refer only to the new provisions of the Lisbon Treaty (Art. 2 and 3 TFEU), but in a more specific way to any sphere where de facto or de jure decisions or actions by the member states are precluded by the European Union.

Negotiations imply an exchange among actors endowed with capacities for veto that require them to compromise with other veto players, driven by the search for common solutions. Here, the picture is more fragmented. The ordinary legislative procedure (OLP) as introduced in the Lisbon Treaty (Art. 294 TFEU) provides for majority voting in the Council, while the European Parliament (EP) adopts decisions by a majority of votes cast or of component members, which represents a rather high degree of hierarchy as in both institutions minorities are forced to accept a decision, while their interaction is guided by negotiation in which both sides have to agree, and thus act as veto players. Nor should the role of the Commission be forgotten: on the one hand it holds the legal initiative, while on the other it may impose unanimity upon the Council if it deviates from the Commission position at the second reading (Art. 294 (9) TFEU). The institutional triangle is thus characterized by a process of negotiations between the Council, the EP and the Commission, with a high degree of hierarchical elements within each of these institutions that may be described as *supranational decision-making*.

Still, the ordinary legislative procedure is far from being the only procedural variant (Wessels, 2005a; 2005b). In a number of cases the Council may act by unanimity or by majority coupled with no EP participation, or with the mere communication of information to or consultation of the Parliament, while in other cases consent by the Parliament is coupled with unanimity or majority voting in the Council. These variants hint at highly mixed *forms of joint decision-making*, where hierarchy is combined with elements of trans- or intergovernmental negotiations, making it difficult to locate its precise place on the map of governing modes.

The picture becomes easier to assess when we turn to *inter- or transgovernmental negotiations* with limited influence from the Parliament and the Commission, as is the case in the Common Foreign and Security Policy (CFSP)/European Security and Defence Policy (ESDP) or in particular areas of police and judicial cooperation in criminal matters. Here, the European Council, the Council and member states dominate the decision-making process, while at the same time processes of socialization, Europeanization and 'Brusselization' are at work, hinting at 'soft' ways of forging common understandings, procedural routines and an emergent common identity which goes well beyond the features of a purely intergovernmental bargaining system (Diedrichs, 2007). The increasingly important role of the High Representative for Foreign Affairs and Security Policy or of special representatives may be described as a process of institutional pooling and delegation, within the limits of the Council's guidelines. Within the area of the ESDP in particular, emergent and cautious elements of coordination and competition among member states' procurement systems have been triggered off, thus revealing different modes within this area (Diedrichs, 2007). In the budgetary field, decisions resemble a mixed negotiation system much more than a clear-cut intergovernmental set-up, as the EP has an important say.

Coordination plays a prominent role when it comes to the debate on new modes of governance, and has been praised as an innovative model for dealing with policy problems beyond any supranational methodology. The Open Method of Coordination (OMC) may be the most prominent case here, reflecting not so much a process of negotiation among the actors, but rather a process of constant adaptation, benchmarking and reporting driven by the attraction of best practice, and by the fear of naming and shaming. This process is not characterized by efforts to arrive at common decisions but rather at adjustments by and in the member states.

The Lisbon Treaty refers to this method in a particular category of competences. Art. 2 (3) TFEU stipulates that '(t)he Member States shall coordinate their economic and employment policies within arrangements as determined by this Treaty, which the Union shall have competence to provide'. As laid down in Art. 5 TFEU, the main instrument for the coordination of economic and employment policies shall consist of (broad) guidelines and initiatives to ensure coordination. Furthermore, Art. 2 (5) TFEU provides that '[i]n certain areas and under the conditions laid down in the Treaties, the Union shall have competence to carry out actions to support, coordinate or supplement the actions of the Member States, without thereby superseding their competence in these areas'. It is also stipulated that no harmonization of member states' laws or regulations shall be implied by legal acts in that area (Art. 2 (5), sentence II, TFEU). Coordination has thus been upgraded to a particular sphere of action according to the treaty, demarcating it basically from exclusive and shared competences and thereby indicating that the member states' sphere of autonomy shall be fundamentally respected.

Competition is not a particular mode of EU governance as such, but should be seen as a conditioning factor for driving and shaping the emergence and evolution of EU governance. It refers to the process by which international pressure can be imposed on national governments to adjust and reform traditional institutional and/or policy structures in crucial areas – such as social security, educational or tax systems – which are core competences of the member states and where there is no EU regulatory power in place. Competition may lead to a call for 'European solutions' in an attempt to avoid unilateral adaptation by establishing common rules. Thus, the shadow of competition may be regarded as a powerful factor encouraging the establishment of EU-wide procedures and institutions.

Starting from this categorization, I will now turn to the analysis of the legal and the living architecture of the EU in order to find out in which way the institutional and procedural space for modes of governance has undergone changes and shifts. Thus, when trying to assess the question of new modes of governance, the perspective should be focused upon the dynamics of the evolution of the EU system which opens possibilities and imposes constraints upon the emergence and evolution of governing modes.

New and Old Modes of Governance: The Dynamics of Change

Modes of governance having been categorized in the way described, the question of how to assess new and old modes of governance becomes urgent. Basically, new modes of governance may be described as specific *single models* of decision-making whose emergence as such provides sufficient proof of change. However, change and transformation may also be grasped in more complex and multi-dimensional directions. New modes of governance may be defined as a code for a transformation of the dominant model of decision-making in a given EU policy area, within one or several dimensions related to the composition of the actors, the principles of interaction or the instrumental features. It may thus imply the rise of private actors or regulatory agencies as key players in a policy field, but it may also hint at a shift from non-hierarchical to more hierarchical modes of interaction between the same players, or at the adoption of new policy instruments in an area, for example, from soft to hard law or vice versa, so that key features of governance are redefined as durable patterns that are resistant to ad hoc pressures over time. This definition also reveals that new modes of EU governance are much less an overall, cross-sector and uniform phenomenon, but have to be analysed in a policy-specific and time-dynamic perspective. Private actors may represent an innovative element in one policy area, but not in another with different traditions and constellations. Soft law may be rather familiar in one area, but exceptional in another.

As already noticed, modes of governance may be found not in a pure and isolated form, but instead in mixed compositions, and this is even more true for changes of such modes. Thus, new modes of governance, when and if they emerge, will probably reveal features of 'new' and 'old' in a mixed proportion and in comparatively swiftly changing composition. Thus, it becomes crucial to identify such phases of emergence and define their particular features.

ASSESSING THE DYNAMICS: THE LEGAL AND THE LIVING ARCHITECTURE OF THE EU

Modes of Governance in the Legal and the Living Architecture of the EU

I focus upon the legal and living architecture of the EU in order to assess its impact on the emergence and evolution of modes of governance. Primary law provisions (the legal architecture) offer constraints and opportunities for the adoption of different ways in which institutional actors, private and public, interact in order to arrive at decisions (the living architecture) on the adoption of instruments. From the Single European Act (SEA, 1986) until the adoption of the Lisbon Treaty (2007), the EU was subject to two decades of reform entailing substantial adjustments to its institutional and procedural set-up. Ever since the evolution of the EU system has revealed signs of differentiation and expansion, in terms of decision-making capacities.

The legal and the living architecture of the EU are closely interrelated in a feedback process which defines the major institutional and procedural provisions for decision-making, and thus for modes of governance (see Chapter 1 by Diedrichs, Reiners and Wessels). Treaty changes since the 1980s have been inspired and driven by the experience gained with and conclusions drawn from implementing the existing legal base, while the adoption of a new legal base has injected new dynamics into the use of the treaties. Modes of governance emerge and evolve in this field of tension, defined by the provisions of the treaty base and its translation into political reality. They may even find expression in the wording of the treaties, as they do with the inclusion of 'coordination in economic and employment policies' within the Lisbon Treaty (Art. 2 (3) TFEU). Thus, the development of the EU system, regarding its major institutional features, the decision-making rules and the distribution of competences, constitute major conditioning factors in the development of the EU's living architecture that has to be taken into account.

The Legal Architecture of the EU: The Lisbon Treaty in Perspective

The Lisbon Treaty has substantially adjusted and reformed the institutional and procedural landscape of the EU, without shaping a fully consistent and transparent legal order. Its provisions do, however, reflect a number of trends and tendencies which are of importance for the assessment of the EU's modes of governance.

EP participation in legislation has been strengthened by extending the OLP to new cases and policy areas, applicable also in areas such as asylum and migration, thus fostering the emergence of bicameral legislature consisting of the Council and the EP. The increase in the co-decision/ordinary legislative procedure has been the most dynamic compared to any other form of participation by the EP from 1958 to the coming into force of the Lisbon Treaty. At the same time, it also becomes evident that other decision-making provisions have not disappeared, but have also either steadily increased or decreased recently, such as 'no participation', consultation or cooperation (which was entirely abolished). Figure 9.1 contains a comparison of treaty provisions on decision-making procedures over that period.

While increased parliamentary rights for participation appear as the form of decision-making that is developing most, with clear potential for hierarchical modes of governance, it also becomes evident that it is far from being the dominant procedure. Taken together, the two strong parliamentary procedures providing the EP with a veto capacity (co-decision/ OLP and consent) are still outnumbered by cases of no or weak parliamentary participation under the Lisbon Treaty. In the Nice and previous treaties, this ratio is still higher: here, the weak procedures outnumber the strong ones by far. Figure 9.2 draws together the treaty provisions on decision-making procedures, dividing them into weak and the strong parliamentary procedures in order to describe their proportions.

Based upon these figures, Figure 9.3 shows the ratio between strong and weak procedures on parliamentary participation.

Starting from extremely low values, the ratio reaches almost 0.7 with the Lisbon Treaty, thus still far from a balanced relation in quantitative

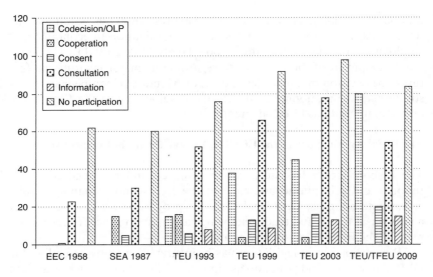

Source: Hofmann and Wessels (2008).

*Figure 9.1   Treaty provisions on the participation of the EP, 1958–2009:
absolute numbers of provisions*

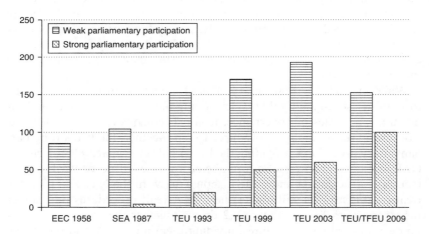

Source: Adaptation from Hofmann and Wessels (2008).

*Figure 9.2   Strong versus weak EP participation in EU decision-making
as specified in the treaties, 1958–2009: absolute numbers of
provisions*

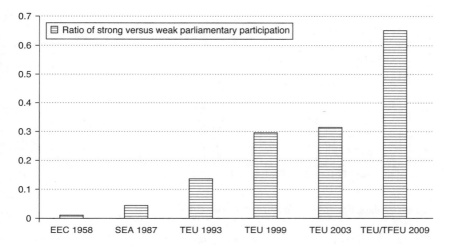

Source: Calculations based on Figure 9.2.

Figure 9.3   *The ratio between strong and weak parliamentary participation procedures as based in the treaties, 1958–2009*

terms between provisions on strong and weak EP participation. The trend of growing parliamentary participation as taken from the treaty provisions becomes obvious, although the existing cases indicate that most provisions still do not allow the EP to play the role of a veto player. From these figures, the picture appears to be mixed. Thus, while the European Parliament has gained more new powers, they do not dominate the legal architecture of the Union. Hierarchical elements in decision-making have gained ground, while not reaching out – as far as the EP is concerned – to all cases of decision-making.

As far as the Council is concerned, it is of particular interest to analyse the legal provisions on the use of qualified majority voting (QMV) (see Figure 9.4).

There is a clearly visible tendency which hints at an steady increase of treaty provisions on QMV since 1958, so that during the last 50 years the opportunities for the use of majority voting – and thus a hierarchical voting procedure – in the Council have been increasing. At the same time, the number of cases where a special QMV (lifting the requirements for majorities and thus less hierarchical than 'ordinary' QMV) is applied, has also shown sharp growth, though on a much lower quantitative level. The treaty provisions on unanimity reached a peak with the Amsterdam Treaty, while simple majority voting remains on a generally stable, though low,

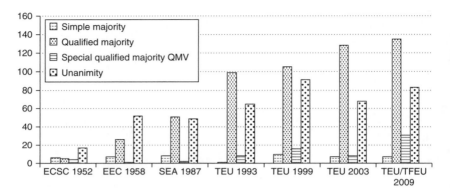

Source: Adaptation from Hofmann and Wessels (2008).

Figure 9.4   Treaty provisions on voting modalities in the Council, 1958–
            2009: absolute numbers of provisions

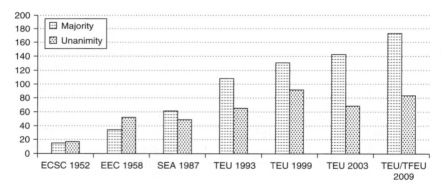

Source: Calculations based on Figure 9.4.

Figure 9.5   Treaty provisions on majority voting and on unanimity in the
            Council, 1958–2009: absolute numbers of provisions

level. Taken together, the provisions on majority voting (simple, qualified, special qualified) outnumber those on unanimity, as Figure 9.5 shows.

The ratio between provisions on majority voting and unanimity in the Council have developed in a dynamic way in favour of the former, reaching around 2:1 for the Lisbon Treaty (see Figure 9.6).

The data presented so far suggest that in both the EP and the Council dynamic change has been at work, giving more weight to decision-making

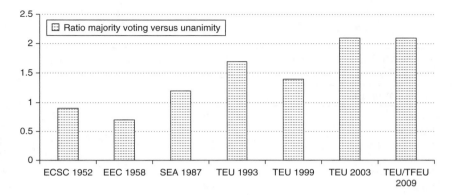

Source: Calculations based on Figure 9.5.

Figure 9.6   *The ratio between treaty provisions on majority voting and unanimity in the Council, 1958–2009*

procedures that enhance parliamentary participation – without these becoming the dominant procedural variant – while, in parallel, majority voting in the Council is evolving as the dominant voting modality.

It is particularly helpful at this point to investigate the interrelation of EP participation and Council voting modalities in order to assess the opportunities for and constraints upon the emergence and evolution of particular modes of governance in the two organs.

Table 9.2 provides an overview of different combinations of these elements in the Lisbon Treaty.

Under the Nice Treaty, the picture looked different (see Table 9.3). In particular, the disappearance of the cooperation procedure reduced the number of combinations.

These data seem to indicate that there is no clear relationship between voting procedures in the Council and parliamentary participation, but a rather multifaceted picture prevails. Taking up the modes of governance from Table 9.1, supranational decision-making (consent combined with majority voting and co-decision/OLP combined with majority voting) is of less quantitative importance than forms of joint decision-making. The trans-/intergovernmental form, where weak or non-existent formal parliamentary participation is coupled with unanimity voting in the Council, plays a less important role under the Lisbon Treaty. In Figure 9.7, the combinations are ordered according to their level or hierarchy: three groups of combinations are established. The first contains those combinations which link a weak or non-participation of the EP with unanimity in

Table 9.2   Combination of EP and Council modes of decision-making specified in the Lisbon Treaty

Voting Modality Council	Simple majority	Qualified majority	Unanimity	**Sum**
Participation EP				
OLP	0	80	0	**80**
Consent	1	5	14	**20**
Consultation	2	21	31	**54**
Information	0	14	4	**18**
No participation	4	48	34	**86**
Sum	**7**	**168**	**83**	**258**

Source: Adapted and updated from Hofmann and Wessels (2008).

Table 9.3   Combination of EP and Council modes of decision-making specified in the Nice Treaty

Voting Modality Council	Simple majority	Qualified majority	Unanimity	**Sum**
Participation EP				
Co-decision	0	42	4	**46**
Consent	0	6	25	**31**
Cooperation	0	4	0	**4**
Consultation	1	44	25	**70**
Information	1	3	1	**5**
No participation	10	56	31	**97**
Sum	**12**	**155**	**86**	**253**

Source: Wessels (2008: 338).

the Council, representing the trans-/intergovernmental version of governance, such as decision-making in the CFSP/ESDP. The second, the joint decision-making mode, contains the cases where strong parliamentary participation is combined with unanimity in the Council or where weak or non-participation of the EP is coupled with majority voting requirements, while the third category refers to the supranational decision-making model, represented by majority voting in the Council and consent or co-decision/OLP procedures.

This overview stresses the point that the prevailing (in quantitative terms) mode of governance as taken from analysis of the legal provisions

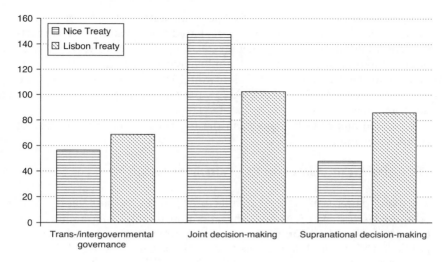

Source: Adapted and updated from Wessels (2005a).

Figure 9.7   *Modes of EU decision-making according to treaty provisions in the Nice and Lisbon versions*

of the treaties is based upon cases of mixed joint decision-making where no clear-cut relationship is established between voting in the Council and EP participation. While the trans-/intergovernmental mode has remained comparatively stable between Nice and Lisbon, the joint decision-making mode has lost ground, but still remains the dominant model. The supranational decision-making mode has increased in (quantitative) importance, but does not even account for one-third of the cases under investigation here. It may be assumed that the dynamics observed in the institutional development regarding the EP and the Council, at the interinstitutional level of decision-making procedures, is not being translated into a single dominant mode of governance, but rather feeds a complex and not very transparent mix and combination of decision-making procedures; more hierarchical modes of governance have been strengthened, but have not so far become the prevailing model, as far as the treaty provisions are concerned.

This balance is further confirmed by the fact that the newly introduced categories of competences in the Lisbon Treaty (Art. 2-6 TFEU) do not allow for clear interrelations with regard to procedural aspects of decision-making. The findings indicate that the observed mix is running across different competence levels of the EU; in the sphere of exclusive competence as defined by the TFEU, parliamentary participation is rather weak, while it is stronger in the area of shared competence, or in supporting, coordinating and complementary actions. Remarkably, in the area of coordination of economic and employment policies the picture offers more than the mode of coordination would let us expect. Cases of OLP are also embedded, while in general low parliamentary participation does not come as a surprise.

Thus, the mix of policy modes in the EU runs mainly across areas of competence and policy fields.

The Living Architecture of the EU: Patterns of Activity

The major patterns in the legal architecture of the European Union having been analysed, I will now turn my attention to the living architecture, trying to find evidence on the way the legal provisions are translated into political reality. I look first at the European Parliament's use of different procedures from the SEA until the Nice Treaty. Table 9.4 reflects decisions and resolutions by the EP under consultation, cooperation, co-decision and consent in that period. It reveals a high level of activity under the consultation procedure, where the Parliament's rights of participation and rights to shape decisions are extremely limited. In the whole of the period, around half of all EP resolutions and decisions fell into the category of consultation, while co-decision (first, second and third readings) accounted for around a quarter.

To be analysed and evaluated, these figures need some more refinement. When comparing the intensity of the use of different procedures, the time frame must be compatible. Thus, it makes sense to have a closer look at the period after 1993, when co-decision came into being, in order to get a coherent picture. Figure 9.8 reflects the use of the procedures by the EP from 1993 to 2006.

In order to compare the use of the different procedures, a look at the dynamics is revealing. Thus, the trend lines for the different procedures reveal that the weak parliamentary procedures (consultation and cooperation) have been suffering a decline since 1993 (see Figure 9.9).

On the other hand, the data for the strong parliamentary procedures (co-decision and consent) reveal – despite interim volatility – an upward trend, while the use of the consent procedure is slightly positive, close to stagnation (see Figure 9.10).

Thus, while the actual share of resolutions and decisions by the EP based upon the consultation procedure amounts to more than 50 per cent (in 2006: see Table 9.4), whereas co-decision sums up to a little over 25 per cent (in 2006), the use of the two procedures as expressed in the EP's

Table 9.4 European Parliament proceedings, 1987–2006: resolutions and decisions adopted

Year	Activities of the European Parliament									
	Consultation	Cooperation			Co-decision			Withdrawn or failed	Consent	Sum
		Reading 1	Reading 2	Completed	Reading 1	Reading 2	Reading 3			
1987	152 *75.6%*	13 *6.5%*	9 *4.5%*	7 *3.5%*					20 *10.0%*	**201**
1988	131 *47.0%*	45 *16.1%*	45 *16.1%*	44 *15.8%*					14 *5.0%*	**279**
1989	128 *40.0%*	55 *17.2%*	71 *22.2%*	63 *19.7%*					3 *0.9%*	**320**
1990	159 *47.3%*	70 *20.8%*	49 *14.6%*	56 *16.7%*					2 *0.6%*	**336**
1991	209 *67.4%*	62 *17.2%*	37 *10.2%*	50 *13.9%*					3 *0.8%*	**361**
1992	243 *53.8%*	70 *15.5%*	66 *14.6%*	62 *13.7%*					11 *2.4%*	**452**
1993*	199 *53.9%*	50 *13.6%*	46 *12.5%*	52 *14.1%*	5 *1.4%*	0	0	9 *2.4%*	8 *2.2%*	**369**
1994	168 *50.6%*	33 *9.9%*	21 *6.6%*	21 *6.6%*	18 *5.4%*	34 *10.3%*	23 *6.9%*	3 *0.9%*	11 *3.3%*	**332**
1995	164 *54.5%*	26 *8.6%*	12 *4.0%*	10 *3.3%*	35 *11.6%*	19 *6.3%*	16 *5.3%*	2 *0.7%*	17 *5.6%*	**301**
1996	164 *45.1%*	31 *8.5%*	34 *9.3%*	25 *6.9%*	34 *9.3%*	37 *10.2%*	31 *8.5%*		8 *2.2%*	**364**
1997	154 *49.0%*	19 *6.1%*	15 *4.8%*	17 *5.4%*	34 *10.8%*	27 *8.6%*	32 *10.2%*	1 *0.3%*	15 *4.8%*	**314**

Table 9.4 (continued)

Activities of the European Parliament

Year	Consultation	Cooperation Reading 1	Cooperation Reading 2	Cooperation Completed	Co-decision Reading 1	Co-decision Reading 2	Co-decision Reading 3	Withdrawn or failed	Consent	Sum
1998	215 *50.5%*	38 *8.9%*	24 *5.6%*	24 *5.6%*	41 *9.6%*	43 *10.1%*	36 *8.5%*	1 *0.2%*	4 *0.9%*	**426**
1999	177 *48.1%*		17 *4.6%*	17 *4.6%*	69 *18.8%*	34 *9.2%*	37 *10.1%*		17 *4.6%*	**368**
2000	113 *37.5%*				60 *19.9%*	53 *17.6%*	50 *16.6%*	11 *3.7%*	14 *4.7%*	**301**
2001	190 *48.2%*				85 *21.6%*	51 *12.9%*	51 *12.9%*	1 *0.3%*	16 *4.1%*	**394**
2002	136 *38.6%*				90 *25.6%*	56 *15.9%*	66 *18.8%*		4 *1.1%*	**352**
2003	129 *40.7%*				94 *29.7%*	67 *21.1%*	11 *3.5%*		16 *5.0%*	**317**
2004	163 *57.2%*				69 *24.2%*	29 *10.2%*	13 *4.6%*		11 *3.9%*	**285**
2005	113 *43.2%*	1 *0.4%*	1 *0.4%*		90 *34.4%*	32 *12.3%*	0		24 *9.2%*	**261**
2006	158 *54.8%*				73 *25.3%*	34 *11.8%*	10 *3.5%*		13 *4.5%*	**288**
Sum	**3265** *49.3%*	**513** *7.7%*	**447** *6.8%*	**448** *6.8%*	**797** *12.0%*	**516** *7.8%*	**376** *5.7%*	**28** *0.4%*	**231** *3.5%*	**6621**

Source: Adjusted and updated from Wessels (2005a).

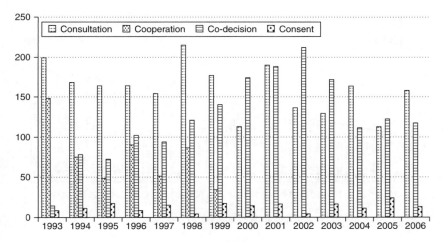

Source: Adjusted and updated from Wessels (2005a).

Figure 9.8 *The use of decision-making procedures by the EP, measured by the number of EP resolutions and decisions under each of them, 1993–2006: absolute figures*

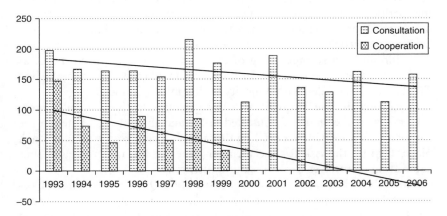

Source: Adjusted and updated from Wessels (2005a).

Figure 9.9 *The use of the consultation and cooperation procedures by the EP, measured by the number of EP resolutions and decisions, 1993–2006: absolute figures and trend line (linear regression)*

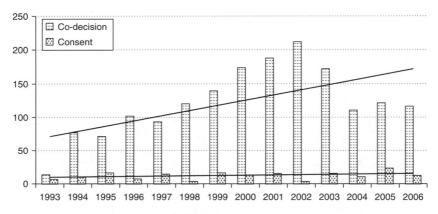

Source: Adjusted and updated from Wessels (2005a).

Figure 9.10   *The use of the co-decision and consent procedures by the EP,*
                 measured by the number of EP resolutions and decisions,
                 1993–2006: absolute figures and trend line (linear regression)

activities from 1993 to 2006 is shaped by very different dynamics. During
that period, the procedures involving stronger parliamentary participation
developed more dynamically than the procedures involving weaker parliamentary participation. There has thus been a cautious trend since that
date, hinting at a strengthening of the more hierarchical procedures, as
co-decision is in most cases under Nice, and in all cases under the Lisbon
Treaty's OLP, coupled with majority voting in the Council.

Regarding the use of qualified majority voting in the Council, Figure
9.11 portrays the share of contested votes and uncontested votes in the
Council between 1999 and 2004, in those cases where voting actually took
place, bearing the risk for the member states of losing a vote and thus
submitting themselves to a procedural hierarchy.

First of all, the share of legal acts based upon QMV has remained basically stable in the period under investigation, increasing slightly between
1999 and 2004, and representing almost 70 per cent of all legal acts adopted
by the Council in this period, while legal acts based upon unanimity
account for slightly over 30 per cent. Of all legal acts falling under QMV,
around 20 per cent were contested in 2004, remaining comparatively stable
since 1999. These figures suggest that, even under QMV provisions, the
Council prefers to refrain from contested voting in favour of searching for
consensus; on the other hand, it also shows that at the same time a considerable share of votes are contested, and that share might even increase

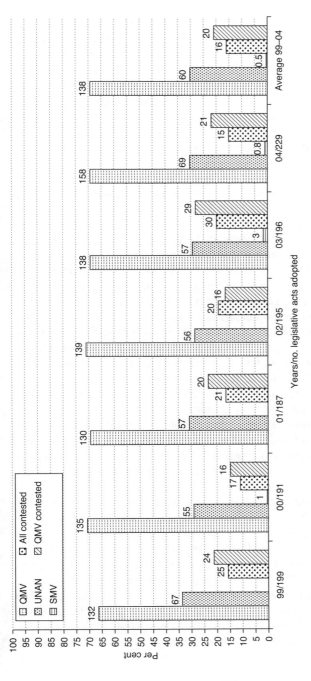

Notes:
QMV: share of total definitive legislative Acts that have a legal basis for QMV.
UNAN: share of total definitive legislative Acts that have a legal basis for unanimity.
SMV: share of simple majority of total definitive legislative Acts.
All contested: contested votes as share of all decisions on definitive legislative Acts under all voting rules.
QMV contested: contested votes as share of all decisions on definitive legislative Acts under legal basis QMV.

Source: Hayes-Renshaw and Wallace (2006).

Figure 9.11   Shares of contested and uncontested votes in the Council and of different voting rules, 1999–2004:
percentages

given the latest enlargement of the EU (figures for the years since then are not yet available). The use of consensus in cases where QMV would apply according to the treaties leads to the emergence of less hierarchical modes of joint decision-making, although in the shadow of hierarchy, that is, of majority voting, which confirms trends towards mixed modes of joint decision-making. In fact, the real patterns of the living architecture reveal a less dominant trend towards hierarchy than the legal architecture would allow for, reflecting a preference for consensus-building in the Council that would correspond to the notion of a concordance system (Puchala, 1972; Hrbek, 1981).

Considering the living architecture, apart from looking at the decision-making procedures and their use, it is also extremely important to assess the kind of legal instruments adopted. In particular, shifts away from binding legal instruments towards non-binding instruments call for attention. Table 9.5 contains an overview of the legal acts adopted in the EC/EU from the coming into force of the Maastricht Treaty until the end of 2007, categorizing them into types of legal acts and differentiating them in relation to different policy areas. This compilation has been undertaken on the basis of EURLEX, thus taking over the categorization applied in this database. This overview allows particularly for the identification of regulations, directives and decisions, while non-binding acts such as opinions and recommendations have not been specified, so that the fourth category also includes a number of other instruments (such as CFSP and Third Pillar acts) which call for some caution in interpreting the figures.

On a general level, the shares of the different types of legal acts have undergone some changes since the coming into force of the Maastricht Treaty. The proportions between regulations, directives, decisions and other acts (which include non-binding acts such as opinions and recommendations, legal acts under the Second and Third Pillar, and unspecified legal acts) out of all legal acts adopted under Maastricht, between 1993 and 1999, are shown in Figure 9.12.

Thus, the relative majority of legal acts have been regulations, with almost 50 per cent of all secondary legislation adopted in that period. Next come decisions, while directives only account for a rather modest share of 4.3 per cent of all acts concluded. The main sources of this dominance lie in the fields of agriculture, fisheries and external relations, where regulations are intensively used either for shaping the market or for commercial policy vis-à-vis external countries. Competition policy and external relations account for the high numbers of decisions adopted, the decision instrument being used in particular by the Commission in exercising its regulatory role and for specific trade policy instruments. The picture is much more mixed and balanced in other policy areas. Thus, policy-specific

Table 9.5 Secondary legislation categorized by types of legal acts in the EU in different policy areas, 1993–2007

Policy domains as identified by CELEX	Maastricht Treaty 11/1993–4/1999					Amsterdam Treaty 5/1999–1/2003					Nice Treaty 2/2003–12/2007					Totals 11/1993–12/2007	
Time frame	Total	Reg	Dir	Dec	Oth	Total	Reg	Dir	Dec	Oth	Total	Reg	Dir	Dec	Oth	Legal Acts: total	av. legal Act/year
General, Financial + Institutional affairs	793	86	2	427	278	618	56	1	302	259	1121	141	15	565	400	2532	179.8
Customs Union + Free Mov. Goods	1036	969	1	60	6	469	442	4	15	8	484	459	3	20	2	1989	141.3
Agriculture	5413	3639	145	1600	29	2828	1624	107	1071	26	3593	2035	175	1365	18	11834	840.5
Fisheries	867	662	1	196	8	422	342	0	78	2	609	514	0	93	2	1898	134.8
External Relations	1564	925	6	563	70	1020	531	1	448	40	1322	654	1	602	65	3906	277.4
Competition Policy	1158	30	6	1096	26	1483	13	3	1443	24	1657	26	2	1629	0	4298	305.2
Industrial Policy and Internal market	704	54	193	376	81	415	38	142	174	61	625	125	201	262	37	1744	123.9
Taxation	92	7	13	61	11	81	3	13	61	4	109	11	27	70	1	282	20.0
CFSP	186	22	0	87	77	277	70	0	75	132	693	196	0	220	277	1156	82.1
Area of Freedom, Security, Justice	217	6	1	19	191	192	29	5	76	82	265	46	12	158	49	674	47.2
Freedom of Movement and Social policy	158	22	29	54	53	128	21	21	46	40	162	58	22	61	21	448	31.8

Table 9.5 (continued)

Policy domains as identified by CELEX	Maastricht Treaty 11/1993–4/1999					Amsterdam Treaty 5/1999–1/2003					Nice Treaty 2/2003–12/2007					Totals 11/1993–12/2007	
Time frame	Total	Reg	Dir	Dec	Oth	Total	Reg	Dir	Dec	Oth	Total	Reg	Dir	Dec	Oth	Legal Acts: total	av. legal Act/year
Right of Establishment + freedom to provide services	70	5	39	10	16	50	8	24	7	11	88	19	36	29	4	208	14.8
Transport Policy	158	44	53	41	20	143	29	44	37	33	236	116	49	50	21	537	38.1
Economic and Monetary Affairs	122	36	3	39	44	145	57	4	26	58	303	65	4	83	151	570	40.5
Regional and Structural Policy	406	35	4	356	11	217	49	0	159	9	101	63	2	36	0	724	51.4
Environment, Consumer, Health	413	114	70	161	68	451	141	57	186	67	667	258	94	262	53	1531	108.7
Energy Policy	142	9	12	97	24	105	5	4	53	43	81	9	13	41	18	328	23.3
Science, Information, Education, Culture	183	13	5	103	62	100	6	3	50	41	174	44	4	84	42	457	32.5
Law relating to Undertakings	41	22	4	8	7	32	17	6	1	8	91	47	18	10	16	164	11.6
People's Europe	7	0	3	0	4	3	0	1	0	2	9	1	2	3	3	19	1.3
Sum	13730	6700	590	5354	1086	9179	3481	440	4308	950	12390	4887	680	5643	1180	35299	2507.0

Source: EURLEX data 1993–2007.

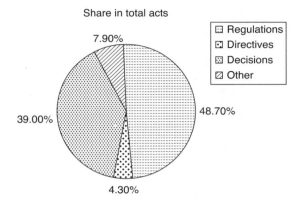

Share in total acts

Source: EURLEX data 1993–2007.

Figure 9.12 *The shares of types of EC/EU legal acts of secondary legislation adopted under the Treaty of Maastricht, 11/1993– 4/1999: percentages*

peculiarities play an important role in assessing the mix between different legal instruments.

Under the Amsterdam Treaty, the picture changes, with a considerably reduced share of regulations, in particular in favour of decisions and of legal acts not specified (see Figure 9.13). In particular, the rise of the latter could suggest an increased role for non-binding acts; but it could also be a reflection of rapid development in CFSP and Third Pillar decision-making.

Under the Nice Treaty, until the end of 2007, the trend in the respective shares observed since Maastricht has undergone some modifications, but has remained basically intact (see Figure 9.14).

The share for the adoption of regulations as well as directives has risen slightly, while all other types of legal acts have suffered a decrease. From these general and broad figures, an EU-wide substantial trend towards the use of non-binding, soft law provisions can hardly be justified. The main shift has apparently taken place between the share of regulations and that of decisions, decisions having become the most frequently used instrument ever since the Treaty of Amsterdam. The scope of decisions is much more limited than that of regulations, though both are entirely binding as to their contents. The shift from regulations to decisions in quantitative terms thus may be seen as a reduction of overall binding legislation in favour of more specific and discretionary binding acts. There has also been a general reduction in the share of binding legal acts since Maastricht, which took

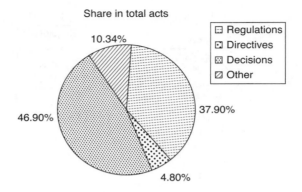

Source: EURLEX data 1993–2007.

Figure 9.13   *The shares of types of EC/EU legal acts of secondary legislation adopted under the Treaty of Amsterdam, 5/1999– 1/2003: percentages*

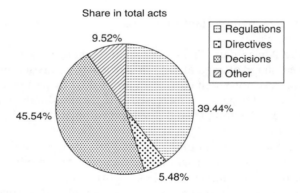

Source: EURLEX data 1993–2007.

Figure 9.14   *The shares of types of EC/EU legal acts of secondary legislation adopted under the Treaty of Nice, 2/2003– 12/2007: percentages*

place mainly under the Amsterdam Treaty, but which has not been confirmed under Nice so far. The impact of enlargement should be taken into account in this context, as it will probably lead to renewed efforts to (re-) define binding legislation so that more representative results could be anticipated over longer periods of time. Taking a broader view, the results appear to be modest, but analysis that takes more policy-specific perspectives on different areas of EU activity may produce more refined results.

CONCLUSIONS: WHICH DYNAMICS IN EU MODES OF GOVERNANCE?

Given the analysis of the legal and the living architecture of the EU, a number of trends can be identified which reveal that modes of EU governance are in a process of dynamic change, although not following a clear-cut model. In general, the revisions of the legal architecture of the EU have opened the way for tendencies for stronger supranational features in governance, thus increasing the opportunities for hierarchical modes. In particular the further expansion of the co-decision/OLP procedure has contributed to a movement in that direction (without, however, prescribing a dominant procedural model). At the same time, the Council enjoys more leeway in adopting decisions by majority voting; it is in the interrelation between EP participation rights and Council voting modalities that (at the level of the legal architecture) differentiation and mixture come into play; there is so far no clear-cut unidirectional trend towards a combination of hierarchical elements between the Council and the EP, although the OLP as introduced by the Lisbon Treaty no longer provides for cases of unanimity in the Council, thus making the procedure more consistent. Apart from this, a wide variety of combinations cutting across areas of competence and policy fields is in play, and characterizes the features of EU governance for the time to come.

In the living architecture of the EU, the use of treaty provisions suggests that the use of majority voting in the Council has been rather cautious, while the EP has increasingly been using the co-decision and consent procedures since Maastricht (although these only account for around a quarter of its resolutions and decisions). Consultation still plays a very important quantitative role in decision-making for the EP. Thus, while the trend is towards the use of procedures that shape decision-making into a more supranational and hierarchical mode, this has so far not become the overriding tendency, leaving much space for mixed forms of joint decision-making.

Regarding the use of different legal acts, the Treaty of Amsterdam has apparently led to some overall shifts from regulations to other instruments, and particularly to a strengthening of non-binding legal acts, but there is no indication that – particularly after Nice – this trend has turned around the use of binding versus non-binding acts. Here, policy-specific perspectives promise to allow for more differentiated and refined results, as the overall dominance of regulations and decisions in the use of legal acts may be attributed to a number of particular areas such as agriculture, fisheries, external trade policy and competition policy.

Taken together, our findings are as follows.

- Treaty changes provide opportunities, incentives and constraints for decision-making in the EU and are thus to be considered as important milestones for the analysis of EU modes of governance.
- For the European Parliament, since the creation of the three original communities, the ratio between strong and weak treaty-based participation rights has undergone a change, until a more balanced relation has been reached under the Lisbon Treaty, with a particular dynamic being injected by the Treaty of Maastricht.
- The analysis shows that increasing parliamentary participation rights and more possibilities for Council majority voting based on the legal constitution have not led to a dominance of clear-cut models which would provide a framework for more hierarchical modes of governance per se. Thus, while the legal architecture has strengthened the foundations for the use of the supranational decision-making model, it has also opened up the space for combinations, so that in terms of the legal provisions, the supranational decision-making mode is far from being the dominant one. Institutional elements of hierarchy and non-hierarchy are frequently combined in the legal provisions, particularly in the Lisbon Treaty. There is no clear relation between the newly introduced areas of competence and specific procedures, not even under the 'coordination of economic and employment policies' or under the 'supporting, coordinating and complementing actions'.
- The analysis of the living architecture of the EU has shown that the treaty provisions are used intensively by the actors; since Maastricht, the EP has been more dynamically engaged in co-decision and consent than in cooperation and in consultation, revealing that the new provisions on enhanced parliamentary participation are of growing importance; at the same time, they do not cover the majority of EP activity up to date. In the Council, the use of qualified majority voting has been handled with a high degree of caution, not as yet driving a major dynamics; thus, the potential for hierarchy is not being fully exploited by the member states in the living architecture. Rather they have favoured a mode of governance based upon consensus. It remains to be seen how far the last enlargement will substantially change that rationale, as consensus will be much harder to achieve.

- The use of specific legal instruments has undergone changes, primarily with the entry into force of the Amsterdam Treaty, while no major shift from binding to more non-binding acts on the overall EU level can be detected. Regulations and decisions dominate the picture, due in particular to some policy areas where they are in frequent use. A more policy-specific analysis of the practice of governance will lead to more refined and differentiated results.

- Thus, shifts in modes of EU governance are subject to dynamics which are is more incremental than 'revolutionary', leading to new institutional and procedural solutions triggering off a process of differentiation. Instead of a consistent, clear-cut architecture we find elements of mixture and combination, with trends in the direction of more supranational, hierarchical modes in the context of complexity and evolutionary enhancement.

REFERENCES

Bähr, Holger, Oliver Treib and Gerda Falkner (2007), 'Von Hierarchie zu Kooperation? Zur Entwicklung von Governance-Formen in zwei regulativen Politikfeldern der EU', *Politische Vierteljahresschrift*, **40** (2007), pp. 92–115.

Börzel, Tanja (2007), 'European Governance – Verhandlungen und Wettbewerb im Schatten der Hierarchie', in Ingeborg Tömmel (ed.), *Die Europäische Union, Governance und Policy-Making*, PVS-Sonderheft 40/2007, Wiesbaden: VS Verlag, pp. 61–91.

Börzel, Tanja, Yasemin Pamuk and Andreas Stahn (2008), 'The European Union and the promotion of good governance in its near abroad: one size fits all?', SFB-Governance working paper series, Berlin: SFB 700.

Diedrichs, Udo (2007), 'Neue Dynamik in der Europäischen Außen- und Sicherheitspolitik: auf dem Weg zu einer Security Governance', in Ingeborg Tömmel (ed.), *Die Europäische Union, Governance und Policy-Making*, PVS-Sonderheft 40/2007, Politische Vierteljahresschrift, Sonderheft 40/2008, VS Verlag, Wiesbaden.

Hayes-Renshaw, Fiona and Helen Wallace (2006), *The Council of Ministers*, 2nd edn, Basingstoke and New York: Palgrave.

Hofmann, Andreas and Wolfgang Wessels (2008), 'Der Vertrag von Lissabon: eine tragfähige und abschließende Antwort auf konstitutionelle Grundfragen?', *Integration*, **1**, 3–20.

Hrbek, Rudolf (1981), 'Die EG ein Konkordanzsystem? Anmerkungen zu einem Deutungsversuch der politikwissenschaftlichen Europaforschung', in Roland Bieber et al. (eds), *Das Europa der zweiten Generation, Gedächtnisschrift für Christoph Sasse*, Vol. 1, Baden-Baden: Nomos, pp. 87–103.

Jachtenfuchs, Markus (2001), 'The governance approach to European integration', *Journal of Common Market Studies*, **39**, 245–64.

Kohler-Koch, Beate and Bertold Rittberger (2006), 'The "Governance Turn" in EU studies', *Journal of Common Market Studies*, **44**, Annual Review, 27–49.

Puchala, Donald J. (1972), 'Of blind men, elephants and European integration', *Journal of Common Market Studies*, **10** (2), 267–84.

Scharpf, Fritz (2000), *Interaktionsformen. Akteurzentrierter Institutionalismus in der Politikforschung*, Opladen: Leske & Budrich.

Schuppert, Gunnar F. (ed.) (2005), *Governance-Forschung. Vergewisserung über Stand und Entwicklungslinien*, Baden-Baden: Nomos.

Tömmel, Ingeborg (2007), 'Governance und Policy-Making im Mehrebenensystem der EU', in Ingeborg Tömmel (ed.), *Die Europäische Union, Governance und Policy-Making*, PVS-Sonderheft 40/2007, pp. 13–35.

Wessels, Wolfgang (2005a), 'Emergence and evolution of modes of governance: designing a treaty-based framework – towards an index of integration', paper presented at the NEWGOV Plenary, Cluster 1 meeting, Florence, May 2005.

Wessels, Wolfgang (2005b), 'The constitutional treaty: three readings from a fusion perspective', *Journal of Common Market Studies, Annual Review 2004/2005, The European Union*, pp. 11–36.

Wessels, Wolfgang (2008), *Das Politische System der Europäischen Union*, Wiesbaden: VS Verlag.

Index